# THE WAY WE WERE

# The Baby Boomer Story

## MICHAEL F. KASTRE

The Way We Were – the Baby Boomer Story

Copyright © 2021 by Michael F. Kastre. All rights reserved. No part of this publication may be reproduced, stored in a retrieval system or transmitted in any form or by any means, electronic, mechanical, recording or otherwise, except for citations for scholarly, reference, or book review purposes, without the prior written permission of Michael F. Kastre at michael@michaelkastre.com.

This is a nonfiction book. The places and times are real. The characters, however, are fictional, unless actual historical figures, because the author has created composite characters to tell The Way We Were—The Baby Boomer story.

The Way We Were – the Baby Boomer Story
ISBN 978-1-7356527-4-0 (paperback)
ISBN 978-1-7356527-5-7 (electronic book)
Library of Congress Control Number: 2021912178

Published 2021 by:

Saint Michael's Press
4 Weems Lane, No. 133
Winchester, VA 22601, United States
(stmichaelspress.com)

Printed in the United States of America.

Cover and interior book design by Deborah Perdue, Illuminationgraphics.com

Cover: Author with his first hotrod, 1962.

# Dedication

To my wife, Nydia, who makes all things possible and life complete with her love, support, and encouragement. And, a big thank you to our daughters, Natalie and Veronica, for their invaluable insight, suggestions, and encouragement.

Also, a special heartfelt thank you to Mr. Tony Testa for providing the forward to this book. As the leader of the Duprees, he has been instrumental in ensuring that their harmony and love songs have been an important part of the soundtrack of baby boomers for over 50 years. Mr. Testa's charismatic and engaging stage presence lights up every performance of this classic musical group as they blend big band and doo wop to create classic romantic songs that remind all of us of the timeless power of love.

# Other books by Michael F. Kastre

*The Minority Career Guide*
(Published 1993 by Petersons Publishing, Princeton, NJ)

*Walking in the Clouds – Colombia
through the eyes of a gringo*
(Published 2014 by St. Michael's Press)

# The Way We Were

*Memories light the corners of my mind*
*Misty watercolor memories of the way we were*

*Scattered pictures of the smiles we left behind*
*Smiles we gave to one another of the way we were*

*Can it be that it was all so simple then?*
*Or has time rewritten every line?*

*If we had the chance to do it all again tell me would we?*
*Could we?*

Written by Alan Bergman, Marilyn Bergman & Marvin Hamlisch
Song recorded by Barbara Streisand, 1973

# Baby Boomer Humor and Wisdom

*All generations have their sense of humor. We are no different. There are so many things that BBs say that make us laugh or think. Here is a smattering of BB humor and wisdom. Just some thoughts . . .*

We enjoy an advantage that those who followed us do not—that is, we did much of our stupid stuff before the Internet.

If things get better with age, then I must be close to being magnificent.

If I shouldn't eat at night, then why is there a light in my refrigerator?

You don't stop having fun when you get old. You get old when you stop having fun.

Old age is the time when you finally get your head together then your body starts to fall apart.

Life is what happens to you while you are busy making plans.

I've reached an age when my train of thought often leaves the station without me.

I'm not getting old. I just can't remember stuff because my brain is full.

Inside every old person is a young person wondering what happened.

They call it gray hair. I call if stress highlights.

As for age, I'm really 16 years old with 50 years of experience.

"To do is to be." Nietzsche
"To be is to do." Kant
"Do be do be do." Sinatra

Christmas is just plain weird. What other time of the year do you sit in front of a dead tree and eat candy out of your socks?

I'll never be over the hill because I'm just too darn tired to climb it.

Have you ever had a memory that sneaks out of your eye and rolls down your cheek as a tear?

# Contents

About the Author ............................................. viii
Author Notes ................................................. ix
Foreword by Tony Testa, leader of the Duprees ............. xi

Introduction ................................................. 1
Chapter 1 – Learning to Walk (1946 – 1951) ................ 18
Chapter 2 – Starting Real School (1952 – 1955) ............ 48
Chapter 3 – Sock Hops & Beginning to Rock (1956 - 1960) ... 72
Chapter 4 – High School Days (1961 - 1963) ................ 97
Chapter 5 – Off to College (1964 – 1966) .................. 123
Chapter 6 – Protests of a Generation Divided
   & the Man on the Moon (1968 – 1969) ................. 147
Chapter 7 – We Prevail – The War Ends (1970 – 1975) ...... 165
Chapter 8 – Financial Nightmares, Disco Days,
   and Saturday Night Fever (1976 – 1979) .............. 185
Chapter 9 – Me, Me, Me (1980 – 1984) ..................... 203
Chapter 10 – It's All About Money or
   Living in a Material World (1985 – 1989) ............ 216
Chapter11 – Scandals, Culture Wars
   & Middle Age (1990 – 1999) .......................... 231
Chapter 12 – Becoming Senior Citizens
   & the New Millennium (2000 – 2008) .................. 243
Chapter 13 –The End of Normal and the World
   as We Know It (2009 – Present) ...................... 258

# About the Author

Michael F. Kastre is a leading-edge Baby Boomer (BB) born in 1946. He has written over 750 magazine and newspaper articles and columns published in various magazines, newspapers, and online covering a spectrum of topics, ranging from health, lifestyles, and terrorism to technology, culture, food, business, and the workplace. He covered Capitol Hill for seven years as a military affairs correspondent. He also traveled extensively in South America, working as a photojournalist. He is the author of *Walking in the Clouds – Colombia Through the Eyes of a Gringo* and *The Minority Career Guide*.

More importantly, growing up and coming of age he lived, studied, and worked in Michigan, Arizona, California, Ohio, Maryland, Virginia, Washington, DC, New Jersey, and New York. He has also worked and traveled abroad, including the US Coast Guard expedition to the Antarctic as part of Deep Freeze 67. In addition to writing, he worked as a consultant to the Department of Defense and served as an adjunct faculty member for several universities, teaching undergraduate courses in advanced research and writing, business, and communications. He also worked at The Johns Hopkins University's Applied Physics Laboratory, developing advanced electronics for medical and space applications. He resides in the Potomac Highlands of West Virginia with his wife, Nydia, who writes children's books with a nutritional theme.

He loves to hear from readers. Please feel free to contact him at michael@michaelkastre.com.

Also, please visit him at www.myhealthyseniors.com and check out his useful blogs about life and living as we all attempt to age gracefully.

# Author Notes

Based on the multi-decade nature of *The Way We Were – The Baby Boomer Story* and the countless things that were happening, often simultaneously, I offer these notes for clarity and book organization.

- **The voice of the book, and your guide, as you travel on this journey is James Michael Bennett**, or Jimmy to friends and family. In every sense he is real—he lived the times—but since he is a composite character there is no such single person.

- Most BBs will recognize the major events and things referenced in the book. For other readers, though, I have provided footnotes to define things that they may not be fully familiar with from a historical perspective since they didn't experience them during that time.

- To have a canvas against which to illuminate and share this story, each chapter starts with the events, fads, movies, music, and trends that were prevalent during the time. Woven into this cultural backdrop is the personal story of Jimmy and other baby boomers he interacts with to capture what it was like to be a BB. In the very early years (primarily Chapter 1), the book covers mostly the times, but, as Jimmy gains his voice and starts to become of age (beginning in the early 1950s) succeeding chapters increasingly capture his personal story of what it was like for him and others during those times. His story covers what many of us were doing, feeling, and experiencing during that time.

- I would suggest that you visit online sites (like youtube.com) and check out some of the music noted in *The Way We Were – The Baby Boomer Story*. Who knows, you may discover some new favorites, rediscover old favorites, or, at the very least, it will give you a better flavor of the time and the soundtrack of our lives.

- Although I have included footnotes to summarize key events and things, I highly recommend some online research to gain a deeper understanding of them for any of those items that pique your curiosity. Often, certain events like 'Watergate,' for example, had a profound impact on our country. And, fully understanding them can help put everything else in context.

- Finally, what is described in this book is how I, and my narrator, recall the times; however, since BBs are such a diverse and geographically dispersed group and so much was going on, I may have overlooked some of the moments or particular events that defined some of us. It was not, however, my intention to slight anything or anyone. And, if I have done so, please accept my sincere apologies.

# Foreword
## by Tony Testa

The over 50-year history of the Duprees is a remarkable story that I'm proud to have been a part of shaping. For over 30 years I have been privileged to lead the group. It has been a journey of evolution and discovery, just like *The Way We Were – the Baby Boomer story*. Along the way, our music has been an important part of the soundtrack of baby boomers as they came of age and matured. After all, the sound of the music is a direct conduit to our memories. I still find it amazing that a single song can bring back a thousand memories. And, we are still doing our thing just like the BB generation.

*The Duprees. Tony Testa bottom center, then clockwise Jimmy Spinelli, Tommy Petillo, and Phil Granito.*

I feel privileged to be able to write this forward for the book. It's a story that spans the decades of one of the largest, most diverse, and privileged generations in American history. It is a book about the past, but one which is still relevant.

As writer William Faulkner once noted, "The past is never dead. It's not even past." Or as American patriot, Patrick Henry, said, "I know of no way of judging the future but by the past."

Despite the endless waves of change described in the book, musical groups like the Duprees' timeless classics have endured and impacted countless lives. Indeed, the Duprees first big hit called *You Belong to Me* in 1962, was about journeys to faraway places, longing, and love. It still resonates with people because we all want stability and a sense of belonging. It tracks what many leading-edge BBs were experiencing at that time.

As the book details, during those tumultuous decades, the times were far from perfect as the BBs went from the innocence of the 1950s to the chaotic 1960s when events and cultural changes caused seismic upheavals in the US across the cultural and political spectrums. Such things as the pill and the resulting sexual revolution, the assassination of President John F. Kennedy, the draft which obligated young men to serve in the military and fight an unpopular war in Vietnam, the Civil Rights act of 1964, the assassination of Martin Luther King, race riots and countless protests across the country. It was also a time of the hippie counter culture and the rise and height of flower power.

The book's characters were also far from perfect. As you will see, the protagonist is a troubled character in many ways, which is no wonder. At school, for example, he and his fellow students often found themselves crouched under their desks in preparation for a nuclear attack from the Russians which never came.

Later in the story, much to the disapproval of his parents, he struggles to maintain relationships as he and other BBs made divorce mainstream with about half of all their marriages ending in divorce.

Like many BBs, though, despite what was happening, he maintained a large measure of optimism and hope. At heart, he was a good person trying to find himself and more typical of his generation than not. Also, like most BBs, despite what was happening, he maintained that positive attitude troughout his life.

Baby boomer parents were from the Greatest Generation and had mostly conservative ways. This put them largely at odds with most BBs as they became sexually adventurous and rebellious against the old norms. Add to this the BBs flirtation and indulgence in mind-altering drugs and it was a truly chaotic time.

Growing up, BB kids were not tethered to their parents with

things like smartphones. They had a lot of freedom and were expected to behave themselves, which they didn't always do. This sense of independence would eventually lead them into the streets to protest against the establishment for a wide range of causes from equality to anti-war.

Follow the cast of characters as they journey from youth to old age. As the BBs matured and evolved, so did much of the music, from doo wop and rock and roll to techno, disco, rap, and beyond. But our music was still there. Many thought the old music would die, but of course, it didn't. It continues to be well-received, proving that classics never fade away because we all need songs that remind us of the unending power of love.

From the early years to middle age and on to the present, the BBs were different. Accordingly, along the way, they established many "firsts" and "lasts." Things like the first generation to make protesting mainstream. The first to be sexually liberated because of the pill. The last to make dancing a part of their lifestyles. The last to write physical letters as a primary way of communicating. The last to have meatloaf and mashed potatoes as a primary part of their diets. And, the list goes on.

Part of the power of the book is that it is not just a snapshot or segment, but follows the BBs through to today. How they are seeing and coping with a world so radically transformed with things like pollical polarization and the rise of fake news, including how they view the future. It's the way they were and the way they are.

No matter if you are a BB or not, I hope you enjoy this unique journey. The story is a distinct chapter in American history. It is a trip well worth taking and I'm proud to be associated with it.

*Tony Testa*

# Introduction

We all have our time machines—memories take us to our past and dreams transport us to our future. Just like it is never good to fret too much about the future, it's never good to dwell too much in the past, but a little nostalgia can be good for your mind and soul. Reflecting on the past puts things into perspective and reminds us of the events and times that shaped our lives and made us who we are. After all, the richness of life lies in the memories we have made.

Maybe you didn't go to Woodstock[1] or participate in campus protests. Perhaps you never wore bell-bottom pants, love beads, or flowers in your hair.[2] But if you were one of the 77 million born in the United States between 1946 and 1964, you're a Baby Boomer because we were the post-World War II baby boom. It was the most fertile period in U.S. history. It was also a time when everything changed at an increasingly dizzying rate. Not just in America, but in the world.

For the U.S it was an extraordinary time. We had no bombed-out cities like in Europe and elsewhere. Most people had savings

---
[1] 1969 music festival in upstate NY attended by over 400,000. (Discussed in detail later in this book.)
[2] All traits of hippies and flower power of a generation whose rallying cry was "love and peace."

in the form of war bonds. It was money just waiting to be spent. Our industrial power was running at full throttle. American companies merely had to stop making bombers, tanks, and battleships and transition to making cars, washing machines, refrigerators, and a host of other conveniences for a public weary of war and hungry to improve their lives. The war had not only devastated the economies and industrial infrastructure of Europe but had also laid waste to countries like Japan and China, so American companies faced little competition. For America, it was prosperity on a scale never seen.

Technology and shifting demographics propel change today. For us BBs, though, change was driven not merely by a combination of technological advances and population shifts, but explosive cultural transformation as well. Our times were marked by a country always on the move. From ponytails and flat tops with ducktails,[3] we went on to become hippies, yuppies, and yuppies.[4] Along the way, we went from drive-in movies to drive-through banks and from crew cuts, American Bandstand, and hula-hoops to finding ourselves, Vietnam, middle age, and becoming senior citizens.

It was a wild ride. The 1950s were a time of innocence, the 1960s the age of the pill (birth control), protest, and change, the 1970s a decade of disco and discovery. The 1980s were characterized by money, Wall Street, and three-piece suits. By the 1990s and the new millennium, many of us were sliding into middle age and worried about such things as thinning hair, playing catch up with our retirement plans, and serving as the vanguard in the global struggle against a new brand of terror. Even the youngest BBs were faced with these inevitable realities.

The first decade of the millennium saw us enter the perfect storm. That is, the most significant financial calamity since the Great Depression—insufficient retirement planning and savings,

---

[3] Classic BB hairstyles of the time. The ducktail was a cut that was flat and short on the top with long sides slicked back with pomade hair gel.
[4] A term coined in the early 1980s for a young professional person working in a city. Similar to yippie, a yuppie was short for "young urban professional" or "young upwardly-mobile professional" They were also young professionals working in a city. There was eventually a backlash against this group of BBs over concerns with such issues such as gentrification as they took over sections of major cities, displacing whole segments of poor population.

anemic returns on 401K accounts, unsustainable mortgages, a collapse in housing values, a near-bankrupt federal government with threats of Social Security and Medicare cuts, and an economy with scarce employment opportunities. Throughout it all, despite different locations, politics, and economic backgrounds, there are memories and lessons learned that all BBs share.

As for age differences, leading-edge BBs share this journey from the beginning; but no matter, younger BBs will relate more personally during their time. Our children may never have used a telephone party line, dialed a rotary phone, wound a watch, owned a 45-rpm record, shifted a three-speed gear shift on the column of a vintage Chevy or Ford, gone to a sock hop,[5] or clacked the keys on a manual typewriter,[6] but we did. Until the arrival of our kids (Generation X – those born between 1965 and 1981), we were the most privileged generation in history.

Shaped by the times, we grew up in a dangerous world over which we had no control. Indeed, leading-edge BBs grew up under the iconic mushroom cloud that symbolized the explosion of an atomic bomb in a world chilled by a cold war and divided by an iron curtain.[7] There was no escape. By the time many of us were starting school in the 1950s, we had seen the atomic bomb tests on TV and the all too familiar mushroom cloud was indelibly etched into our minds. We became the first generation with a legitimate fear that there would be no tomorrow. Even our name, 'boomers', conjured up something explosive and volatile. It wasn't until later that our voices would be heard as we rebelled against the establishment. Nonetheless, ours was still a world shaped by a large dose of hometown hope and optimism.

Fed by our parents' hope for us, our expectations were high. Unfortunately, those expectations would eventually turn into a sense of entitlement for too many of us. Even though we shared dreams with them of something better, our youth was vastly

---
[5] We had dances in school gyms and were not allowed to wear shoes on the hardwood floor, so we boogied in our socks.
[6] If you didn't want to write longhand you used a manual typewriter. They were found in all homes and offices before the advent of personal computers.
[7] It was an era of MAD (Mutually Assured Destruction) which was the arms race of atomic weapons everyone was afraid to use because you would not only destroy the other country but yours as well. The Iron Curtain was a dividing of the world between Communists and primarily western democracies.

different from that of our folks. After all, they didn't grow up with TVs, computers, and the pill. They weren't neglected but weren't like today's all-consuming instant gratification society. Their understanding of the world was gained in a more orderly—perhaps thoughtful fashion—because they weren't bombarded by today's 24-hour breaking news cycle and continual commentary. Politics and public discussion were more genteel and civilized. That, of course, would all change.

It started when our parents brought home the first television sets. These one-eyed marvels produced an eerie light that washed over us but didn't illuminate our being. No matter, it was magic. It helped shape our image of the world and spawned many of our myths and hopes. It talked to us, provided our role models, and brought us together—although sadly not to converse since as it turned out it went a long way towards destroying conversations in our homes, as well as family meals.

TV shows were aimed at our parents and us. Many had strong parental role models. These were often males. Remember watching *Father Knows Best, Leave it to Beaver*, and *The Nelsons*?[8] Looking back, they may have been a little low on reality, but they were usually high on morality and so-called traditional values.

Although the world always seemed to be spinning out of control, on a lifestyle level we shared constant things. We not only watched the same TV shows—there were only three channels—but also followed the same professional sports teams. There were no free agents. Johnny Unitas was a Baltimore Colt, Mickey Mantle and Roger Maris were New York Yankees, Ted Williams batted for the Boston Red Sox, and Ernie Banks was a Chicago Cub—period.[9] Players were drafted and usually stayed with the same team throughout their careers. This made it easy to identify with our sports heroes and the teams they represented.

---

[8] Father Knows Best was a chauvinistic program with a strong father role model about the idealized typical American family and how we lived, or were supposed to live, our lives. The parents were wise and imparted life lessons to their kids (it aired from 1954-1966). Leave it to Beaver was about the life lessons and misadventures of 8-year old Theodore 'Beaver' Cleaver in an Ohio family (from 1957-1963. The Nelsons were another idealized typical family. It showed how parents Ozzie and Harriet raised their sons Ricky and David through the teen years, navigating teen issues, like dating. Ricky was also a teen idol with his top selling records we all enjoyed on the radio and bought on vinyl (it was on the tube from 1952-1966).

[9] All legendary sports figures when we were young.

Early on our idols sang about innocent love, tenderness, and cars. There were never thoughts about the need for warning labels or ratings on music or TV shows. This started to change in the 1960s with songs like *Happiness is a Warm Gun, I Shot the Sheriff,* and *The Bitch is Back.*

Everyone said we had it made so we didn't talk about hardships. We weren't allowed. Our parents and their 'Great Depression' and war stories had first rights to that. Funny thing, though, our parents remembered, but they didn't complain or view themselves as victims. Respect for our elders was the way it was. Everybody was a Mr., Mrs., ma'am, or sir. Our parents didn't try to be our friends. It was strictly a parent-kid relationship. Maybe they knew something we would never learn. We BBs on the other hand would later want to befriend our kids and the results would be mixed at best.

In the early years, life wasn't a Norman Rockwell[10] painting, but many of us thought it was. But the conformity of the 1950s covered up smoldering embers of social and cultural tension that helped ignite the flash fires of the 1960s when BBs as a generation were torn apart over race, culture, war, and politics.

No matter the personal roles each of us played, collectively we changed the world. Some of these changes were positive—others were not. We helped end what was deemed an 'imperial presidency,' when Richard Nixon resigned the presidency over the Watergate scandal,[11] protested and fought the first war (Vietnam) the country ever lost, shook the political structure to its foundation, altered sexual values forever, made environmental issues mainstream, and elevated materialism to a lifestyle. We rocked, shared doo-wop, and folk music, and pranced around disco clubs on platform shoes.[12] We witnessed the beginning and end of Camelot[13] and the man on the moon. We

---

[10] An American artist whose unique paintings captured life in the US with his inspiring artwork for nearly five decades from the 1920s into the 1970s. His covers for *The Saturday Evening Post* magazine were iconic. His paintings were a chronical of American history during this period.

[11] The President Nixon administration's scandalous cover up from 1972 to 1974 of a burglary of Democratic National Committee's headquarters in Washington, DC that led to the disgrace and resignation of him before he could be fully impeached and removed from office.

[12] Men wore platform shoes with heels and soles several inches thick during those times as well as baggy pirate shirts with flower designs.

[13] John F. Kennedy's popularity and romanticized brief time in office before he was assassinated led to it being called Camelot suggesting the tales of King Author. Jackie and John were young and glamourous and presided over a time that to some seemed like the manner of a mystical king and queen.

watched and saw our share of scandals, including Watergate, Iran-gate, Travel-gate, and finally Zipper-gate.[14] Ironically, the star of the latter was President Bill Clinton, one of ours.

To be sure, there were differences in BBs. Not everybody was a greaser with tight jeans and a pack of cigarettes rolled up in a white tee shirt sleeve like James Dean.[15] And, not all of us fought or protested. Nor did we all drop acid or become hippies and yuppies. But there is more that connects us than separates us. Whether we were 'far out' or 'in like Flint'[16] or just plain groovy,' we were the first generation to be so tolerant of those things that did separate us.

Continual change has radically transformed the country and continues to do so. As a transition generation, this gap between the old and the new was perhaps wider for us and our parents than between any other two generations. Things like the sexual revolution, the rise of personal computing and the Internet, and countless other things had a dramatic impact on culture, lifestyles, and the workplace between what our folks experienced and what we underwent. It moved the country from what was a "traditional" tradition level to something altogether different. Not since events like the 1920s, for example, which saw more Americans living in cities rather than rural areas, had there been such transformation.

Even education changed. In our lifetime we saw the rise of not only racial equality and the abolishment of segregated schools but women's rights and gender equality as well. Early in our lives, schoolgirls took Home Economics to learn how to cook and boys went to shop classes to learn how to make things. The system had a built-in gender bias. It prepared women to be homemakers and men to be breadwinners.

Consider just how much things have evolved over the last century. Most younger folks today have an awareness of this, but perhaps not a comprehensive understanding of how much. To

---

[14] Refers to President Clinton's sordid affair with young intern Monica Lewinsky in the White House.
[15] The actor was the quintessential bad boy teen idol and nonconformist—the cigarette always dangling out of his mouth, raw masculinity and devil may care attitude made us want to imitate him. We saw him as a real rebel and when he died in a car crash at age 24 this myth was permanently etched in our memories.
[16] Cool sayings of the time. In Like Flint refers to the 1967 movie starring James Colburn as a suave cool secret agent.

put all of this into perspective and context of what led to the baby boom requires a very quick peek back a century.

In 1905, the average life expectancy in the U.S. was only 47 years. That is relatively young in today's world. Life was certainly a lot different. Only about 15 percent of homes had a bathtub, less than 10 percent had a telephone. Communications were out of reach for the average person; for example, calling from New York City to Denver for three minutes cost over 10 dollars—which would be the equivalent of $259 in 2016 dollars! Unbelievably, there were less than 10,000 cars in the country, and they went nowhere fast since the maximum speed was 10 miles per hour. Unlike today, not that many people lived in California, and out of 45 states, 20 of them had more population. The average wage folks earned was about 22 cents an hour. Twenty percent of Americans couldn't read or write and only about 5 percent of people graduated from high school. No doubt we became better educated, although perhaps less wise.

Over 95 percent of Americans were born at home, not in hospitals. Over 90 percent of our doctors had no college degree, but rather merely studied in medical schools without graduating. You could buy sugar for about 4 cents a pound and coffee for 15 cents a pound package. There were few personal products. Women washed their hair about once every month, using home concoctions.

Surprisingly, drugs we now consider dangerous, like cocaine, heroin, and morphine, were available without a prescription over the counter at drug stores. That, like most things, would change after WWII when everything changed.

Our parents were hardy and hopeful in a stoic way, having successfully navigated a devastating economic depression and a global war, they saw the country enter a period of overwhelmingly overt optimism. It was a time of new opportunity with technology and cultural shifts driving dramatic change that would come in constant waves, washing over our parents and us.

When we are young, we tend to think time won't pass and we will be forever young. But, of course, it does. As the inevitable happens we humans just change our standards and definitions. As French novelist Victor Hugo once said, "Forty is the old age of youth; fifty is the youth of old age."

*The Way We Were* is a front-row seat as an entire generation traveled through a lifetime of constant transformation. For better or worse, these transitions shaped our world. Some of the times were fun and joyous, others were sad and tense, but the one constant of the period BBs shared from 1946 to the millennium and beyond is that it was increasingly turbulent. This is the story of *The Way We Were,* and the way are and the journey that defined our lives. Sometimes looking back is the best way to remember what matters most.

Baby boomers grew up differently because the rules were different. We were the product of what many today would consider the Parenting Stone Age. Many of the things our parents did that shaped who we became would never be done today. With the Internet, a million online opinions, dissemination of information at lightning speed, the world is different than when we were kids. We were raised by the same rules our parents were raised by our grandparents and so on from generation to generation.

Today's kids seem more protected, but less safe. We had broad limits but were essentially free. Well before cell phones and being able to reach out and connect instantly with someone, we were allowed to roam. Our imaginations fed what we did because we were short on gadgets, toys, and virtual reality but were free. Our parents let us go off and explore for whole days at a time as long as we were home by dark or a set curfew. Today's parents would never do that. Just imagine today's parents not knowing exactly where their kids were and what they were doing most of the day?

Consider that we could pretty much drink as many sodas as we could get our hands on and eat things like processed snack lunches and colorful cereal. Indeed, prepackaged and processed lunch and snack foods became ubiquitous when we were kids. Now with things like childhood obesity and diabetes rising dramatically and an increasingly health-conscious public, more parents view things like excess sugar as a real problem. In my house, my mom would bake bread and can foods. So, in many ways, my diet was less processed and more homemade.

On the entertainment front, the rise of on-demand video and the ability to stream content, for example, has turned radically changed how much time kids and parents alike spend online and perhaps being less active. It has tended to create more couch potatoes. As we transitioned from kids to being adults, movie night used to consist of going to the video store and renting a single movie. Now you can just sit on the couch and continue to stream as many as you want, sometimes for hours or whole weekends. Add to that the rise of video games.

Self-entertainment for us required getting plenty of physical activity along the way. Today, the most exercised parts of the body are likely a person's thumbs as they work job sticks and tap letters into text. Who knew we would go from pedaling bikes, walking, playing in the streets to just wiggling our fingers while sitting stationary for hours or even days at a time?

We played in mixed-age neighborhood groups most days after school until dark. We played weekends and on those long summer days. Sure, there were times we were bored, but we knew it was up to us to find ways to overcome that boredom. We had the time and opportunity to get into trouble. But we also had the time and the challenge to figure out how to get out of trouble. It was problem-solving 101. We had time to daydream, to immerse ourselves in whatever hobby we liked. It was not just a physical difference.

Various studies strongly indicate that the rise in mental disorders, like depression and anxiety, may be the result of a lack of childhood freedom. Despite that, today's establishment seems to be pushing for more school, more homework, more standardized testing, and less play. Perhaps that is damaging to both the mental and physical health of people. Baby boomers were all athletes to some degree. It was pickup games as opposed to the organized team sports of today—which has shut out a lot of kids from the action.

One has to wonder if the lack of activity and constantly being online is having a negative impact on our young. It would appear so. Kids today are heavier and slower by any measure; for example, it takes them a minute and a half longer to run a mile than kids did a mere 30 years ago.

It doesn't appear that today's increasingly strong push for less recess, more school classes, and standardized testing is yielding the results that were envisioned. Baby Boomers had the advantage of two educations, playing and social interaction in informal settings and the classroom.

Today's kids know more, but that is a two-edged sword. Smartphones and computers give kids access to not only encyclopedic information but social media and dangerous material like pornography. Today parents must grapple with how to control and protect a kid who is not home but has a smart device. The result is more kid rules and less freedom and less need for imagination. Our parents never had to supervise us when we were looking up information for school in an encyclopedia. After all, it was a physical book. How much trouble could we get in? This is not the case with being online.

So, from skills development to behavior and physical conditioning we were fortunate. One vivid reminder of this is the disturbing school shootings we now see. We were not exposed to that level of violence. Today, though the average American kid will see 200,000 violent acts and 16,000 murders on TV by age 18! That doesn't even account for the majority of video games where kids shoot virtual people for hours at a time.

We only had one theater in our town, no multiplex. If you wanted to go to the movies you had to see whatever was playing. I was probably about 9 or 10 when my parents took me to see a black and white movie about Cesar and ancient Rome. I imagine that my parents thought a little history might be good for me. The one scene seared into my memory is when Cesar's colleagues stabbed him multiple times to murder him. It gave me nightmares for many months. Unfortunately, most kids today would just take it in stride, and it wouldn't be as traumatic as it was for me.

More studies are done today than when we were kids. That said, it doesn't take a social scientist to start connecting the dots as we become more desensitized.

Across the board and in myriad ways our environment and how we were treated shaped our habits, character, and view of the world. *The Way We Were* is set against a backdrop of changing culture, norms, and politics as seen through my eyes. I'm Jimmy Bennett. I was there from the beginning. Like many American families, mine lived and worked and attended school in various parts of the country as people became more mobile.

I shared the times with classmates, acquaintances, and friends, including stereotypes like jocks, book worms, goof-offs, early feminists, Vietnam draft dodgers, those who went off to college, those who stayed behind in their hometowns, those who would go on to become professionals and blue-collar workers, and every other type of BB. I had a bird's eye view. I not only experienced the times and saw the impact on others, but I viewed the BB saga from different geographic regions as my generation chose different life paths.

Our parents were ingenious and frugal. The environment they created wasn't a disposable throw-away one. Mom washed aluminum foil after she used it to cook and reused it again. My dad was happier to get his old shoes re-soled or new heels put on than buying new ones. This was a time when people subscribed to the "waste not, want not" approach.

There was no green movement or green buildings or the various green initiatives that exist today. Being a steward of resources was more local and personal. Our parents' generation fixed things or had them repaired, including everything from clothes and socks to radios and appliances. They reasoned, "Why throw things away when they had more life?" Like their possessions, they were in it for the long haul.

Some things, though, remain the same. Like all kids, being a BB child could be confusing for me. Some memories didn't make sense at the time, but my dad still liked to give me confusing advice. For instance, he was a faithful husband to mom, but he did seem to appreciate attractive women. If we saw an attractive woman in the store or passed her on the street and he would say, "Son it's okay to read the menu as long as you don't order . . ." Okay, I didn't understand that at all when young but today I can see what he was trying to teach me.

Today you probably would not hear someone comment on that but those were different times.

We were more basic or just naïve. Rightly or wrongly, we had two genders—male and female. The concept of gender fluidity never occurred to us. It was a matter of biology not feelings.

Although my early real memories started when I was about four or so, listening to adults later gave me a real sense of things even before I developed any in-depth awareness. When World War II ended in the spring of 1945, national pride was heightened by a sense

*Post WWII Wedding*

of euphoria and everyone across the country stood a little taller and straighter.

The folks in Philadelphia, Pennsylvania, certainly felt like that. The streets of working-class neighborhoods were once again alive with young men, many of them still in uniform. It was a welcome change from the years that saw mostly old men sitting around diners sipping coffee or gathered at corner stores and parks speculating about the war. As the boys flooded home it brought a renewed vitality to the American scene. And, it set the stage for the largest baby boom in U.S. history.

It started at a few seconds past midnight on January 1st in 1946 when Kathleen Casey was born at Philly's St. Agnes Hospital. This first BB weighed 7 pounds and 5 ounces. The event marked a sharp reversal of a century-long decline in the national birth rate. Births began to shoot off the charts, creating demographic chaos that transformed everything.

It was an era of unprecedented national economic stability—something that was not true of world security and stability. Later you will see that our coming of age was typified by a vain search for satisfaction, even though we had every advantage. It didn't matter how much we had, we wanted more. This would at times lead to narcissism and greed. For the

*BB Boom Stamp*

present, though, my parents and others were optimistically creating their futures.

I was born in a house in Muskegon, Michigan in January of 1946. This was not unusual because most kids were not born in the hospital but at home. My parents named me James Michael Bennett. My father, Ralph, returned from World War II early in 1945 after being wounded. My mom, Molly, graduated from a secretarial school and volunteered as a hostess at the USO[17] where they met at a dance for service members.

Their relationship blossomed and within months they were married. I was born nine months later. Even with his new responsibilities and work, as a young father, Ralph used his G.I. Education Bill[18] benefits to become the first in his family to graduate from college. During that time, he worked part-time in a hardware store to make extra money while my mom contributed by working as a secretary for a company that manufactured furniture. Her mom, my grandmother, took care of me during these times.

After graduation dad became a teacher and mom became a full-time homemaker. Another son, my brother Paul, was born in 1951 and my sister Molly, named after mom, came along in 1953. I was happy to have siblings and we all settled into trying to live the American dream. A later diagnosis of asthma for my brother Paul would ultimately take our family to Arizona. My dad's teaching career, though, would then bring us back east to Ohio.

Yet, no matter the region, this was being repeated almost countless times throughout the county. The predictable and stable nature of our parents became our shared start. They stayed together and tended not to divorce, unlike us. The pattern played out as they pursued their version of the American dream, including a cross-section of BBs who would make up our generation and some even passing through my life as I came of age.

Families like Brian's whose parents, Pete and Grace, lived in a narrow red-brick row house at the end of the block on Fourth Street in Hoboken, New Jersey. They had become infected with

---

[17] These clubs provided a venue for military personnel to socialize, dance and just unwind.
[18] The original post WWII G.I. Bill provided free funds for ex-service members to attend college, and, they flooded into colleges and universities by the tens of thousands to get what they saw as free education.

the typical 'can do' feeling of optimism that permeated the country. Pete, a corporal in the U.S. Army Infantry, had returned from Europe at the start of 1945 after taking a bullet in the shoulder from a sniper as his unit had approached the outskirts of Berlin. Grace had been grateful that it hadn't been more serious. After a couple of months convalescing in a veteran's hospital in nearby Newark, the young couple was finally reunited for good.

Pete gained almost instant employment with an office supply manufacturing company. He didn't mind the repetitive nature of the assembly line that produced staplers and paper punches. It was steady employment. The money was more than he was used to making, and it was good honest work. He would maintain such an attitude throughout his life. His sense of satisfaction increased when, like me, his son Brian was born January 1946, almost nine months to the day after his discharge from the hospital.

He never questioned the wisdom of his wife, a graduate of a local secretarial school, for quitting her job after the birth of their son. They had only discussed it briefly and it seemed normal and the way it should be. They had married in a simple civil ceremony in 1944 and Pete had been shipped to Europe virtually the next day. Grace had gone to work the same week for a shipping company and liked it from the beginning, but she never once complained about giving up her modest career. She firmly believed it was her responsibility to take care of the home and their growing family.

At the same time in Long Beach, California, a slightly different version of this scenario was being played out. It was the start for a girl who would later become an early feminist. In 1945, her father Ed had been released from his commission as a lieutenant commander in the Navy and taken a job as a federal civil servant at the sprawling Long Beach Navy Yard. After a brief three-month courtship with Gladys, a girl who worked in her family's florist shop, they had married.

Both of their parents helped scrape together the necessary funds for a down payment and the young couple bought a small bungalow a few blocks from the beach. It cost a whopping thirteen thousand dollars. At the time Ed wondered how he would make the $85 a month mortgage payment, but those fears quickly passed as he settled into his new life. By June 1946, they were the proud parents of a cute baby girl named Kathy, named after her grandmother, Kathryn.

With the help of the grandmother and a neighbor, Gladys was able to continue working at the flower shop. One day it would be hers and she took great pride in watching it prosper and grow. Her independent attitude would later do much to shape the character of Kathy.

In the meantime, a young marine named Charles, or Chuck to his friends, returned to McKeesport, Pennsylvania, after the war ended, along with his enlistment. His life was set in this union town as one of his brothers and his father got him his old job back in the small steel mill. He rekindled his relationship with Barbara, his high school sweetheart. Within a year they were married. In July 1948, the family celebrated the birth of a bouncing baby girl named Sally.

Further west in the high desert of Arizona, Joe's dad, George, had just graduated from college. Denied military service because of medical problems, the young accountant took a job at a local department store in Tucson. He continued to date Ruth, a young woman who worked as a nurse at the University of Arizona's medical school hospital. After he felt settled into his new job, he proposed to her and they were married within two months. George's father made the generous offer of providing them with a modest house and they set about selecting furniture.

Ruth was in no hurry to have children and it became a sensitive topic around the household. After several years and considerable discussion, they decided to start a family, but George agreed that Ruth would continue to work at least part-time at the hospital. She reasoned that she was on her way to becoming the head nurse in her assigned wing.

Their son Joe was finally born in October of 1951. Both young couple's parents were tremendously relieved and proud. Ruth took three months of maternity leave without pay. In the back of his mind George believed that because of the life-changing event, she would not return to her duties as a nurse. He was wrong, however, and his mother became an important part of Joe's life. Ruth would deliver the little boy to her mother-in-law's home in the morning and pick him up in the evening. It set a pattern for daycare for many young families of the day. It was a family thing.

We were all different but united in many things. And, my path would intersect with this diverse variety of BBs. You will meet them as *The Way We Were* unfolds. Our paths would cross, and our lives intertwine as our generation grew up and came of age. We would become everything from friends and casual acquaintances to coworkers, loves, neighbors, and—gasp!—senior citizens.

By the time one of our peer group, Bill Clinton, gained the White House in 1993, we were becoming more alike as we faced looming middle age and the task of trying to take care of not only our sons and daughters but our aging parents as well. Others of us were starting to experience the 'empty nest' syndrome as our kids left home. Yet, still, other BBs were beginning to discover that their children had become 'boomerang' kids. Those that left home but weren't quite able to make it and returned to our spare rooms or basements. Many of us found it a bit disquieting to have 20 or 30 somethings living in his or her old room as if they were still teenagers.

The realization that we had finally become the establishment was unnerving. Some of us clung to the past, listening to 'oldies' on the radio and trying to ride fading professions to the finish line. Others embraced king technology and tried to join the cyber-techies and e-generation, buying stocks online and chatting with friends and strangers on the web by joining social media to stay connected. Many of us became obsessed with the ultimate toys, like the latest computers, cellular telephones, and luxury foreign cars.

Our parents have been called 'the greatest generation' because they survived the Great Depression and won a world war. Growing up we never faced such formidable challenges and never had to rise to the occasion. That, of course, would all change as we entered the millennium and the age of global terrorism and financial, political, and cultural calamity, along with racial tension.

The destruction of the World Trade Center on September 11[th,] 2001, the hit on the Pentagon, a hijacked plane downed in a field in Pennsylvania, and the threat of deadly anthrax in our mail thrust us suddenly and spectacularly into the challenge of our lives. Overnight we went from a generation without strong tethers, who envied the resolve and spirit of the greatest generation, to facing unprecedented tests of our own.

We would be overwhelmed with random and spontaneous shootings in schools and the public square, widespread acts of global terrorism, and unimaginable and unmanageable waves of immigrants and refugees that would threaten many cultures and ways of life. It would tend to polarize us politically and heat up the clash between the haves and have nots. Such turmoil would ultimately lead to an era of unimaginable political and cultural craziness—like fake news and a post-truth world.

Our lot in life would be further compounded with the crash of the housing market and the global financial meltdown. Many of us saw whatever wealth we had vanish or become greatly reduced. But I am getting ahead of myself. Let's begin at the beginning to experience how it happened. Enjoy the journey because the past starts here . . .

# Chapter 1

# Learning to Walk (1946-1951)

In 1946, my parents and many others were reading Dr. Benjamin Spock[19] and his common-sense book of baby and childcare. When I was born, our parents were also huddled around console radios listening to shows and plays. They were not the sleek brushed metal and plastic compact models of today. Instead, they were usually wooden cabinets several feet tall with a heavy woven cloth over the speakers. To us kids, they were beautiful and mysterious. Except for newspapers, they were our most immediate window to world events, information, and entertainment. Everything was on the radio—soap operas, quiz and game shows, variety hours, mysteries, talent shows, situation comedies, sports, news, music programs, and superheroes like Superman, the Green Hornet, and Planet Man who was an intergalactic troubleshooter for an organization known as the League of Planets.

---

[19] Dr. Spock was an American pediatrician whose book was one of the bestselling in history. It was the child rearing bible of the day. Ironically, in 1957 he revised it, admitting he had given advice that was too permissive and offered new advice for more structure and discipline for their children.

*Typical 1950s family*

So, while popular, the news didn't come just from newspapers. From these magic boxes, our parents learned that the war didn't leave Russia and the U.S. on very good terms. That the hot world conflict had simply been replaced by the beginning of the Cold War. We were in diapers and weren't aware of that but would later learn what it meant. Winston Churchill toured America and warned of an iron curtain that had descended over Eastern Europe after the victorious allies divided up Europe into sectors.

Our parents, though, were confident about the future because America was the predominant country in the world. It reinforced the belief in American exceptionalism, which would later be challenged, and we would be labeled by some as elitists, racist, and a whole bunch of other negative connotations.

*Vintage 1950s Radio Console & Stereo*

Our parents started to become fascinated by the emergence of technology that would eventually do much more to shape our world than theirs. In 1946, for instance, the copy machine was invented and the Eniac electronic brain was built at Pennsylvania University. It was a glimpse of how the computer would come to dominate our lives and lifestyles. In their wildest imaginations, though, I am not sure anyone could have appreciated how profound the impact would be. The invention of the transistor marked a milestone in the development of modern electronics. But for our part, we were still snuggled in our cribs untouched.

In 1947, some of us were taking our first steps. Our parents were starting to buy TVs. When *The Howdy Doody* Show [20] debuted in December 1947 by asking what time it was, our parents never dreamed it would run for 15 years and help frame our generation. We were still too tiny to see the dangerous world that was emerging and would eventually be ours. This same year saw the CIA chartered. Our parents started to see flying saucers and UFOs. In Congress,, the U.S. House of Representatives Un-American Activities Committee (HUAC) started investigating Hollywood for communist subversives.[21]

Meantime, America was gearing up to feed Europe and the Russians were auditioning for their role as the world villain by stopping road and rail traffic between Berlin and the West in a divided Germany.[22] Truman signed the Selective Service Act, creating the first U.S. peacetime draft of young men into the military. This would come back to haunt us later. Further atom bomb tests were conducted at the Bikini Atoll in the Pacific Ocean. Oddly, the name of this tiny island would soon popularize the two-piece bikini swimming suit.

In 1947, Jackie Robinson joined the Brooklyn Dodgers and became the first African American to play major league baseball. They played the Yankees that year, who won the series in seven games.

---

[20] Wildly popular with kids, it was the first nationally televised American TV show. It ran from 1947 until 1960.
[21] McCarthyism was a period in the 1950s when US Senator Joseph McCarthy of Wisconsin investigated and held televised hearings in an effort to expose alleged communist infiltration of the US government. It also impacted the entertainment industry where many famous celebrities were blacklisted from working without due process.
[22] The US controlled West Germany and the Soviets had Eastern Germany. Likewise, Berlin was divided but was landlocked within Eastern Germany so the only route in for the US and its allies was by air.

I was only two, but in California what would become one of our cultural icons emerged as the first McDonald's drive-in opened in San Bernardino. The LP record (Long Play) became available, and our parents were listening to Nat King Cole's velvet voice as he crooned *Nature Boy*. Fats Domino, Ray Charles, and Little Richard produced their first records and Miles Davis' jazz album called *The Birth of the Cool* came out. There was something for everyone as Pete Seeger and Burl Ives were instrumental in helping folk music emerge.

Yet, all was not normal, and our parents got a disturbing glimpse of the future when George Orwell wrote *1984*.[23] They also got a startling glimpse of themselves when Alfred C. Kinsey[24] wrote about human sexual behavior.

By 1948, many of us were perched on the laps of our parents as they watched the Ed Sullivan television show[25]. That year when they went to the movies our folks saw tough guy Humphrey Bogart star in *The Treasure of the Sierra Madre* and *Key Largo* with sultry Lauren Bacall. We would rent these films years later at the video store and marvel at the power of these black and white classics.

The MovieTone News Reel[26] before the picture show highlighted world events, including the Gandhi assassination, the founding of the People's Republic of China, and the USSR tests of its first atomic bomb. It was unlike the Internet instant 24-hour news of today, but nonetheless a major source of news at the time.

Some of our parents were reading Nelson Algren's *The Man with the Golden Arm*. Later, as young teens, we would see a movie about drug addiction, starring Frank Sinatra.

Our world was changing, and we didn't even know it yet. We older BBs were only four when President Truman authorized

---

[23] The British novelist's book about the consequences of government over-reach, totalitarianism, and mass surveillance within society. It was a glimpse of the big brother nanny state.
[24] Kinsey was an American biologist, professor of entomology and zoology, and sexologist who studied and researched sexual behavior. His findings were titillating and shocking to our folks at the time.
[25] Sullivan hosted this variety show from 1947 to 1971. It was one of the most popular entertainment shows ever and showcased and introduced a number of entertainers, including Elvis Presley and the Beatles.
[26] In those days, there was always a news reel and a cartoon before the screening of the feature movie. Along with radio and newspapers, it was a major source of information for many Americans.

production of the H-bomb. The military got $12 billion out of a total $40 billion U.S. federal budget. That's hard to fathom with today's trillion-dollar expenditures.

Senator Joseph McCarty announced he had a list of 200 State Department employees who were communists. Dubbed "McCarthyism," the practice of blacklisting artists and celebrities suspected of being communists or communist sympathizers started and was seen by many. Alger Hiss[27] was convicted of lying and spying for the USSR. North Korea invaded South Korea. We sent troops and some of our fathers were absent.

My dad was called up and I remember asking mom when he was coming home so many times that she started either crying or becoming irritated with me. So, I just stopped and waited like everyone else.

China occupied Tibet. Ironically, almost 50 years later our kids would be attending things like the Tibetan Freedom Concert. The Rosenburg's[28] were charged with espionage and prosecuted. Ugly events were taking place around the globe. Truman called Russia a worldwide aggressor that was bent on world domination and the cold war became official.

TV started to give us color images in 1951. *I Love Lucy*, starring red-haired funny lady Lucille Ball, premiered on the new sets. Our parents saw Marlon Brando on the big screen in a *Streetcar Named Desire*. Salinger's book *Catcher in the Rye* was popular. Little did we know that the book would be required reading for us in school years later.

On the lighter side, Rodgers and Hammerstein's musical *South Pacific* was a smash on Broadway. It would be years later that I would get to see a play there, but just the mention of the name "Broadway" was synonymous with the faraway glamour of live theater.

Our parents listened to *The Tennessee Waltz* and *Rudolph the Red-nosed Reindeer*. Everyone was glued to the tube and there were 1.5 million TVs in the U.S. If our family didn't have

---

[27] Hiss was an American government official and spy for the Soviet Union. Before his trial he was involved in the establishment of the UN as a State Department official.
[28] Julius and Ethel Rosenberg were US citizens convicted of spying for the Soviet Union, providing vital top-secret information about sonar, radar, jet propulsion engines, and nuclear weapons when the US was the world's only nuclear power.

the magic box, we visited the neighbors or relatives. TV shows like *You Bet Your Life* were popular. In 1951, the first of us—me included—started kindergarten.

In the meantime, our dads (those were male chauvinist times, that was the reality) were going to college in record numbers on the Servicemen's Readjustment Act, known as the G.I. Bill. While wives and moms primarily stayed at home to cook and clean. Although not paid and often unappreciated, these homemakers kept the family together.

The G.I. Bill called for unemployment benefits of around $20 per week. Also, the feds were to underwrite up to $500 a year for tuition. For the more entrepreneurial vets, loans up to $1000 were available to help start or acquire a business.

They told our dads that it was a reward for them and the millions who fought and won World War II. In reality, though, it was aimed at keeping veterans out of the job market as long as possible because leading economists of the time were predicting a return to the Great Depression as soon the war ended. It did the job; plus, it resulted in a better-prepared workforce.

I vaguely remember my dad and uncles talking at the kitchen table about how it meant that better-educated vets would make more money and therefore pay more taxes. The point being that the investment would ultimately pay for itself. Given my age, of course, I didn't understand the discussion or realize the cynical nature of those conversations.

The program was not without its critics and opponents, though. Some politicians opposed it on the grounds of cost and the underlying welfare state quality. Surprisingly, even some academics opposed the plan, fearing it would flood schools with undeserving and under-prepared students. These fears were born out of sheer numbers. After all, more than 16 million Americans served in the war. They poured into colleges and trade schools, peaking in 1947 when almost 50 percent of enrollees were vets.

The program, of course, cost far more than the original government estimate but turned out to be a great investment, nonetheless. We had a more skilled force capable of making all types of things for domestic use and exports. This enabled them to make higher wages, which in turn allowed them to buy new things like appliances and cars. All of this powered the American economy to new heights.

The success of all this help for veterans played a major role in fostering what would turn out to be the longest sustained period of economic growth in our history. This allowed us BBs to grow up during a period of economic prosperity unparalleled in world history. This era started just after the end of the war and lasted until the oil shock of 1973.[29]

Elsewhere during this period in America actor Ronald Reagan, a handsome leading man in Hollywood was elected president of the Screen Actors Guild in 1947. This would set the stage for his eventual transition to mainstream politics, first as governor of California and then as president of the United States. No one had the slightest idea that this would later become reality or that he would play a leading role in bringing the cold war to an end. At that time, though, he was busy with his film career. Two of his movies during this period have since become classics—*That Hagen Girl* where he acted opposite Shirley Temple in 1947, then *Bedtime for Bonzo* in 1951 in which he co-starred with a chimpanzee.

One constant reminder that we Americans were special and privileged occurred regularly at the dinner table. Mom would serve. Sometimes I would leave food I wasn't particularly fond of on my plate. She always looked at me and said something like, "Eat all your green beans, Jimmy, people are starving in China."

This always completely baffled me. I never understood how me cleaning up my plate or overeating was going to help those starving Chinese folks. Why I didn't ask the question I will never know. Perhaps I sensed to do so would be to challenge her authority. Or maybe I should have known and just didn't out of ignorance and was too embarrassed to admit it.

Much later when I had a child of my own, I told her to eat her veggies because it was good for her. That she would grow up big and strong. Even though I didn't always use mom's words, I did

---

[29] This happened when OPEC started an oil embargo and production cuts, which drove the price of oil up almost 400%. This caused shortages of oil needed to feed gasoline refineries. The price of gas skyrocketed but there still wasn't enough fuel for our cars at any price.

remember countless other sayings she used to indoctrinate me—like when something would go undone or wrong and my daughter would tell me she had good intentions. I could hear mom's words in the back of my mind as she said, "Jimmy, the road to hell is paved with good intentions." It was a bit dramatic, but when I said it, it usually got the kid's attention.

Quite simply our parents brainwashed us, starting at an early age. Whatever you want to call it, they did a consistent and thorough job. We were not only brainwashed but completely indoctrinated to be guilt-ridden—about everything from sexual feelings to anything else that was deemed to be remotely pleasurable or excessive. Later, as we aged, that faded, but many of us still harbored a deep-seated sense of guilt.

*Author (in hat) & friends gather for a birthday party (circa 1951).*

In the 1950s, our parents were bigger than us and not just physically. They knew what they were doing and didn't want or need our input when making decisions. Our opinions didn't matter much. They didn't tend to bend down or get on their knees to make us little people feel more comfortable when talking to us. Or as if they were petitioning us while asking us something, like, "Do you think you can stop playing video games for a minute so I can talk to you?"

In general, today's parents seem more apt to ask their kids to do things and the children take their request under consideration. Today's parents also seem to talk more to their kids, do more for them, and take more interest in them. We were ordered to do things. It was 'just do it' before that became a popular slogan.

In contrast, our parents towered over us. They didn't do this because they weren't considerate because they were. They knew something some of us BBs never learned—they were the parents. Our feelings and opinions were putty to be shaped by them. It wasn't as though they thought we weren't smart. They did. That's why they only said things once. They told us what to do and we did it because they said so. That was reason enough. They didn't have to justify themselves. They knew better than us. It's no wonder we took what they said to heart.

Our parents told us many things, many of them over and over. Some were profound, some full of humor. "Go to sleep. I'm tired." Or, how about "That's not worth a tinker's damn." What was a "tinker" anyway? I never knew. Then there was "A lick and a promise." Again, I am unsure what that meant." I think it was doing something halfway.

I did understand, "Just wait until your father comes home." That most likely meant I was in for a spanking or at the very least a good dressing down with strong words. And, "Don't stir up the mud" meant knock it off. "Going to hell in a handbasket' was also self-explanatory. It meant if I continued on that course it wasn't going to end well.

They used the "F" word, but it wasn't obscene, and it didn't refer to a sexual act. It was, "I FORBID it." This was the ultimate no and a sign that whatever it was I wanted, it wasn't going to happen.

Beyond discipline, there were clear sayings and words that were meant to instill in us a sense of right and wrong. What was not clear to me at the time, or even today, is whether they did this unconsciously or consciously. Ironically, they always accused the communists of their use of propaganda, but they were Masters of it in their own way as well.

Specifically, when you did something wrong the ultimate weaponized words were: "I am not mad at you. I'm disappointed." That hurt. It meant you should have known better and had failed. When those words were said I wished they were angry because at some point over time they would cool off and get over it. But disappointed meant that they had lost some trust in me. I had proven myself inadequate. I knew they wouldn't get over that without me later proving myself to them.

Talk about guilt. To disappoint your parents could mess with your head on many levels. You had let them down. You had possibly embarrassed them in front of other adults. You were not worthy to be trusted and on and on. In essence, it gave you the ultimate guilty feeling. Imagine this on top of our parents conditioning us with their sayings?

Looking back later I find it interesting how many BBs used these same words on their kids to shame them into better behavior or compliance. I, for one, must admit that I am guilty of doing that.

Based on our parents' no-nonsense approach of not coddling us and our run-free lifestyles, we were hardy and healthy. Just like free-range chickens, which are supposedly much healthier than those in a cage. Notwithstanding our shortcomings, the dangers of the day, and our brainwashing we survived and thrived, both physically and mentally.

Consider that there were no seatbelts, children's car seats, or airbags. No real official car inspections so we were often riding in cars with bald tires and questionable brakes. When little we most likely slept in cribs with lead paint. There were no child-proof lids on medicines or on kitchen cabinets. Drinking water was not purified and in plastic bottles. We drank it from the tap or even from the garden hose. We climbed trees and sometimes fell out of them and broke bones. It was just part of life. We got hurt playing physical games, like baseball in the street and falling on hard asphalt or running into an unmovable fire hydrant. I don't recall anyone getting sued but do remember a lot of scraped elbows and knees.

Most people smoked and so we breathed a lot of secondhand fumes. Cigarette ads of the day touted the practice as healthy and invigorating. No wonder many of us would smoke later. Not only was it cool, but it was healthy too! For instance, one ad said, "Each Camel at mealtime adds cheer . . . stimulates digestion . . . increases alkalinity. So, for digestion's sake smoke Camels." Or how about "For a treat instead of a treatment smoke Old Gold."

One brand, Phillip Morris, used the slogan, "When smokers changed to Phillip Morris every case of nose or throat scratch —due to smoking—either cleared completely or definitely improved!"

Another featured a picture of a baby in diapers and stated, "Gee dad you always get the best of everything . . . even Marlboro!" And added, "Yes, you need never feel over-smoked . . . that's the miracle of Marlboro!"

*1950s Cigarette Ad.*

A Pall Mall ad advised: "Guard against throat scratch . . . enjoy the smooth smoking of fine tobacco—the finest quality money can buy!"

Cigarettes were even touted for weight control. One Lucky Strike ad showed an obese runner alongside a fit athletic runner with the caption: "Face the Facts! When tempted to overindulge reach for a Lucky instead."

There we even cigarette ads featuring pregnant women. The thought being it would help soothe them during a difficult time.

As a kid, I remember how persuasive the radio, print, and TV ads were. I especially enjoyed the voice on the radio when a young boy sang: "Call for Philip Morris." You couldn't help but sing along. The TV version featured a young hotel bellhop in uniform with a pillbox hat, presumably standing in the lobby singing the jingle. Most of us kids liked to imitate it just for fun.

Celebrities were often front and center when it came to smoking. Famous actress of the day, Hedy Lamarr, for example, touted smoking as, "A good cigarette, is like a good movie—always enjoyable that's why it's Lucky Strikes for me."

A great many of the ads featured very attractive scantily clad women, which always gave us boys a thrill. There was some benefit for everyone; for example, an ad for cigarettes, called Juleps, at the time said, "New miracle mint in Juleps freshens the mouth at every puff. Even if you chain smoke, your mouth feels clean, sparkling all day long."

Smoking knew no politics. Future president, then actor Ronald Reagan, was featured in ads with him saying, "My cigarette is a mild cigarette . . . that's why Chesterfield is my favorite."

[*On reflection, in the 1970s and 80s, I think actor and comedian Bob Newhart best captured the lunacy of these ads years later with a standup comedy routine that went something like this. In his deadpan voice, he started by asking his audience to imagine a phone conversation between Sir Walter Raleigh—credited with discovering tobacco in The New World—and the head of the West Indies trading company based in England. Then he went on to describe the conversation.*

*Trader:* "I'm not sure what tobacco is Walt, but you say you bought 80 tons of it?"

*Raleigh:* "It's a leaf. You can stuff it up your nose and it makes you sneeze."

*Trader:* "Oh."

*Raleigh:* "Or you can chew it and it makes you want to spit every few seconds."

*Trader:* "Oh."

*Raleigh:* "Or you can shred it and wrap it in paper."

*Trader:* "Please don't tell me you stick it in your ear."

*Raleigh:* "No you put it between your lips then set it on fire."

*Trader:* "You're kidding? Then what?"

*Raleigh:* "You cough."
*Trader:* "Walt I think we are going to have a rather tough time selling people on sticking burning leaves into their mouths . . . "

*Raleigh:* "Well it's going over really big here in the American colonies:*

*Trader:* "Well then alright. Let's give it a try."

*Remembering Newhart's routine never fails to make me smile.*]

And although our diets were often questionable by today's standards, we were mostly skinny and fit. My mom told me regularly that I was as skinny as a green bean. Even later in life, she would tell me this. This even though we consumed some questionable things; for example, we ate baloney sandwiches on doughy white bread slathered with mayonnaise. It was zero fiber and nutrition with lots of fat. Mom fried our eggs in the bacon grease left in the skillet. We wolfed down Twinkies and Ding Dongs and a host of other things considered junk food today.

There were lots of ads for lard to make sure we consumed our share. Yup, that artery-clogging white grease was a mainstay. One ad featured a smiling attractive young family in swimming attire. It said: "They're happy because they eat lard." That was obviously a stretch, but that's what it said.

Another showed a glamorous couple in formal evening wear sipping what appeared to be wine, it remarkably said, "They're young . . . they're in love. They eat lard." I suppose the message was the reason for their good fortune and looks was lard, a somewhat tenuous connection but people didn't seem to notice.

My favorite was a poster from the N.K. Fairbanks & Company featuring a large hog dressed like a matronly mother looking down at her piglet that proclaimed, "Lard will fatten the youngsters."

I suppose this was a sure sign that childhood obesity was almost nil. How things have changed. Although we didn't realize it, our secret was endless physical activity. Perhaps our folks knew. I don't know. My mom's instructions to me on most summer mornings were, "Be good and come home when the streetlights come on."

So off I went on my bicycle for a good adventure. Or I would collect my glove, baseball, and bat in search of a pickup game in the street or at a nearby park. I also had a canvas bag full of little olive-green GI Joe figures a couple of inches tall and along with friends, we would stage epic battles.

We understood that our parents bought us very little in the way of toys, so we appreciated everything we had. We also understood that if we broke something, we weren't getting a new one anytime soon. It either had to be fixable or we would have to do without it.

One Christmas my folks gave me a shiny silver metal cap pistol. It looked real. The barrel would release on a pin and swing down. Then you could load in the caps. These consisted of rolls of sturdy red paper with bumps on them that contained real black powder. So, when you fired it, it sounded like a gun. One of our favorites was playing cowboys and Indians. We would chase each other around yelling and shooting like there was no tomorrow. I seriously doubt today's parents would buy those for their children even if they were available.

Back then we loved our guns. In fact, as young teens, during hunting season, many of us who lived in rural areas would take our rifles on the school bus. They were then stored in the principal's office. Then on the way home, the bus driver would drop us off a few miles from our homes and we would hunt rabbits and other animals as we walked home. I hate to think what would happen to a boy today if he tried to board a school bus with his gun. I'm sure someone would call the SWAT team.

Most boys also carried a knife in their pocket, even to school. They were called "jackknives" and they varied in style. They had wooden or bone handles. They usually featured both a big and a small blade that could be pulled out individually. They weren't huge like hunting knives, but we thought they were indispensable. We could cut things and whittle or slice up an apple. The most dangerous thing that happened with our jack knives was that if you weren't careful, it was easy to close the blade on a finger. If that happened, you could suffer a pretty good nick or cut.

The thought never crossed my mind that they were in any way a weapon. Like most of my friends, I saw them as a tool. I felt special because after having several regular jack knives my granddad gave me a Swiss army knife for my birthday one year. Talk about cool. In addition to the blades, it had a pair of small scissors, a screwdriver, and a small pair of pliers.

I was the envy of my friends. My routine was to wipe the tools with machine oil that dad kept in the garage to keep any rust at bay. I'm not sure any parents or grandparents would buy a kid a knife today as a present.

Those of us fortunate enough to have a stand of trees close by would scavenge wood and cardboard and built a fort. And, most of us had one. They were ubiquitous. Close to my house was what my parents called "the grove." It was a deserted wooded area at the end of our street. I would often crawl through it on make-believe adventures, climb the old trees, and have bicycle races with my friends, with the trees acting like an obstacle course. Sometimes we would screw up and crash into a tree incurring some damage to our machines and us. We didn't worry, though, because we knew our dads could fix them up with a hammer, wrench, and a few other basic tools. The scratches and dings would just add to our exaggerated legends.

We were untouchable and unreachable. No beepers or cell phones, so our sense of freedom was complete. We were in charge of our time and what we did. There were rules, of course, like no physical fighting with other boys. Those rules were not to restrict our freedom but to keep the peace. If there were lapses in our civility towards each other it usually resulted in a little pushing and shoving, posturing, and name-calling. Things like "Your Grandma wears combat boots . . . " That saying was meaningless to me, but I knew it was insulting so I used it. We were more likely to get a black eye in school than we were in our local neighborhoods where we were surrounded by neighbor kids. Our loyalties in those days were first to our families and then to our neighborhood. It was our world.

I was starting to remember other things and more specific events like drive-in movies. We would pile into the family car. As we got in line, I could see the giant screen with images, and I was thrilled. Dad would navigate the rolling humps that would place the front of the car at the perfect angle for viewing. Mom would caution dad to be careful not to scrape the metal poles that protruded everywhere. Each pole contained speakers.

Dad would find the place he wanted, roll down the window, hang the speaker on the glass and adjust the volume. This usually led to a prolonged discussion about how loud it should be. Dad liked it blasting and mom wanted a more normal level. As always, though, they would settle on a compromise.

Then I would go with dad off to the concession stand for popcorn and sodas. He held my hand as I stood next to him. Often, he would make me feel important by giving me the money to pay the person serving us. I would hold out both hands as they counted the change then carefully turn so dad could take it and slip it into his pocket. He would usually wink and leave a nickel behind with instructions to put it in my pocket and deposit it into my piggy bank when we got home to save for a rainy day.

It was a time when scenic American towns started to give way to small mass-produced suburban housing and business developments. Most towns had a section where this occurred. Although thrown together, the houses were affordable and had all the modern conveniences. Often the only difference between neighboring houses was the color of the front door. It was the beginning of cookie-cutter communities like Levittown[30] on Long Island and it started to impact our impressions of the world.

Such communities and neighborhoods were made possible in part by a portion of the GI Bill that dealt not with education, but types of loan guarantees to buy real estate. The banks were happy because they had nothing to lose since it was backed up by the federal government. This had a positive impact on the real estate market for years. Our parents enjoyed rising house values and acquiring something unheard of for average people. That is, capital and financial assets they could eventually pass along to their kids (us BBs!).

My first memories were also my increasing awareness of my environment. These include recollections of Formica[31] tables and shiny silver toasters. But not all of these memories were benign.

Those early memories include the fear our parents expressed when I nagged them to go to the local community swimming pool. Usually, they said no. They were worried about the crippling

---

[30] In 1946, the Levitt Company bought 4,000 acres of potato fields 25 miles east of Manhattan on Long Island and mass-produced thousands of row after row of modest houses. The first ones cost $6,990. This 'cookie cutter' approach to building opened up a new chapter in affordable housing for all.

[31] Formica was a hard laminated surface used for counters in kitchens and as tabletops, usually if was a yellowish color.

disease known as polio.[32] I saw kids shuffling along with steel and leather braces, but our parents' fear didn't hit home. After all, it was happening to others, not us. To this day, though, I shudder when I think of images of young kids encased in iron lungs.[33]

I remember hearing my parents talking about current events as mom cooked and dad sat at the kitchen table drinking coffee or nursing a beer. I didn't know why, but it scared me. When I expressed this mom and dad would pat me on the head and assure me that everything would be okay. I believed them because they were so confident. We were protected by ignorance and childhood innocence.

While our dads were going to college in record numbers on the G.I. Bill our moms stayed home and cooked and cleaned as homemakers. That's the way it was, and no one complained. The words *feminism* and *male chauvinist* hadn't been coined yet. The first of us were five and about to start kindergarten, a milestone on our journey.

My brother Paul was born in 1951. Mom was a picture of calm and composure throughout the 9 months. The only complaint I ever heard her voice during that time is that her ankles tended to swell. In the evening she would recline on the sofa and dad would rub her feet. The doctor would stop by periodically to check things out, but there didn't seem to be any complications. Yes, they visited patients at home; they didn't go to his office.

I quizzed dad about how this miracle happened. He then proceeded to give me some confusing mumbo jumbo about the birds and the bees. It didn't make sense, but I didn't push too hard. It was enough that I was going to have a younger sibling.

One day mom calmly informed dad she was starting to feel twinges and contractions. The evening before Paul's birth the midwife came and stayed with mom. She slept in the spare bedroom. I heard her all night, getting up to check on mom. I caught bits and snatches of hushed conversations and drifted in and out of sleep. The doctor came in the morning and I remember dad calling into work to take the day off.

---

[32] Polio was a common infectious disease that caused muscle weakness, making it difficult to move. It commonly impacted the legs but could also strike the neck and diaphragm. It was devastatingly crippling.

[33] Iron lungs were a type of ventilator that enclosed a person's body, leaving only the head exposed to enable people to breathe.

I admired how the doctor always wore a suit and tie. He looked professional and sharp to me. I lived in a middle-class blue-collar environment. The only time I saw people dressed in suits was at church on Sunday or if we would go downtown where people had offices, like lawyers and accountants.

While the whole birth thing was going on upstairs, dad sat on the porch and fidgeted with an unlit cigar. I sat on the steps and tried unsuccessfully to engage him in some sort of conversation. He didn't say much but did ask me if I wanted a brother or a sister. At that time there was no way for doctors to determine the sex of a baby. I diplomatically told him either one would be great.

When the big moment arrived, we heard the baby crying when he got slapped on the bottom. Shortly after the doctor appeared on the porch. As he was unrolling his shirt sleeves—he had only taken off his suit coat and tie—he congratulated dad on the birth of a healthy son. Dad just beamed and offered him a cigar, which he accepted. He plopped into the lawn chair next to dad. I watched them light up. I was happy but felt sort of like the invisible man. I listened to them chatter about the routine nature of the birth and a discussion of names.

Finally, not being able to stand it any longer. I asked when I could see the baby. The doctor assured us as soon as things were cleaned up, we could go upstairs to visit mom and the new son. That it wouldn't be long. The fact that I now had a younger brother made me feel important. I was a big brother now.

Memories, of course, can be elusive, but the snippets I have at that age are vivid. Things like one night when the living room lights were off, except for a lamp in the corner. In the dim light, dad pulled up a chair to the radio console. The lights of the radio dial flickered on and I heard a whine as he intently fiddled with the dials. Then a sardonic voice said something like this, "Welcome to the Perfect Alibi. In tonight's episode, LA private investigator Johnny Seltzer, played by Jack Webb, is approached by a beautiful would-be heiress who offers him $50,000 to help her escape the clutches of a local hoodlum. Johnny falls hard for this temptress, and he thinks he has the perfect scheme to win them both what they want. But given the Whistler's penchant for a story with a sting in its tail, Seltzer's plans are almost certain to fall flat in some unforeseen manner."

The Whistler was the invisible voice of the narrator. All-knowing and all-seeing. Each episode began with the sound of footsteps and a person whistling. You could just imagine a figure with a fedora sauntering down a dark street as he passed through shadows and pools of lamplight.

In the late 1940s and early 50s, it seemed, only the cosmic audacity of the Whistler could foil the success of the sort of tough-talking private-eye then ubiquitous on the airwaves. Webb himself starred in three such series. He would go on to become the iconic voice of Sergeant Joe Friday on Dragnet.[34] This well-written, well-acted show ran from 1942–1955. It was narrated cynically by the eponymous shadow-lurker who saw all and told all a bit at a time, taunting and mocking the modern fools whose criminal schemes he chronicled.

I could see nothing of the show, of course, it was just a voice in the dark, except for the images it conjured up in my head. Yet, hearing this gave me goosebumps. For reassurance and comfort, I looked over at mom who was sitting calmly on the couch by the lamp knitting for the baby. I was sitting on the floor but snuggled closer to dad who smiled down at me. The show fascinated and scared me at the same time. I knew it was make-believe but somehow it seemed real. My imagination usually ran wild. I knew it was a story, but it sounded real to me. I loved when my dad would take his old leather pouch and pack his pipe. As the aromatic cloud of smoke enveloped me it would add to my sense of protection and wellbeing. It was like a magic fog.

This type of ritual was repeated many times with shows like *Amos and Andy*, singing cowboy Gene Audrey's *Melody Ranch*, funny man Jack Benny, and *Mr. District Attorney*. (You might want to check such classics out on YouTube.) There were dozens of shows from mystery and singing to cowboy, comedies, and variety. Watching them now I realize how different times were by current standards. I'm not sure how a younger audience would react to them.

---

[34] Dragnet was popular on radio then TV from as we followed Los Angeles policeman Sergeant Joe Friday and his partner as they went about the business of solving crimes and apprehending criminals. Who could forget that droll voice as Friday said, "The facts, ma'am, just the facts."

They might sound corny by today's entertainment standards. There were no mind-boggling special effects. To be sure there were crude audio effects—like the clopping horse hooves or the creak of a door closing. The magic, though, happened in the listener's mind. Not a bad thing when you think about it.

*

Despite the importance and power of the radio, TVs keep invading and changing more homes. My parents were not immune to this. Dad finally splurged and bought a small RCA set with a slightly oval screen. Then something remarkable happened.

It was a Saturday. I was playing with my Lincoln logs on the living room floor. My dad called me. "James Michael come here."

This got my attention at once. When your parents called you by your formal name and threw in your middle name, you knew it was something serious. You were either in big trouble or they wanted to tell you something profound.

I cautiously peeked into the kitchen where dad stood by the door to the garage. He motioned for me to follow him. He looked both serious and excited and I wondered if I was in trouble for something I did or didn't do. Was I supposed to sweep the garage and had forgotten? We went to the garage and he solemnly took his sacred brown canvas tool bag down from the shelf. He unzipped it and took out a couple of screwdrivers.

"The picture on our set is rolling," he said. "And you and I are going to fix it."

I had no idea what he was talking about, but I knew I wanted to be part of it. I tried to look all-knowing and nodded. Then I followed him to the living room. First, he removed the rabbit ears from the top of the set. When viewing the tube, you had to move the two slender silver antennas around to get a watchable picture. Sometimes it was almost as though one of us had to stand there and touch them to have a static-free picture.

We slid the console out from the wall, and I watched as he removed the screws from the back of the TV set. One by one he handed them to me. I clutched the screws, but my hand was getting full, so I finally placed them in my trouser pocket. Heaven forbid if I lost any of them. Fascinated, I watched as he began removing vacuum tubes one by one from the set. He set them carefully on the living room rug and warned me not to step on them. I remember wondering how my dad had become so smart and knew about everything. He told me to get a small cardboard box from the kitchen. When I returned he placed the tubes in it.

[We had plenty of boxes because there were no plastic bags. Instead, groceries were typically loaded into the boxes that products were shipped into the store.]

"Now son, we are going to the drug store."

Were the tubes sick? Of course not, but by this time I was mystified. Just learning how to read, I was a big proponent of former President Abraham Lincoln's advice where he stated, "Better to remain silent and be thought a fool than to open your mouth and remove all doubt," so I said nothing as we climbed into the family sedan and off we went. I don't remember the exact model year, but it was a black 1940s Plymouth sedan with a sloped back. It had a three-speed shifter on the steering column. I watched as dad skillfully worked the clutch and gas pedal, hoping when my turn came to drive, I would be as good.

I thought the dashboard instruments were modern looking, but obviously, they were not by today's standards. They were just cream-colored gages with regular black numbers and hash marks on them. The steering wheel was flat and made of some type of hard material with a chrome ring on the inside. The dashboard itself was metal—imagine smacking your head on that? There were no seat belts. If your parents had to stop abruptly, their right arm would shoot out to try and hold kid passengers in place. Not a very safe or effective system but it was what it was. We made it to the drugstore without any mishaps, such as me bouncing my head off the metal dashboard.

In the corner of the drug store was a big metal console with various plugs in it. I had seen them before but never really thought much about their purpose. I held the box as one at a time dad plugged the tubes in and fiddled with the controls. Finally, he pointed at the analog gage, which had green and red sectors.

"Ah hah. Just as I thought, it is the horizontal output tube."

Boy was I impressed. A store clerk helped us find the right

tube in a cabinet close to the tester. Dad paid cash because the use of credit cards was almost nonexistent. (The first credit card was Diner's Club in 1950, but it was limited to paying for meals in certain restaurants.) Then, off we went home where he replaced the tubes. I carefully handed him the screws and he put on the back panel.

Later I would brag to my friends. "Yup, it was the old horizontal output tube." I didn't know what I was talking about. All I knew was that it had a silver metal tip on the top where a wire was attached but had no idea of its purpose in the TV. That didn't stop me from acting all-knowing. To this day if I had a vacuum tube TV that is the first tube I would check . . .

When dad had turned on the set and it warmed up, he seemed delighted and said, "Jimmy, we did it. Look, the picture doesn't roll anymore."

I hadn't done anything, but my sense of pride made me feel taller. I felt an almost conspiratorial companionship with dad. We had done something together that only he and I shared. It was my first real awareness of how the technology worked—even though I had no idea how any of it worked.

In my later life, I would do the same thing. The ensuing years were a time when regular folks could still fix things. This practice extended into the 1970s. At that time and for years to follow every drugstore in America had tube testers. It was empowering that despite our lack of technical knowledge we could still fix things.

With time, though, things got more complicated, or simple, depending on your perspective, as we unconsciously began to transition to a modular and throw-away world. This was great for manufacturers but not so much for the environment. New materials, such as plastic, coupled with engineering advances, meant if it broke you just threw it in the garbage or set it by the curb. It was a time when TV and radio repair shops began to disappear from main street along with other specialty stores. And, of course, tube testers in drug stores disappeared, too.

I remember the 1967 movie, *The Graduate* when a young Dustin Hoffman is told by an older friend or relative that the future was in plastics. Boy was he right, although things like the proliferation of plastic bags and bottles have become an environmental nightmare. Perhaps one day a return to paper and glass will signal a concession to the old ways.

My generation experienced all levels of technology from yesteryear to today. You didn't have to be an electrical engineer to appreciate the advances in shrinking size and increases in picture and sound quality. Imagine the feeling of seeing everyday electronics go from vacuum tubes to the invention and rise of transistors and circuit boards with discrete components where they were mounted along with resistors and capacitors to power our lives? Years later this was followed by the tiny plastic modules known as integrated circuits. They contained everything needed to power modern life in sleek little packages.

BBs saw this evolution from crude electronics to miniature powerful circuits that provided the public with radios, TVs, cell phones, tablets, computers, and more. It was so overwhelming that at the time most of us could not process what was happening. I still shake my head when I think about the incredible progress over the years made possible by some very smart and clever engineers.

In our early years, we had such things as transistor radios for music, cathode ray tubes powered by thousands of volts for video, and pencils with erasers to do our math problems. Today's kids have calculators, electronic tablets, cell phones, flat displays, and screens to stream not only audio but video and e-books. Of course, the side effects include a shrinking attention span and a tendency to read less and spend more time on social media. The result is less human contact and people seem less content.

No matter, I was still basking in the glory of helping dad fix that pesky rolling picture. Later the day of our triumphant repair job, dad said we deserved a special treat and invited me to Caruso's Ice Cream and Soda fountain. In those days, soda fountains were bars for kids. Caruso's was no exception. It had a long marble bar. Behind it usually a couple of "soda jerks" worked. Yes, that was their official job title. They typically had dark slacks, crisp white shirts with a black bow tie, and white paper hats—much in the style of those worn by soldiers during World War II.

We sat at the bar on fancy wrought iron stools. Dad asked, "What would you like, son? Anything you want."

Talk about pressure. Usually, our parents would dictate or strongly suggest to us what to order when we went out. I wanted to maximize the opportunity and immediately opted for my favorite, a root beer float.

I watched as the soda jerk filled a tall elaborate glass—much like a fancy beer glass with a base—with vanilla ice cream. Next, he went to the soda taps with large intricate knobs and slowly added the root beer. He let it settle for a minute. After the foam receded, he added more. It was a masterpiece. He then gave me a long-handled silver metal spoon and paper straw and it was ready.

My dad watched my obvious anticipation and delight with a smile. He said, "That looks so good I think I will have the same."

Then we just sat there in comfortable silence and slurped the marvelous concoctions. I felt close to dad. We were partners.

It was a time of momentous events. It also marked the beginning of many other adventures. Things changed when mom and dad kept reminding me that I would be starting school. They started talking about getting me clothes to start kindergarten.

They took me shopping on main street with its specialty shops. There was a shoe store. Another one sold men's and boy's clothing. Sears and Roebuck was the place to buy underwear and socks. The five and ten cents variety store was the place to get school supplies and a book bag.

They bought me two sets of slacks and cotton long-sleeved shirts. Next on the list was a sturdy pair of oxford shoes. I wanted brown, but dad advised me to get cordovan—a sort of classy dark reddish color—because it was better than brown or black as it would go with any color of slacks and shirt. I filed that away as good advice. And, to this day, I prefer cordovan for their flexibility to use with any color of clothes.

I would try on the shoes and mom would put her thumb on the tip of them to see where my big toe was. She always insisted on buying my shoes a size or two too big. "You will grow into them over the school year," she would say.

I was never thrilled because I thought they made me walk funny, sort of like a duck. So, I would end up with oversized oxfords for what she called "Sunday and school dress" and a pair of high-top Keds tennis shoes for play. They had to be high tops because mom informed me that they would give my ankles better support. That might have been true, but I always lobbied for the low cuts, which I perceived as cooler, and what all the hip kids were wearing. It wasn't until I was about in the 6th grade that I won this battle.

This back-to-school ritual would be repeated for many years. You only had one chance to shop. That was it unless you tore your clothes, and they couldn't be mended.

Starting school drastically changed my lifestyle. It introduced responsibility, a new word, into my vocabulary. Up to that point, I was allowed to roam free around not only our yard but the neighborhood as well. I went from my Western Flyer tricycle, with bright streamers at the end of the handlebars, to a small bright red Schwinn bicycle with training wheels at about age 5. I also gave up my little red metal wagon, which I pulled everywhere.

Now my bike was my freedom. No helmets needed. Just jump on and pedal and I could go anywhere. That "no schedule carefree existence" was suddenly threatened and apparently about to change. The whole family seemed to know I was about to become a schoolboy. This was heady stuff for me and the introduction of lots of new words and ideas.

My Uncle Chuck, mom's brother, even stopped over one day to give me some advice. "Now boy you listen to your teachers and do what they say. Be your own man and don't follow any boys who think it is okay to be rude and disruptive." (It was the first time I could recall that anyone ever called me a man without "young" before it.)

"I'm not worried about that, Uncle, but what if I'm the only one that doesn't understand the lessons?"

He grinned. "Jimmy, you are smart as a whip. You won't have any trouble learning."

I could never figure out why whips were smart, and I didn't entirely share his confidence, but it did make me feel better. Seeing my frown, he tousled my hair and said, "It's going to be great. You will see."

Then he reached into the pocket of his trousers and pulled out a quarter. "You always need some money in your pocket. There will be unexpected times when you're with your friends and they will want to have a soda or buy some penny candy and you don't want to be embarrassed. So, keep this in your pocket for those times. It will help you build self-confidence."

[Up to that point, the only money I had was generated by picking up empty pop bottles and taking them to the corner grocery store for pennies.]

Self-confidence? I wondered silently. Then I said, "I am not sure what you mean."

"That feeling knowing you can do anything your friends can do. In fact, you can probably do it better. You can handle it. Never forget that. Know you can be competitive with your peers."

"It sounds like a game. And who are my peers?"

"Your age group and the people you will find yourself with. It starts with standing tall, both physically and mentally. Don't ever lie or do something that will embarrass you or your friends. And don't forget it is nice to be popular, but more importantly, be true to yourself. And yes, in many ways it is a game."

"How do I know I'm being true to myself?"

"Do you ever feel icky when you tell your parents a lie or you do something you know is not right?"

"Yes."

"That shameful feeling is what I'm talking about. You know when you are being a good boy. You want people to respect you and think you are someone to be trusted and counted upon."

I looked straight into his eyes and nodded. I remember wondering if mom had put my favorite uncle up to giving me what was turning out to be quite a lecture. I would realize later that this was the beginning of learning about integrity and morality. Something his generation seemed to value highly. Was it their bombarding us with their sayings and clichés, coupled with these mini-lectures and lessons that shaped our morals? I often wonder if I was as diligent in instilling such values in my child many years later. I wasn't an ideal dad, but I hope I did.

I also wonder if young parents are doing that today? I don't get the sense that they are to the extent our parents did. I could be wrong but that is my perception.

Another difference is that today it seems to be the era of participation trophies. Events where there are no winners and everyone gets rewarded for participation. I wonder if this is an incentive or if it creates apathy? After all, in life, you won't always be rewarded just for showing up.

In any case, this was heavy stuff for a five-year-old. It was something I knew I would need to carefully ponder. Starting school was going to require a new level of thinking on my part. I was going to part of a larger group and was going to be judged on my behavior. I hoped I was up to the challenge and would be able to pull it off.

Despite any fears or doubts, by this time I was starting to feel important. My uncle was talking to me like I was an adult. I found myself more aware and tried not to slouch, but to make myself as tall and straight as I could.

Ironically, it wasn't weighty moral issues and ethics that shaped my entrance into formal school. It was puppy love. Indeed, my first memory of kindergarten was marked by developing a crush not only on my teacher but a little red-haired girl. I remember that my heart ached. Carrying her books home from school was the best. During nap time on our mats in class, I would position myself so that I could see her while I was laying there. My parents didn't seem to notice that I was in puppy love, but I was.

I know I started to be much more aware of my surroundings—people and things. I was so proud and in awe of my classroom. It was magical. The rows of small desks with built-in seats. The innocent graffiti I saw carved into them, which was mostly the names of kids who had gone before me. Should I carve my name there too? I debated this for weeks but decided, in the end, it showed disrespect to the school. I loved to see the green border around the room with the letters of the alphabet written in white chalk. Instinctively, but unconsciously, I started to memorize them. I silently moved my mouth as I said the letters to myself.

The mats we lay on to take a nap were made of woven straw. It left marks on your face if you lay your head on them for too long. I soon realized that laying my head on my arm would eliminate this embarrassment.

Unlike today there was no "graduation" from kindergarten. The school year just ended mysteriously. Some kids were labeled slow, and others were seen as qualified, and sometimes your path in life started with that label. Adults then were not careful how they expressed themselves about kids, either in front of them or at parent conferences. Kids were talked about as if they were adults. Everyone was not rewarded as a winner. We just did the best we could and what was expected of us and that was that.

After the last class of the year, we gathered with friends outside the school and said a short goodbye because we all knew we would be seeing each other around the neighborhood as we returned to our "free-range" lifestyle. There were no such things as "play dates" with other kids. Why would we need such a thing when we all ended up together and interacted with each other in streets, back yards, and parks anyway? We would naturally gravitate towards other boys and girls we liked and invent or find shared activities and games to play.

If your parents were friends with other adults whose kids were your friends, they would visit. And, while the adults sat on porches or in yards to chat, we kids would organize our games and activities. This usually involved games of tag or hide and seek as it got dark. It was exciting enough for us and didn't require any special equipment or adult supervision. We were expected to entertain ourselves and we did.

Successfully navigating kindergarten was satisfying. I didn't see my little redheaded girl crush that summer because she had moved to another neighborhood. I didn't forget her but my feelings for her somehow seemed to melt away. She might as well have been a thousand miles away. We had no way of staying in touch and I had to accept that.

It was a time of old-fashioned rotary telephones, the kind where you put your finger into the round dialer and rotated it around for each number. They were all black and set on a surface and plugged into the wall. There were no wall-mounted or wireless phones. We shared our line with three other neighborhood families. For these "party lines" you knew when it was a call to your house by the number rings. One ring was ours and we would answer. Two rings signaled it was for the next house and we just ignored it and so on.

It was a very efficient system, but if you were noisy and liked to listen to gossip you could pick up the phone and listen in on other folk's conversations. This tended to discourage people from having private and personal conversations with anyone because you never knew who might be listening.

Then towards the end of summer—which passed all too quickly—my parents told me that I was going to enter real school in the fall. They could have fooled me. I thought I had just completed 9 months of real school, but apparently, that was just a dress rehearsal. I started to worry and wonder all over again what it would bring. I didn't voice this to the adults in our family, but it was definitely on my mind. I even speculated about it with my friends. That is when the myths and legends, fueled by older kids and siblings, started to impact my life.

There were the usual stories about legendary mean teachers to avoid. David, our neighbor's son who was starting 4$^{th}$ grade typified this. "You have to avoid Mrs. Kirkland at all costs," he told me. "If she doesn't like you, she will have you sent to the principal's off and he will spank you with a big wooden paddle."

"How big?" I wanted to know.

"Big," he assured me. "And it has holes in it to make it hurt more."

I cringed a little and then some common sense kicked in. "How do you know this?" I asked.

"I survived it," he replied.

Well, that gave me something to think about. He never told me what got him unceremoniously delivered to the monster who ran the school for this scary punishment. When I would ask, he would just smile. I thought he was so wise and strong for having survived this and hoped if my time came, I would be as brave.

I was overwhelmed by all the talk about 1$^{st}$ grade and gradually thoughts of all the things that could go wrong blurred together. I suppose I unconsciously decided that my only choice was to be cautious and take it as it came. Things were changing, our clothes, what was popular, and what we were doing. My horizons were expanding. Movies, for example, exposed me to things that impacted how I saw myself. My dad had always been my hero, all-knowing and seeing. Suddenly there were others seen in movies and elsewhere who I also wanted to imitate.

So, tentative but undaunted and feeling important, yet vulnerable, I was off to school for the big kids. The first-day mom dressed me in new khaki slacks and a checkered shirt, and I slung my empty bag (except for a pad of paper and pencils) over my shoulder and I was ready to face this brave new world. I stood in the driveway in my too-big oxford shoes and took a deep breath.

I almost forgot my lunch, but at the last moment, mom gave me the little tin box. It was painted to feature a colorful Roy Rogers and Dale Evans at the entrance to the Double R Bar Ranch. Roy cut a dashing figure astride his horse, Trigger. Although Roy was popular with boys my age I wondered if they would have the same box or something else.

Looking back was that the beginning of pressure to conform? Or perhaps a devil may care attitude that it didn't matter because as my Uncle Chuck had told me, "I was my own man."

# Chapter 2

# Starting Real School (1952 – 1955)

Despite the astonishing advances in technology and the education I was receiving, it was the Wild West, an era long past, that powered my life. By the early 1950s, like many other young boys, I saw myself as a cowboy. All things for me were the wild west—movies, cowboy shirts, cowboy hats, cap pistols, and boots.

I immersed myself in it as I learned to read. I even went through all the western-themed books in our small-town library, checking them out and savoring them one at a time. My favorite was the Zane Grey[35] series, including Riders of the Purple Sage, The Rainbow Trail, and The Lone Star Ranger. They featured strong silent heroes who against all odds successfully dealt with greedy ranchers, outlaws, and unscrupulous lawmen. They were usually loners. There was always a beautiful woman involved and she invariably fell for the hero. This was well before I began to transition into my James Dean period.

---

[35] Author and dentist, Grey wrote western adventure stories about rugged cowboys that idealized the American frontier. He is credited with 110 films based on his books.

For the moment, though, I made it to first grade. It wasn't the beginning of any new math, only 2 + 2 = 4, phonetics and penmanship. The Cold War was hot, and I started to learn about air raid sirens and bomb shelters and sitting under one's school desk. Did anyone believe this would provide protection from an atomic bomb? Instinctively I knew that the school, including the desks and us, would have been vaporized in an instant.

Some Saturdays we got to spend a dime and see the serials at the local movie theater with our older siblings or parents. Westerns were big and film cowboys like Roy Rogers, Gene Audrey, The Lone Ranger and Tonto, and the Cisco Kid fascinated us. They were, of course, the strong silent types we seemed to love, and they always got the bad guys. That was a given. They could even fight and never have their hats knocked askew.

*We were all cowboy (author with his siblings and dad, early 1950s)*

We heard our parents laugh as they watched Jackie Gleeson and *The Honeymooners* on the tube or listened to *Amos and Andy* on the radio. Years later, of course, such shows would be politically incorrect because they would be considered racist, sexist, chauvinistic, or all three. Our parents didn't seem to notice or even care. We certainly didn't.

By 1952, Jonas Salk was testing his polio vaccine. It wouldn't be long before we would get vaccinated. For many of us, it would be our very first shots. By that time, though, nearly 60,000 of us would be in wheelchairs or walking with braces. Some were in iron lungs because the dreaded disease prevented them from breathing normally. Later, kids would not take the shots, but rather receive their doses in sugar cubes. This was the beginning of a lifetime of sugar-coated medicines and remedies for us BBs.

Cars were big and heavy with plenty of room and chrome. Most Saturdays we helped our dads wash them lovingly because they represented the freedom of the open road. It was a father/son ritual. Dad would park in the driveway and have me drag the hose around. He would spray the car and put me to work washing the hubcaps and tires while he cleaned the roof and hood. Then we would soap up the sides. There was still plenty of time for trips to the park.

When we traveled, it was usually by car and we stayed in highway motels, not city hotels. That year the first Holiday Inn motor hotel opened in response to our parents' love for inexpensive road travel. Those of us who lived in the city, though, still remember the trains. We asked our parents for metal toy cars and miniature trains so that we could feel connected to the real toys of the grownups. TV started to mix in a little more of the gritty side of life as we continued to watch and listen to Jack Webb ask on the crime show, *Dragnet*.

In 1953, the Korean War was in our living rooms on the tube. I would squirm around. It was disturbing to watch two armies trying to blow each other up right after we had eaten dinner. I watched the explosive images and asked dad lots of questions after he had returned from the conflict. Years later M*A*S*H[36] would become a smash hit with Baby Boomers—even though none of us ever fought there. Atomic bomb explosions were also televised, and the distinct mushroom cloud was more permanently seared into our memories. It's an image that would come to increasingly haunt older BBs, including me.

It didn't seem to bother the grownups at the time, though. Or perhaps it did, and they just had a more stoic attitude about it. Our parents were strong and confident. Everyone knew his or her role. It was a time when many of our parents went on a buying binge and the stock market soared. We heard our folks talking about the death of Russian dictator Stalin. Some guy named Khrushchev took over the Soviet Union and grownups speculated what it meant.

---

[36] This was a popular show that was both serious and comedic about a group of zany doctors treating the wounded during the Korean War.

Years later he would visit the U.S. and during a televised meeting he took off his shoe and banged it on the table and told the world how he would bury America. It was classic stuff that gave me nightmares for a long time. My dad just laughed at him and said, "Just let them try and see what happens." They took the Russian leader to a major league baseball game and he chided our president for staging such an event like it wasn't real.

Musical hits included *How Much Is That Doggie in the Window* and Tony Bennett's *Rags to Riches*. We heard them on the radio. The men talked about boxing and Rocky Marciano was the champ. Marlon Brando was *The Wild One* on the big screen and Marilyn Monroe appeared in the movie *Gentlemen Prefer Blondes*.

Reality started to set in as lung cancer was officially attributed to cigarette smoking. Most of our parents, though, still smoked. They puffed up everywhere, including stores and movie theaters. Some even scoffed at the latest link between smoking and the dreaded disease.

Actor Fess Parker was *Davy Crockett* on the Disneyland TV show. I pestered my parents to buy me a coonskin hat and other goodies. Albert Einstein died. Looking back, maybe it was a sign of the coming times, but Thorazine, the first major tranquilizer, which was later proven to cause birth defects, was invented at this time. Bill Haley and the Comets sang *Rock Around the Clock* and Elvis recorded *That's All Right Mama*. I couldn't buy records yet, but I still heard such hits on the radio.

Alienated and disaffected writers of the young "Beat Generation," like Allen Ginsburg, begin to flock to San Francisco. Not surprisingly, they were called Beatniks.[37] But heck, the oldest of us were only nine and it did not mean much to us. It was just an expression we heard. We fell in love with *Captain Kangaroo* kids' TV show. *The Lawrence Welk Show* and its Champaign music was hot for our parents. *Cat on a Hot Tin Roof*, *Bus Stop*, and *Damn Yankees* lit up Broadway marquees.

Chuck Berry rocked live and recorded *Maybelline*, his first hit. I hummed along and played my air guitar. I enjoyed the

---

[37] They marched to a different drum. These hip folks were about artistic self-expression and the rejection of conventional society.

dismayed look on my parent's faces as they struggled to accept this new form of music. It was the beginning of my feeling like a true rebel. I loved how I could get a cringing reaction from my folks by imitating these revolutionary entertainers.

Disneyland opened, but unless we lived in Southern California odds were, we didn't see it for a long time if ever. Our folks speculated what it would be like to answer the $64,000 question on TV. "Wow, imagine all that money," they kept saying. Matt Dillon was the Marshall on *Gunsmoke* and reminded us that men were supposed to be strong and righteous. Fats Domino sang *Ain't That a Shame*. That wild and crazy Little Richard sang *Tutti Frutti*. Our parents wondered what was becoming of music. Singer Pat Boone's mellow hits were popular and he also had an impact on fashion and style. We pestered our parents to buy us white buck shoes to be like him. I had mine.

On TV we continued to watch *Father Knows Best* and everyone seemed to want to believe that was the way life was supposed to be. *Lassie* was also a favorite and we wondered why our mutts couldn't be that smart. *The Blackboard Jungle* about juvenile delinquency reminded us that there were bad boys out there. Some concerned moms refused to buy certain comic books because they didn't want us to get any funny ideas and end up as juvenile delinquents or worse. I remember my mom, for instance, when she caught me with a red bath towel tied around my neck like Superman's cape while I apparently contemplated jumping off the kitchen counter in an effort to fly.

A whopping $50 billion out of a total U.S. budget of about $72 billion went to the military. This was caused mostly by the Korean War. Ultimate bad boy, James Dean, died at age 24 when his Porsche crashed on California Highway 101. His movie *East of Eden* was out, but *Rebel Without a Cause* and *Giant* hadn't been released yet. He immediately became one of our first romantic heroes. For BBs, it was a time of little league and girl scouts.

My sister Molly was born in 1953. Mom was delighted at the arrival of her namesake. Her birth mirrored that of Paul's with the midwife and doctor delivering her at home. Our folks were so calm under pressure. They truly "just did it".

Stability meant tradition. Before we became a transient nation, most everyone knew everyone else in their neighborhood. Many people lived in the same neighborhood for generations and the adults knew their neighbor's children and often their extended families. It fostered a sense of closeness and community that has tended to disappear over the years.

Summers were magical with picnics and local baseball games. Autumn and Halloween were also special times. No one worried about poison candy or razors in fruit as we would later with our children.

*Group of kids enjoying watermelon in the park.*

For us, it was still the age of innocence. Some of us still believed in Santa Claus—although even by then there was more than a smattering of cynics among us.

The summer had been full of surprises. Paul had been diagnosed with asthma. The doctor said he needed a drier climate. My parents were somber and there were many hushed conversations about what to do. I felt bad that I couldn't play ball or even catch with my brother. I could tell he sensed my unease and that I didn't want to hurt his feelings or embarrass him.

Nonetheless, life was magical even though I felt guilty that it was for me and not my brother. It was a series of familiar things. Trees to climb, the occasional trip with mom and dad for a 15-cent hamburger. Swapping 45 RPM records with a friend so we could drive our parents crazy by playing our favorite songs over and over, big cardboard boxes to cut a door in and create our make-believe cars or use it to build a fort in the back yard. I was still too small to cut the grass with a push mower, but I kept dad company as he cut the neat narrow rows.

The days were the same, but somehow different. Sometimes I wore my cowboy holster with a shiny six-gun and had quick draw contests with friends. If I had collected enough pop bottles, I bought candy cigarettes and pretended to smoke, even mimicking blowing smoke rings. Sometimes I would switch it up and buy packets of baseball cards with a slab of bubble gum the same size. We all had our favorite teams, and it was fun to swap player cards with friends. Mine was the Detroit Tigers. Dad even bought me a Tigers cap from the five and ten cent store. I liked to wear it when we could get enough of the guys together for a spirited game.

The sounds were familiar and comforting as the neighborhood girls would use chalk to draw hopscotch boxes on the sidewalk and play this for hours when they weren't using their jump ropes. Or they played jacks. It was just laughter and kids chatting, but it was the soundtrack of those days. My friend Ricky's dad had given him a little Brownie camera and he captured some of those moments. Although he was allowed to shoot only a limited amount of Kodak rolls because they cost money to process and produce photos at the camera store.

When it rained we would get together indoors to build. We would take our Tinker toys or Lincoln logs and create something. My favorite was my erector set. It had metal ribbons you could bolt together. I liked it because you had to use a screwdriver and small wrench or pair of pliers to tighten up the screws and nuts it required. More than once I was reprimanded for not putting dad's tools back in their proper place in the garage.

We listened to our parents and other adults as they went about their lives. As life changed, they complained in a good-natured way. Mom would say something like, "I never thought I'd see the day when all my kitchen appliances would be electric. Now they are even making electric typewriters." Dad would reply, "If cigarettes keep going up in price, I'm going to quit. A quarter a pack is robbery." Or, "If Joe thinks I'm going to pay 50 cents for a haircut, he can forget about it."

Mom would often touch on cultural changes and dad would nod knowingly. I remember one night at the dinner table. She said, "It is too bad that things are so tough these days. Some married women are having to go to work to make ends meet."

We were completely indoctrinated in the traditional role models where mom took care of the home and kids and dad worked and "brought home the bacon."

Hollywood itself was pushing changes, too. As dad observed, movies were more daring, more liberal. I remember him telling mom they had to be more careful about what I saw. "Ever since they let Clark Gable get away with saying 'damn' in *Gone with the Wind*, it seems every new movie has either 'damn' or 'hell' in it."

(I'm not sure what they would say in today's society where adults and kids frequently use the "F" word.)

And mom would agree and fret even more about the bad examples Hollywood was setting, "Marriage doesn't seem to mean a thing anymore. Those Hollywood stars seem to get divorced and remarried like they change their socks."

These things seemed to make them even more determined than ever to make sure our moral compasses were firmly guiding our lives. They did their part in brainwashing us and pulled out the big guns on Sunday when we went to church.

It was one constant year-round activity. Terms like "no beginning and no end" were incomprehensible to me. I pondered it but just couldn't understand. For many of us, there were no questions like, "Does God exist and if he does, where did he come from?" He did because our parents said so. The fact that we couldn't see him was a minor point to our parents. As dad told me, "You can't see the wind, but you know it's there." Still, that didn't stop me from pondering these weighty questions from time to time, but I already knew what they would say about faith and the way it was, so I just didn't ask.

On Sunday mornings I would put on dark slacks, my only white shirt, and my single tie. Dad would help me tie the knot. I would then snuggle into my only sports coat. It was dark blue. Dad and I dressed the same. I even had a small fedora like him. We were sort of generational twins.

The women all wore hats, many with a sheer veil, or a lacy scarf over their heads. When we went to church there were no blue jeans, shorts, cut-offs, tee shirts, or any of that. Everyone was decked out in their Sunday finest. Us kids felt special to be in such company.

I understood little of the sermons, except that if you didn't behave you were going straight to hell. Nonetheless, it was still a comforting ritual. I was proud that so many people seemed to know and respect my parents. They would approach them before and after church; the men most often tipping their hats to both mom and dad and engage them in pleasantries. They always looked down at me and said how I was growing and that I was a handsome lad. This seemed to be their stock observation. It made me shuffle my feet and not know exactly how to respond, but my parents would beam with pride.

Beyond some semblance of organized religion, including many sermons about morality, church seemed to keep most of the community somehow connected with a certain regular comradery. I felt this and sensed a real link to our town. My biggest fear was that I was somehow sinning and would go to hell. Ironically, this tended to scare the hell out of me. I still believe it was all part and parcel of the guilt that adults of the day used as a tool to make us behave and mold and shape our characters.

Most Sundays we kids had to attend a religious education class. I heard a lot of bible stories. Our teacher, usually a learned older man or woman from the congregation who volunteered time to teach, would endeavor to explain what the Bible stories meant in a language we could understand. Still, it was often confusing and complicated, but since I wasn't ever planning on becoming a preacher when I grew up, I sort of sleepwalked through it.

There was one lesson I remember with total clarity, though. We were learning the Ten Commandments. The kindly old woman who was teaching said, "The Ten Commandments are not multiple choice. You don't get to pick and choose which ones to obey. You must obey them all."

As those words were uttered, she looked directly at me and held my attention. Maybe I was just feeling paranoid or guilty, but her eyes seemed to pierce my soul. I will never know if she just happened to be looking at me when she said those words. Or she saw something in my eyes. But the effect was absolute. Did she know something I didn't about my future life? Whatever the reason for that penetrating look at me, it left a lasting lifelong impression on me. That moment still makes me wince a little.

Other things that made me cringe from that time were not as ominous. Not everyone was on key, for instance, when it came time to join in singing hymns. People, including my family, tended to sit in the same pews Sunday after Sunday. There was a middle-aged widow who sat behind my family who sang off-key.

I was no Pavarotti or Caruso, but I knew enough to sing softly when I couldn't hit the high notes. I just sort of moved my mouth until the song got into my range and I would resume my normal volume. Not her, undaunted she just belted it out, completely flat and extremely loud. Had neighborhood dogs been allowed in the church, they would have howled in protest.

※

In the fall the moment I had dreaded was there. I was off to school. As mom had instructed me, I stood in front of the house on the sidewalk next to the driveway. She said to wait, and she would be out before the bus arrived. I was suddenly uncomfortable in my trousers and a new shirt. Perhaps it was having my shirt buttoned up all the way. I undid the top button. Although a couple of sizes too big, my new shoes also seemed too tight. Even more alarming was the fluttering sensation in my stomach. I didn't know why, but I felt scared. My routine was going to change again. What if the kids picked on me or didn't like me? What would we talk about? What would I say? What if I failed?

I was truly terrified. My thoughts were interrupted as mom called from the porch. "I'll be right there, Jimmy. Just stay put and don't get your clothes dirty."

I glanced back and realized that no matter what happened this first day, mom wouldn't be there to make it right. I held my breath and choked back tears as my eyes watered. I remember muttering to myself, "I have to be brave." As I heard mom approach, I could see the bus coming down the street. It stopped to pick up Johnny a few doors down and then continued its way towards us.

Mom had her hand on my shoulder and was telling me how proud she was of me. She looked down at me and said, "I know you will do well. Just listen to the teachers and do everything they say."

All I could think of was what if the other kids were smarter than me and I looked stupid? What if they made fun of my clothes? These thoughts and more were racing through my mind in a jumble.

As the bus squeaked to a stop in front of us and the door hissed open, mom turned me and grasped me by both shoulders, and gave me a smile and peck on the cheek. As the other kids looked out the windows, I felt myself flush. I turned and trudged up the steps towards the driver. The bus got quiet. The kids all stared at me. I knew some of them and that helped a little. Suddenly they started talking among themselves again. A boy I knew from a couple of blocks over waved at me to join him. Gratefully, I navigated down the aisle and slid onto the seat next to him.

He was shaking his head. "I hear we have Mrs. Kirkland. She is the meanest teacher in school."

I just stared at him. There was that name again. Then I asked, "How do you know?"

"My brother told me. He had her when he started school. Worse, she has a huge wooden paddle."

Just great, I thought, I had a confirmed meanie who liked to paddle kids. As it turned out, though, my fears were unfounded. The worst I was to experience was the occasional swat on the bottom when I was being difficult. But at the moment I knew I would have to behave to stay out of the evil clutches of Mrs. Kirkland. Funny thing was that in reality, the teacher my friend had described turned out to be an ancient (at least to me) lady with her gray hair pulled back in a bun and a look that could freeze hot chocolate, but the disposition of a kindly grandmother.

The memory of her presence would stay with me for a lifetime. Secretly I came to like her. I distinctly recall her gazing at me through thick lenses telling me I could do it or that she knew I could remember something. I think I learned more from her than any other teacher in grade school. I realized I didn't want to disappoint her. I wanted to please her. I suppose this was a sign that my parents brainwashing me was working as expected.

From the first day, I was overwhelmed with doubts and feelings. I would learn later that I wasn't alone or unique in my thoughts. We all tried to look brave and hold back tears as we walked to school with our moms, stood in front of the driveway waiting for the school bus, or rode our bikes as we continued our formal education.

Most of the facilities of the day were basic brick or wooden schoolhouses. Mine was red brick. I liked it. It made me feel important to be part of such a magical and mysterious place. For most of us, the classes were small and basic. Neither the facilities nor the classrooms gave any hint of the high tech that would eventually come to characterize learning centers.

That first day was equal parts exhilarating, scary, and exciting. We were told which classroom to go to and we filed in like sheep to

*Classroom with a vintage typewriter (the early 1950s).*

our homerooms. The first decision for me was whether to sit in the front or the back. I didn't want to be seen by the other boys to be someone angling to be the teacher's pet. Then logic took over and the budding politician in me made me opt for the middle. The desks were one-piece affairs with metal frames painted olive green and the wooden seat and desktop a dark-colored wood. It hardly seemed suitable to me like a bomb shelter, but mine was not to question just to do as I was told.

We all fell silent as a stern-looking middle-aged teacher entered the room. She wrote her name on the board—Mrs. Reilly. Then she took roll call. As she did, she gave each of us one of the most penetrating stares I had ever seen. I didn't avert my eyes but stared right back. She asked a pretty blonde girl in the front row to pass out copies of our class schedule and advised us to memorize it. The shelf under the seat of each desk held a stack of well-used textbooks. English, arithmetic, history, some type of civics book, and a reader.

*The atomic mushroom cloud we all thought would eventually vaporize us.*

I glanced around at my classmates. It seemed to me that they were trying all act the same as I was. Cool and mildly interested. At the end of her sermon about what she expected from us she paused.

"Lastly, when you hear the siren on the loudspeaker, (a wooden box affair mounted high in the corner in the front of the classroom) you will calmly stop doing whatever you are engaged in and crawl under your desk and sit cross-legged on the floor.[38] I will not tolerate any horseplay. Is that clear?" We all nodded. She scanned the room; I suppose in search of troublemakers. "A simple 'Yes ma'am will do."

Like robots, we repeated this.

She then proceeded to guide us through a series of phonetic exercises. I could read some simple words, but truth be told, I wanted to learn how to read proficiently. One of the things that was glaringly obvious to me was that the girls seemed smarter and quicker than the boys at grasping things and raising their hands. I found that interesting. Perhaps something I should discuss with dad during our man-to-man talks.

Recess and lunch periods were uneventful, downright anticlimactic. I'm not sure what I was expecting but it didn't happen. During those first unstructured periods, all of us tended to gravitate to kids we knew. As the school year progressed, these neighborhood cliques expanded to include new friends, which were primarily fellow classmates.

The schools maintained their records and operated with an orderly system of paper and logbooks. There were no computers or computerized files. There were no photocopy machines, only mimeographs where copies were hand-cranked around an inked drum. The results were shiny paper copies with purplish-blue printing. Blackboards were black, not green or white.

A projector was used on the rare occasion when a film with educational value was to be shown. We didn't see many, if any, films in our lives so regardless of the theme, it was exciting. It was mesmerizing to watch the teacher thread the film around spools and channels on the complicated machine. A metal tripod would be placed in the front of the room and the screen unrolled from the bottom, which was then held aloft by a telescoping metal piece behind it. Sometimes the images would be projected onto a bare wall. Invariably, though, at some point in the presentation, the projector bulb would burn out or the film would break

---

[38] These were bomb drills in case those dastardly Russians nuked us.

and flap noisily around. This would either conclude the exercise or there would be a mad scramble as someone ran to the school office for a spare bulb or the teacher spliced the film with a flat mechanical contraption.

At night I often lay awake and heard my parents listen to their radio programs. I often wonder if they had any idea how much I heard at night when I was supposedly tucked into my bed. They not only shared entertainment but talked politics—both office politics and government policy.

Most Saturdays I sat on the edge of the bathtub and watched dad shave. This ritual produced some of my most memorable moments. It was a real connection to this special man. It was a chance to talk to him one on one, besides, I was fascinated by his routine. He would take an old large chipped blue coffee cup from the medicine cabinet. In the bottom of it was a cake of soap. Then he would run hot water and wet his shaving brush, which had a wooden handle and long bristles at the end. He would stir it briskly around the cup and a foamy lather would appear. The smell was fragrant.

At some point, he had traded his straight razor in for a safety razor. I missed seeing him sharpen it on a leather strap that was attached to a towel rack. I asked him about the change, and he told me that Gillette had come out with a safer razor that caused fewer nicks. For the new razor, he would twist the bottom of the handle and the top would flip open. Then he checked the thin, wicked-looking rectangular-shaped razor blade. Satisfied he would put in the stopper and run the sink half full of water. Finally, he would use the brush to lather up his face. I remember those occasions well. But some better than others.

I generally waited until he started the actual process of shaving before talking to him. I am not sure why I did, but I did. Maybe I instinctively didn't want to distract him from his ritual. The dialog varied but not the nature. I considered these man-to-man talks. One such encounter went like this.

"Dad last week they had us hide under our desks at school."

"I'm sure they had a good reason, son."

"I suppose. They are having these bomb drills now. Is someone going to attack us?"

He evidently heard the anxiety in my voice. As he rinsed the foam off his razor in the sink basin by swishing it around, he turned and looked directly at me. "Of course not, Jimmy."

"Then why are they making us hide under our desks?"

"It is just a precaution. It won't really happen."

"Then it seems silly to do it."

"Just do as you are told, and everything will be alright."

"I will, dad." Then I blurted out, "You aren't going to die, are you, dad?"

He put his razor down on the side of the sink and just looked at me. I continued. "Larry's dad died. They sent him to stay with his grandparents for a while."

Dad picked up his razor and resumed shaving and between stokes said, "Yes I know. I went to see Mr. Foster."

"How, if he is not here anymore?"

"When a person dies the funeral parlor has a viewing out of respect before they close the casket so people can say their goodbyes."

"I'm not sure I would like to look at a dead person." Inwardly I shuddered at the fleeting thought of my dad laying there in a box. Dead.

No response as dad concentrated on his shaving. I pressed on, "What happens to us if you and mom die?"

He put his razor down again and splashed water on his face before drying with a towel. Then he put both hands on my shoulders. "Mom and I aren't going anywhere . . ."

I interrupted him, "But Larry's dad . . ."

"You don't have to worry. We will be here."

His tone of voice said that the conversation was over. I could usually tell when it wasn't a good idea to push further. At some point, he would simply say, "Because I said so. That's why."

I remained quiet while I watched him tear some little pieces of toilet paper off the roll and stick them to the few small nicks on his face. And, that concluded our talk.

I still thought about weighty matters like bombs and life and death. It was unsettling, but they were usually quickly pushed to the back of my mind. I had other things to worry about.

At our school, like in most of the country, we drew circles in the playground dirt and played marbles during recess and other playtimes. The concept was simple. A bunch of marbles was placed tightly together in the center of the circle and a player would brace one hand on the ground outside the playing area and put a marble in his shooter hand such that the thumb could propel it. He would then press against the tripod hand to hold it steady. The girls never played marbles. It was strictly a boys' game.

We all had our technique. The shooter marble was bigger than the others. The object was to use it to knock marbles out of the circle and still have your shooter marble inside. Clear glass marbles with slices of color in them, called "cat eyes," were prized. The winner, of course, "took all the marbles." It was competitive, but fun. We all carried our cloth bag of marbles with the drawstring. It was part of our gear.

Yo-yos and spinning tops also easily amused us. The latter were fashioned out of wood and painted bright colors—usually red, green, or blue. We learned to wrap twine around them then put the loop at the end of the string on our middle finger and toss them onto the sidewalk and jerk the string, making them spin for as long as possible. It took some skill but provided hours of fun. Maybe not as sophisticated as today's video or electronic games, but at least it helped kids develop dexterity skills.

The basics were still being taught in school to us BBs. For us, the biggest thing we had to worry about was learning the three "Rs" of "riting, reading, and rithmatic." We were graded on deportment, not conduct. We didn't have any classmates who were on medication. We had never heard of such conditions as attention deficit disorder or other such conditions.

As I quickly learned, bad boys were called to the front of the class and dealt with, often with a swift swat from a wooden paddle. Or worse, they were sent to the principal's office for the supreme punishment which normally included spanking and the obligatory note home to our folks. The embarrassment of bending over in front of the class for a swat on the bottom was worse for me than receiving punishment in the privacy of the school office.

No one thought of suing. You took your medicine. If you were disciplined, your parents took the teacher's side, not yours. It was just assumed that you must have done something to deserve such punishment. On reflection, probably 99.9 percent of those paddled were boys.

Looking back, the lawyers of the day missed out on a bonanza. Of course, lawyers in those days were not allowed to advertise. Perhaps if they had it would have been a different story. The few of us who were truly incorrigible were sent to the principal's office regularly. He or she was the school's ultimate enforcer.

Rightly or wrongly, there were no special schools for either the hardcore unruly or the slow learners among us. Even our most rebellious were usually a little bit intimidated by the stern-faced middle-aged man or woman we were sure to encounter in the school office. If our parents had to be called to the school, we faced an equally scary scenario, as they were sure to side with the school powers. Most of us believed that we had little choice but to behave or willingly face the consequences.

I think it was the second grade that I got an F in deportment, which is now called conduct because I was guilty of passing notes to my buddies in class on numerous occasions. Hey, it seemed harmless when we did it. We were making plans for later. When I presented my report card to my folks, dad expressed his disappointment and mom just looked thoughtful. This made no sense and scared me. The next day she informed me that she would be riding the bus with me to visit the school. I was worried. I couldn't imagine what diabolical plan she had in store for me. I soon found out. It turned out to be an outright ambush.

She marched alongside me into my homeroom to confer with the teacher. After the pleasantries, she got right to the point. "I'm sure Jimmy deserved the mark he got in deportment." Then added, "I just wanted to let you know that if you can't make him behave, I can. And, I'm more than happy to sit in on class to make sure he does."

I flushed from the humiliation as my classmates snickered at me. The teacher restored order to the classroom with just a look. Then said, "I don't think that will be necessary, will it James?" Both the teacher and mom raised their eyebrows and looked at me as I muttered assurances that would not be necessary. Mom wished the teacher a good day and marched out of the classroom. I was stunned. Boy, I didn't see that coming.

Although in different buildings, school complexes were often co-located on the same property. There were no middle schools, just grammar or elementary and high schools. After 8th grade, you made it to the big time. Our high school and grade school were separated by the athletic field with football goalposts and a baseball diamond. So, I frequently saw older kids and wanted to be just like them. Those in upper grades, especially high school were generally held in awe. For me, it seemed so far off that I was sure I would never get there.

One of my first brushes with growing up came in the form of another crush on a member of the opposite sex. For me, this puppy love caused a genuine heartache and a stirring of things to come. I experienced it but didn't understand it. I sure couldn't talk to mom about it. It also seemed an embarrassing subject to bring up with dad. After all, I didn't even understand my feelings. Never in my wildest dreams could I imagine that my parents had at one time passed through the same fleeting stage of life.

My knowledge of the biology of sex was woefully lacking when compared to the advancement of today's youth in such matters. To be sure, there were some stories whispered on the playground. Usually, they were told by the more "knowing" kids to those of us who didn't have a clue. Even so, they usually contained more myth than truth and more distortion than fact.

I started to enter another level of awareness in the way I interacted with others. I suppose unconsciously I built on what I had learned in kindergarten and first grade. I begin to see that friendships and mini social groups were formed frequently not only as a function of the neighborhood where each of us lived but how "cool" you were perceived to be by others, but I didn't yet make the connection that our parents' lot in life had a direct impact on our standing in our world as well.

One thing I came to realize more and more, though, was that conflicts could easily become physical. In my limited world, often petty jealousies or emerging hormones and raging testosterone ended in a playground fight. Sometimes the result was a bloody nose, a shiner in the form of a black eye, or even a few loose teeth. Whether they involved me or someone I knew, or even kids out of my circle, these encounters made me uncomfortable and sent my heart racing.

Even then I was sure that those who engaged in such behavior also experienced the dual feeling of real fear and exhilaration. This was true for me. The first time I got into a shoving match that was threatening to escalate into real fisticuffs, it seemed as if my pounding heart would burst from my chest.

I wasn't worldly or mature enough yet to articulate or analyze it, but I saw firsthand that reputations began to be formed based on looks, attitude, brains, and demeanor. What wasn't clear to me at the time is that these groupings would propel us into the next stage of our lives where social interaction and self-worth would take on a whole new meaning. At the same time, rattling around in my brain, was the mandate to "be my own man." It was like walking a tightrope.

No matter, my immediate world meant I had to be careful, and I was. Controlling my behavior and picking my fights was difficult to master, a real balancing act. More difficult than that were the actions or nonactions of your friends. Rodger, in particular, caused me a lot of angst. I liked him. He was a steadfast friend and fun to play and hang out with. Unlike 90 percent of the boys of the time, though, was that Rodger was rather pudgy, which invited the school bullies to pick on him. The dilemma for me, of course, was that since Rodger could not or would not defend himself, what should I do?

When this first started to manifest itself, words from the adults in my life, people like dad and my Uncle Chuck and my heroes on the radio and in the movies, started to shape my actions. "Be a man. Do what is right. Stand with your friends." There were times when these thoughts all pinged around in my brain like a pinball machine gone wild.

On top of that, usually, the guys who did the bullying weren't looking for trouble with me, but those close to me. Although slender (skinny according to mom) I was tall and gangly for my age and just wasn't an inviting target. Some of my friends were another matter. In such cases, it would have been easy for me to stand aside or look the other way and remain silent. If I acted, I knew that it meant some sort of confrontation and it was going to land me in hot water with my teachers and the principal, not to mention my mom. Dad for his part would sternly lecture me but I knew from that twinkle in his eyes that he was secretly proud of me for standing my ground.

When I was in Mrs. Follet's third-grade class my first real test was on the playground during recess. Tommy, a big husky kid who liked to throw his weight around, started to tease Rodger.

Tommy said, "The only person who likes fat Roger the dodger is his mother." Then he shoved him. "What's a matter fat boy? Cat got your tongue?"

I approached and stood in front of Rodger. "Come on, Tommy. Knock it off."

Surprised he looked at me and said, "You come on, Jimmy. You aren't really going to defend fat boy, are you?"

"He is my friend, and he can't help it."

I remember the uncertainly in Tommy's eyes and that would have probably been the end of the incident. But instead of fizzling out, some of Tommy's buddies and other kids urged him on and things escalated. With a shrug, he pushed me. I pushed back harder. The shock and hesitation in his eyes were absolute as he staggered back.

I'm not sure what would have happened next. Perhaps one of us would have ended up with a shiner. My legs were vibrating with nerves and I couldn't catch my breath. Boy was I relieved when a teacher yelled at us and approached. He scolded us and escorted us to the principal's office. The result was a swift smack on our butts and a note to take home to our parents.

I knew I would get my parent's dreaded "disappointed" speech. Something to be avoided like the plague. (No, unlike the Middle Ages there was no plague when I was a kid, but it was a popular expression all the same.) On the other hand, although it was a nonevent, it fostered and enhanced my reputation as someone not to be taken lightly. It turned out that I was able to parlay my undeserved stature for the remainder of the school year, so I felt it was worth it.

But I had a more immediate problem. I didn't know was how I should interact with Tommy going forward. Were we now enemies? I was afraid to leave the classroom after the last bell but knew I had to at some point. Was he waiting for me to try and beat me up? I went out into the playground. Yup, he was there. Instead of going in the opposite direction, I approached him. Fortunately, we were alone and unnoticed by the other students.

He eyed me warily. "What do you want?"

I shocked him when I impulsively held out my hand, just like I had been taught. "I don't want an enemy. There is no need for that, and I have nothing against you."

He hesitated and said nothing but finally did shake my hand. I continued. "Rodger is my friend. Do you think it is necessary to pick on him?"

I thought he looked a little embarrassed. "I guess not. I was only fooling around; besides we cool kids have got to stick together."

I had just moved up a notch on the school social ladder. If not a friend, I instinctively knew I had made an ally. Perhaps mom's lesson of "nipping things in the bud" had stuck with me. She certainly repeated it often enough. It was an incident and outcome that became firmly planted in my mind and would serve me in my life, both in my professional and personal activities as I tried to meet challenges head-on, instead of kicking the can down the road. To be sure, I was not always successful, but the approach helped.

Later that day when I was alone at home my legs shook uncontrollably. I realized I had acted impulsively. I had just blurted words out. I admonished myself for a decided lack of control. Did people just say things without thinking them through? It seemed that I did. It was a bit confusing and bewildering to me. Perhaps it was something I should talk to dad about . . .

I did a lot of thinking while lying in bed in the dark. Some nights thoughts of school, girls, and my life were continually running through my mind in an endless loop. For me, social behavior was beginning to take up more thought and time than schoolwork and my lessons. Other nights and depending on the season, I worried if I would make whatever team I was vying for. As it turned out, I was fortunate to enjoy success on the field or court.

I heard my parents and other adults talking more about race and ethnic groups. We had Black kids in our school. I was friendly with them in a casual way, but I sensed some disconnect in the way white kids interacted with them. Most were like me. Although friendly, they did not have any Black friends. We just didn't hang out together. Was that an invisible barrier because of what we heard or saw in adults? I don't know.

The one cross-over point was sports. And, even then it was the formal school sports teams where we came together and found some comradery and not pick-up games. There were exceptions, but in general, that was the nature of things.

At the time, they were not referred to as African Americans or Blacks. Some folks used the term, "colored folks." Some called them Negros because that is what they called themselves. Many of these terms have evolved and rightly so.

Our town was small, but there were well-defined sections. There was an Italian neighborhood. We had a lot of Germans who had settled there for whatever reason and, not surprisingly, there was a large German enclave. The Black community had their part of town. All of these sections were well defined. You could tell where one ended and the other began. There was a poor white section and a more affluent white section with larger homes and nicer cars. My family was neither poor nor rich and like most white families of the day we were working or middle class.

We tended not to visit or play in other neighborhoods, instead, as dad would say, "sticking to our home neck of the woods." Since our social circles tended to reflect our parent's economic status at that time, that is the way it was. Later, of course, that was all destined to change.

Other BBs were being shaped by the same types of events as we all walked along the path on our coming-of-age journey. Like me, by 1955 in New Jersey, Brian was finishing the 3$^{rd}$ grade at St. Anthony's school. He was a favorite of the nuns, not because he was a particularly good student. Indeed, he was average. Yet, he had a certain outgoing charm. Popular with his classmates even at that very young age it was already obvious to Father Daniel, the vice-principal, that the boy had the raw talent to become a gifted athlete. He watched him during recess dominating games of dodge ball or red rover, red rover come over. (You remember the game where two opposite lines of kids were formed. They would lock arms and a member of the opposite team would try to run through the line. If they successfully broke through, he or she could choose a member of the team who would go back and join the other group.)

The good father also attended many of the boy's little league games, where Brian's dad told the priest that he dreamed of the boy one day roaming centerfield for the New York Yankees.

That same year, Sally was only in second grade in McKeesport, but already little boys were becoming infatuated with her. Her mom dressed her like a little doll, and she had more than one boy wanting to carry her books home from school. Although only seven years of age, she was becoming aware of the gender roles of the day. That is, while all kids played, the more strenuous and rugged games were the exclusive domain of the boys and the girls watched and giggled. Her teachers of the day did nothing to discourage this behavior, nor did her parents. In the eyes of her father, she was a precious and fragile doll and the pride and joy of his life.

Out in Tucson, Joe was only four and not yet in school. He was still running the streets and yards with his friends in his upper-middle-class neighborhood.

In Long Beach, Kathy was the top student in her 3rd-grade class. After school, she would play, but also spend time hanging around her mother's flower shop. She loved the earthy fragrant smell. There she would watch her mom working and interacting with customers. She also spent time talking to her mom as she watched the older woman deal with vendors and make floral arrangements. Her mom had a quiet confidence that the girl admired. Not surprisingly, one theme she continually imparted to Kathy was that she could do and be anything in life she wanted. There were no limits. She informed the girl that she had what she termed "an equal partnership" with her father.

Slowly leading BBs were heading towards puberty and becoming teenagers. It promised to be exciting, scary, and confusing in varying degrees. We didn't know it would be a time characterized by rock and roll and rockets that would shoot satellites into space and make some Americans a bit uneasy. This timeframe also provided some of the first glimpses into the radical cultural and technological changes that would follow.

Other events were also muddying the waters of my life. Dad, who by that time was a teacher in a rural school district close to our town, started to have mysterious conversations with someone on the phone. I heard parts of the conversation but was still in the dark as to the nature of things. The big announcement finally came one evening at the dinner table. Before the start of the new school year, were going to move to Arizona for Paul's health. Talk about turning my world upside down.

# Chapter 3

# Sock Hops & Beginning to Rock (1956 – 1960)

For many of us, the early years meant moving from town or city neighborhoods to suburbia. It was a time when we started to notice more detail in our home environments. Naugahyde[39] recliners, pseudo-Scandinavian couches, high fidelity (Hi-Fi) with vacuum tubes encased in fake blond wood cabinets, not to mention the inevitable pole lamps, all typified our parents' homes. By this time, many of us were eating TV dinners on aluminum trays placed on little individual fiberglass tables with unstable legs. Our parents probably didn't realize it or maybe they did—we surely didn't—but they had casually started the end of the centuries-old family practice of sitting down around a table to eat, talk and share news and stories.

Our food was good but basic. It wouldn't be until many years later that I learned there were more than five seasonings, condiments, and sauces—salt, pepper, ketchup, mustard, and gravy. We had a meat and potato diet with lots of things like stew, dumplings, chicken, and meatloaf. For us,

---
39    This was a popular form of fake leather.

with exception of pizza, there were no ethnic culinary adventures. We had plenty of homemade cookies and pies. Looking back, we seldom ate out, but when we did it was a real treat.

Vintage Formica kitchen.

I became more aware of money. Dad always had a roll of cash. There were no ATMs. You either had to go to the bank during normal business hours and cash a check or to a grocery store to buy something and write a bigger check to get cash back. Often the amount you could get back was limited to a maximum of ten or twenty dollars. I loved the trips to the bank with dad because it meant I would get a huge lollipop to enjoy.

Cash was also necessary because door-to-door salesmen were plentiful. You never knew when the Fuller Brush man, someone selling encyclopedias, or a vacuum cleaner salesman would show up.

Dwight Eisenhower, or Ike as he was affectionately known, became the first president I remember as a person. He was everybody's grandfather. He seemed so calm and unconcerned about the state of things. I guess he was relaxed because he always seemed to be playing golf. Everyone seemed to have great confidence in him. After all, he had led America and its allies to victory against the Nazis in World War II.

We were being vaccinated against dreaded polio. Our parents put their newspapers down long enough to watch the new Chet Huntley and David Brinkley *NBC Nightly News*. They reported what, why, when, and where. Imagine this time when newsmen reported the news with no pontificating. Our moms and sisters tuned into two new soap operas—*As the World Turns* and *The Edge of Night*. The beginning of the interstate highway system that would alter our landscape and lifestyles excited our parents.

They boasted was that you would be able to drive coast-to-coast without a single red light. It sounded good, but as multi-lane super-highways replaced often picturesque two-lane roads, they bypassed small towns and cities. This killed mom-and-pop businesses by the thousands, including restaurants and motels. It allowed the big chain eateries and motels to dominate. People no longer stopped in hamlets and small urban areas to rest or spend money.

With the lack of traffic, some towns died, others were transformed into hollowed-out shells of their former selves. It was the beginning of the death of Main Street America. The final nail in their coffins was the rise of shopping malls and big-box stores. Then came Walmart and whatever small specialty shops on Main Street that were left were shuttered and gone. Progress had essentially finished killing small-town America.

We didn't stop to think about what this meant. We were adolescents and had other things to worry about. Later our generation would resent how our parent's generation had let this happen.

For the moment, though, we listened as the Platters reached the top ten pop chart with *Only You* and *The Great Pretender*. Elvis' *Blue Suede Shoes* and *Love Me Tender* and Doris Day's *Que Sera Sera* were also top songs. Elvis' first full-length appearance happened on the Dorsey Brothers Show as he sang *Heartbreak Hotel*. Later he also appeared on the Milton Berle TV show and sang *Hound Dog*. The girls giggled nervously at the slick, swivel-hipped singer. We boys liked the music but didn't get what all the fuss was about.

Actors John Wayne and Susan Hayward shot the movie *The Conqueror* in Utah downwind of the site of nuclear tests. By 1960, 90 percent of the 220-person cast and crew had contracted some type of cancer—eventually, 43 died because of it. Our parents didn't seem concerned by the rumors of the cause. After all, they believed the government would never do anything to hurt us. Hey, they were our parents. They knew best. For the first time, white-collar employees surpassed blue-collar workers.

Our emerging music got a name in 1956 when the term "Rock and Roll" was used by Alan Freed, a New York DJ. Elvis's *Don't Be Cruel* was popular. James Brown (who would later become the Godfather of Soul—and we thought soul was a religious term) recorded his first record. Little Richard wailed *Long Tall Sally*. Harry Belafonte produced his first album and calypso music emerged as hot and different. We loved it all. On TV we watched

*The Price Is Right*. But what grabbed our attention was when *American Bandstand* with Dick Clark started on national TV in 1957. It was a great chance for boys and girls to flirt, dance, and form relationships after school. We were growing up. The oldest of us was only 11 and couldn't drive, but dad had instilled the power of the car and the open road in us. On TV, *Route 66* burst on the scene and we romanticized what it would be like to take to the road looking for adventure. This would inspire many of us later to take at least one summer road trip to do just that.

I remember that my parents and the country were stunned when the Russians launched Sputnik, the world's first satellite. "How dare they? Americans were supposed to be first," seemed the prevailing attitude. We weren't used to playing catch up. We did eventually top them because later that year we sent up one with a dog in it. Although we couldn't tell you why, most of us reflected our parent's concern and felt like the sky was falling. By then we all participated in regular atomic bomb air raid drills. This was the peak year for BB births with over 4 million.

The fledgling civil rights movement was increasingly having an impact on the American scene. In 1957 we watched the drama on TV at Central High School, in Little Rock, Arkansas, when Governor Faubus ordered the entrance blocked by the state's National Guard to keep Black students out of the building. Undaunted, President Eisenhower sent in federal troops to allow their entry. It was tense. Our parents, aunts, and uncles argued over the plight of Blacks. Later race relationships would have a direct impact on my life and all BBs and the country at large.

Before the full impact hit us, though, we were busy perfecting our slow and fast dances, and Frankie Avalon, Paul Anka, and Fabian were hot. The Everly Brothers sang *Bye Bye Love* and *Wake Up Little Susie*. Buddy Holly's first records, *That'll Be the Day* and *Peggy Sue* were released and hit radio stations. He also appeared with his group, the Crickets, on the Ed Sullivan Show. Sam Cooke's first record, *You Send Me*, was also big. That year TV featured *Have Gun Will Travel*, *Maverick*, *Perry Mason*, and *The Real McCoys*. We ate it up. After all, these shows reflected exactly how life was supposed to be. *West Side Story* debuted as a popular play.

We also watched as Elvis was inducted into the Army. Hula hoops[40] were the craze. We heard more about the Beatnik movement as it spread throughout the U.S. and Europe. We were too young to hang out in coffee houses, but the notion affected our lives—even if we were not quite sure what it was. Phrases like "Daddy-o" and "Cool man" became part of our lexicon. The Everly Brothers *Hey Bird Dog* and *All I Have to Do Is Dream* and *The Chipmunks' Song, Purple People-Eater, Lollipop,* and Kingston Trio's *Tom Dooley* were all the rage. The Coasters weighed in with *Yakety Yak* and Jackie Wilson scored with *Lonely Teardrops*. We heard Chuck Berry sing *Johnny B. Goode*, wailing with his guitar. Johnny Otis got us hoppin' with *Hand Jive*, and Bobby Darin's *Splish Splash* was big. We were groovin'.

*Groovin to the jukebox stamp.*

When singers Buddy Holly, the Big Bopper, and Richie Valens were killed in a plane crash near Mason City, Iowa—we romanticized the tragedy as the day the music died. Later singer Don McLean would memorialize this in a song called *American Pie*.[41]

D.H. Lawrence's banned book, *Lady Chatterley's Lover,* was ruled not obscene and was finally allowed into the U.S. Teenage BBs of both sexes tried to find ways to get a copy. Chubby Checker's *Twist* topped the charts. We slow danced to Paul Anka's *Put Your Head on My Shoulder* and Dion's *Teenager In Love*. It fit because many of us teenagers were in love. Bobby Darin sang *Dream Lover* and *Mack the Knife*. On TV we watched *Bonanza* and *Rawhide* in our lingering romance with westerns. At the movies, *Some Like It Hot* with Marilyn Monroe sizzled and to us, it seemed like maybe blondes did have more fun.

Rebel Fidel Castro swept down from the mountains and disposed of dictator Batista and took control of Havana, Cuba. No one

---

[40] A large plastic hoop that is twirled around the waist.
[41] The lyrics were so quintessentially American, including "Drove my Chevy to the levee but the levee was dry. And them good ole boys were drinking whiskey and rye. Singin' this'll be the day that I die . . .

knew he was a communist, but it wouldn't be long before he tipped his hand.[42] South Vietnam asked the U.S. for aid to fight against communist North Vietnam. Even though the oldest of us had become teenagers, we were too young to realize that this conflict signaled one of the defining events of our generation. It was a war BBs ended up fighting. The domino theory[43] that politicians talked about had nothing to do with pizza. It was about communism.

Coal was still king, and I remember it was delivered by a big dusty dump truck and shoveled down a coal chute into our basement. Dad and I would then shovel the big pile into a bin that was used to feed our furnace. Dirty work, but still I felt a real sense of importance to be allowed to work with dad to keep the house warm during the winter.

In our spare time, we were glued to the tube. A study at the time showed that nearly 90 percent of the country watched over 40 hours of TV every week. By this time boys were greasing their hair back with products like 'Dixie Pomade' and were all dancing in the local gym at sock hops. We were not allowed to wear our shoes in the gym for fear we would scratch the hardwood basketball floor.

All the girls wore thick white bobby socks. We wore socks of varying colors, making sure to select a pair with no holes. Nothing was worse than showing up at a sock hop with a hole in your socks. (Many years later when I was dating the woman who would eventually become my wife, I invited her to a Japanese restaurant for our first date. The diners sat at low tables. You had to remove your shoes at the door. And, yup, I had a hole in my sock. It was ironic and brought back some fond memories.)

The girls sat on one side of the gym, the boys on the other side. You had to make the slow walk across the floor in front of everybody to ask a girl to dance. The biggest fear was, what if she said no? Even if she said yes, for a few minutes you would be

---

[42] Almost from the beginning the US worried Castro was too leftist with his reforms. Finally, after about a year in power, he declared, "I am a Marxist-Leninist and shall be one until the end of my life. Marxism or scientific socialism has become the revolutionary movement of the working class." By this time, no one was really shocked by the revelation.

[43] The theory that a communist government in one nation would quickly lead to communist takeovers in neighboring states, each falling like a perfectly aligned row of dominos; however, with the exception of Laos and Cambodia, communism failed to spread throughout Southeast Asia at that time.

out there alone until some other brave souls joined in. The critical number of couples seemed to be three. Once three couples or more were swaying to a slow song or gyrating to fast music then groups of couples would join in the mix. We also danced in diners and cafes to jukeboxes.

Like most boys, I had my 'getting ready' hair ritual. My hair was cut short and flat on the top with the sides long. I would slick the sides back with a hair paste-like Dixie Pomade into what was called a DA (duck's ass, yes that was the name). Invariably we all got pimples at the most inconvenient time. If it happened to me, I would go against mom's advice and pop them. I'm not sure if it really helped but I thought it did and it certainly made them less noticeable. The only consolation was that almost everybody had the same problem.

By 1958, *Seventy-Seven Sunset Strip* was hot on TV. Sauvé actor Efrem Zimbalist Junior was truly the coolest of TV detectives. Teen heartthrob Edd Byrnes played his wisecracking sidekick and womanizer, Kookie. We all ran around trying to imitate the favorite saying about him, "Kookie, Kookie lend me your comb." Singer Connie Stevens turned the catchphrase into a popular song. It all came about because he continuously combed his hair while posturing and admiring himself in a mirror. Years later, this habit would become a trademark of the hip Fonz who stared in *Happy Days*. After all, we had to maintain our ducktails.

※

While all of this was happening, I had nagging thoughts in the back of my mind. A real unease. Foremost was what Paul's condition meant for me. Something was going to change. I knew that the doctor had told my parents that Paul needed a hot dry climate because of his asthma and dad had decided to accept a teaching job in Arizona and we were soon to be off. We started collecting boxes from the grocery store. With our help, mom was systematically packing up our belongings. The big moving van came. Suddenly the house was empty. It was a bit creepy to spend the last night in the house sleeping on the floor in a sleeping bag. I wasn't sure how I felt, except that I know I was unsettled and excited at the same time.

Right before this great change mom had scheduled our annual trip to the Sears portrait gallery for our formal family portraits. We visited the nearest Sears store all dressed in our Sunday finest. It was a ritual performed by most families of the day. The gallery had a wall with various scenes that could be pulled down like window shades. There were generic city skylines, mountain scenes, green forests, and others. My folks generally chose the library scene. It featured realistic renderings of classic wooden shelves lined with a great many books.

The photographer would have us kids sit and pose in chairs and have mom perched on a barstool. Dad would then stand behind and put his hand on mom's shoulder. The result was the classic traditional family portrait. We had framed versions hung around our home and often sent them to grandparents and other favorite relatives, too. We tended to take fewer photos in those days, and they were more posed. They required thought because there were only so many pictures on a roll of Kodak film and it cost money to send them to the lab for processing.

With today's digital cameras and electronic pictures that is not even a consideration. And, with virtually everyone in possession of a cell phone with a built-in camera they can snap stills and videos at will and just store and share them digitally. They can even do selfies. Something we never really thought of. The popularity of studio galleries and their services has waned to the point where the only folks who avail themselves of them today are couples trying to capture some formal event like a wedding. This specific sitting for us was to turn out to be our last one in Michigan as we prepared for the big move.

At this time, dad had a green Pontiac Chiefdom car. It was big with the head of an Indian chief on the hood. When I asked my dad what an Indian chief had to do with our car, he told me the story of the chief. My dad seemed to have more information than an encyclopedia.

"Our car is named after the great Indian chief, Pontiac. He was the leader of the Ottawa tribe and was famous for fighting the British occupation around the Great Lakes."

I listened attentively and couldn't wait to tell my friends. I was sure they didn't know the story. I think most of the boys my age found glee in being a sort of know it all. I sure did. At the time I thought it made me look smart and my parents even smarter.

It was a time of book knowledge. Door-to-door salesmen went house to house to sell encyclopedias. The typical set contained 10 to 30 volumes with information about everything. All parents bought them for their kids. Short of going to the library, they were the definitive source for research. Imagine no Google, just old-fashioned flipping pages to learn something. It was the golden age of paper knowledge as opposed to today's digital universe. The lack of GPS also meant that maps were large, folded things or pages in a book of maps called an atlas.

Dad had been studying maps and kept telling us we would drop south and take Route 40 and head west. He estimated it would take us a week to make the 2,000-mile journey. Somewhere in Missouri, we would change to a more southerly route for the final push. I couldn't read the map he kept folded in his back pocket but was glad he knew the way because I sure didn't.

Construction had begun in the interstate highway system, but our trip was on two-lane roads. There were few bypasses around urban areas, and I got to see main street American in so many towns and cities that I lost count. For me, the trip was a blur. Mile after mile. Every time we would pass some attraction, like some famous cavern or the world's largest teepee, I would beg dad to stop, but he just told me that there wasn't time or money and kept driving. From diner to diner and roadside motel to roadside motel we crept across the country. We only averaged about 40 miles per hour.

When we stopped at gas stations there was no self-service. An attendant dressed in a uniform—usually coveralls with a bow tie—would ask and dad would tell him to fill it up with ethyl[44] and check the oil. They would thoroughly clean not just the windshield but the other windows and side mirrors as well. I was grateful to stretch my legs and was fascinated by the fueling process. Many of the pumps had a large glass bubble at the top. The gas was hand-pumped up into this. I watched as the bubble filled with amber fuel. Then it would drain down the hose into the car's gas

---

[44] This type of gas vastly improved performance by adding lead. Although being diluted to a ratio of one part per thousand, the lead additive produced gasoline without the loud, power-robbing knock in engines. Alas, it also poluted the environment.

tank. Along with Texaco and Sunoco, there was Sinclair, Humble, and Rt. 66 and many other brands. Dad's favorite was Standard Oil, but when he needed gas, he bought whatever was being sold at the next station. They weren't called gas stations, but service stations because you got service. What a concept. Self-service was essentially unheard of.

My parents would usually give me some change and I could buy a bottle of soda pop to enjoy. In Texas, I saw a man take a bottle of pop and pour a small cellophane package of shelled salted peanuts into it. That looked good and I imitated him. Drinking a bottle of my favorite Nehi grape soda while getting a mouthful of peanuts to crunch was delicious. For years that is how I enjoyed my pop. I never saw this in the East and guessed it was a Southern and Western thing. Paul and Molly would sometimes join me, but they mostly slept while I gazed out at American zipping by my window.

We made it to our intended destination in Arizona, which was a town in the high desert about 75 miles south of Tucson. At almost a mile high, dad said it was hot, dry, and the perfect climate for Paul. My parents found a small house typical of that era and after a couple of days in another motel, the furniture truck showed up.

Up to that point I had lived and gone to school with Black kids, but never a single Latino. They were different from me, especially culturally. Not in a bad way, simply different. They saw me differently too; and I learned a new word when they called me, Paul and Molly "gringos." It didn't bother me, but it slowly dawned on me that I was now in the minority because my neighborhood was predominately Latinos. As I looked around that was true of most of the town. They seemed as curious about me as I was about them. Unconsciously I mimicked a version of their southwest Mexican accent as I sought out friendships. I wanted to fit in with them.

Unlike today, I don't remember immigration being a hot-button issue. We lived close to the border and that meant there were a lot of folks of Mexican descent. Maybe economic and security conditions were better south of the border at that time and people didn't feel compelled to migrate north in waves. I don't know.

Nonetheless, looking back, it was a time when all of us, especially BBs, were sorting out our personal feelings about others. Back in Michigan, there were some Blacks in our school. It wasn't a perfect world and there was some overt and covert hostility by white kids. This was mostly in the form of derogatory comments uttered by some. Terms they probably learned from their parents. There was an invisible barrier there. Many of our parents acted and talked in what would be deemed an insensitive manner today. Others were unapologetic racists and didn't see minorities as equals at all.

It didn't fully register with me, but I would realize later that my dad was more enlightened than my mom. I didn't dwell on these often-hidden feelings or invisible walls but could sense them.

For most of us kids, it didn't seem deliberate but both they and us seemed reluctant to expand our relationship boundaries. We were polite to one another but did not truly seek out friendships with each other. Looking back, they tended to hang with other Black kids, and we tended to gravitate towards other white kids. Was this discrimination? I don't know. Would I have even known if there had been subtle discrimination?

The reality is that I now found myself in an environment where most kids were overwhelmingly different from me—at least in appearance. More precisely they were Mexicans. There was not the diversity of the Latin community like today where many are from Central and South America.

I was different with my khaki slacks and book bag. I quickly realized that the uniform of the day was blue jeans and a white tee shirt. My parents were understanding about helping me with this wardrobe change. The only hiccup was when mom pressed my jeans. I was the only kid ever in school who had a razor-sharp crease (like dress pants) on his jeans. This brought me some unwanted attention from the other kids, but once I convinced mom not to do it anymore, it passed.

It wasn't completely smooth sailing, but after the initial posturing and few shoving matches, though, things settled down and they seemed to accept me. I found it comfortable to be part of the crowd. I often wonder if my unconscious acceptance on my part was because I was part of the minority and needed to fit in. I will probably never know. That is just the way it happened.

That didn't mean there weren't unseen dynamics at work. There were, but I wasn't mature enough to even identify these hidden issues. These had nothing to do with us kids, but more about adults. In my home, they surfaced almost immediately. There was a girl in my class. Her name was Angela. I thought she was the prettiest girl I had ever seen. I flirted with her and she seemed to like me back. So, it was a no-brainer when we had the first dance of the year and I asked her to go with me. This was a transition time when school dances started to stop being the girls on one side and the boys on the other side of the room. In a way, we were learning to date. Boys would ask girls to social events. It was casual, nothing heavy. Nonetheless, it was a pairing off as we struggled to understand our raging emotions and the attraction and prevailing social customs.

I had already asked Angela and she had agreed we would meet at the dance and hang out together. I was excited and sitting in the kitchen a few days later watching mom bake cookies when I mentioned it to her. She looked thoughtful then burst my bubble.

"You need to respect everyone, especially your friends."

Confused, I said, "I do mom. What does that have to do with the dance?"

"I'm sure she is a very nice girl. I'm happy you made friends with her, but I don't think you should be dating her."

I was taken aback. "Why?"

"Well, she is not like us."

"What does that mean? Did I do something wrong?"

"No son, but you should stick with your own kind. I think her parents are probably telling her the same thing."

My own kind? This was uncharted water for me. Embarrassed, hurt, and confused I decided to be quiet and talk to dad about it. I changed the conversation and mom seemed content to let it drop for the moment.

That evening I asked dad to play catch with me. After a few tosses, I related my conversation with mom. Dad didn't comment. He just listened and said he would talk to mom. I wondered, what did that mean?

I was all ears that night. Usually, when we kids went to bed our parents would sit up in the living room chatting, watching TV, or listening to the radio. I left my bedroom door ajar. When I heard my name, I got out of bed and sat on the floor close to the door.

"Jimmy talked to me about the dance today," dad said.

"I tried to explain to him earlier about the difference between respect and social boundaries."

"I'm not sure that was the right message."

I was stunned. Were my parents calmly disagreeing? Apparently so.

Mom continued, "I'm just trying to spare him the criticism he is bound to encounter from the adults and the other kids. I'm trying to protect him."

"Things are changing in this country. And it's about time. They need to change. He is not too young to understand that. He needs to know that he can be friends and date anyone he wants."

"But he is just a kid. He is so young. He doesn't understand."

"He understands who he likes."

"You know what I mean."

Dad got up and went down the hall. I suppose he had to use the bathroom. Almost as if he had a sixth sense, he pulled my door closed as he passed. I leaped back into bed.

I couldn't process all of this. It was confusing. One thing it did do, though, was make me determined to keep making friends. When I thought about it, nothing had changed. Us kids played catch and all the other activities like my former neighborhood. One big difference was that my uniform of the day had shifted from slacks and button-down shirts to jeans and white tees. We wore that to play and, as it turned out, just about everything else.

I was still adjusting to my new environment. I was going into fourth grade. I remember the first day I showed up with a book bag, a sort of briefcase for kids. My new classmates, though, carried their books by placing a leather belt around them and slinging them over their shoulders. I got a few odd looks from kids. I only carried my bag the first day and quickly conformed to their way.

I was relieved that dad was teaching at the high school and not my mine. I would have been uncomfortable if the other kids knew my dad was a teacher there. Even worse, I couldn't imagine having him as a teacher for one of my classes. Talk about awkward.

Other things were complicating my life. Almost overnight I seemed to be entering puberty. It happened with alarming speed and was quite shocking. Much to my chagrin, I was starting to get pubic hair. I was fascinated and embarrassed at the same time. I found my feelings towards the girls in my life more intense and agonizing. Not only was I changing physically but emotionally too. I desperately wanted to talk to dad but was unsure how to even bring the subject up.

Seeing advertisements with attractive women in them stirred feelings in me that I neither understood nor seemingly could control. This all coincided with a talk with my new best friend. A boy named Danny who lived in our neighborhood. This one conversation changed my immediate life. It happened at his house while we were looking at baseball cards.

"Have you seen the new Sears catalog yet?" he asked.

"Sure, why?"

"I'll show you." He grabbed the huge glossy paper book from under the coffee table. It was several inches thick.

I must give pause here because before there was Walmart or Amazon there was the Sears & Roebuck catalog. You could buy anything from clothes and a rebuilt car engine to dishes and furniture. There was nothing you couldn't buy from this catalog. If you couldn't find it in a ubiquitous Sears store, you simply ordered what you wanted and had it shipped COD to your home. Since there were almost no credit cards and almost no one used them, things were sent Cash On Delivery. Cash was king. You had to plan to have money available to pay the postman delivering the item. There was no online click and pay. The system our folks used was about as basic and straightforward as it came.

Danny plopped the big book down on the couch and said, "Look at page 319."

Dutifully I thumbed through the pages and was suddenly staring at the 'foundation' section. What today would be called underwear or lingerie. There was page after page of scantily clad women in panties and bras and other garments.

I just stared. "Wow!" It was every pubescent boy's fantasy.

He grinned at me and I looked at him with newfound respect. When I left that day to go home, I couldn't wait to check out our Sears catalog. There were no 'men's magazines available at that time. And even if there were, I had no money to buy any to feed my curiosity. And, where would I hide them from my parents? Yet, my friend had opened a door to help me cope with what seemed to be raging uncontrollably through my body and mind. I suspect that the catalog was titillation for every boy like me in the land.

It was like someone had flipped a switch. In a short time, I had dramatically changed. I started to gain weight and muscle. I had sprouted some peach fuzz on my face. And, even the slightest exertion caused me to sweat. For the first time, I noticed I had body odor if I didn't wash up after playing. Perhaps most alarming was that I began to have mysterious nocturnal discharges. My voice dropped. I wondered who I had become. My head was swirling with thoughts as I tried to understand and put the feelings and physical changes into context. Before I could try and sort things out and figure out how to approach my dad, he beat me to it.

One night he came into my room right after I had slid under the covers. He perched on the side of the bed and looked thoughtful. I was grateful he didn't turn on the lights. In the dim light, I could see his face, but the whole thing had the quality of allowing me some privacy. Sort of like the confessional at church. A talk in the dark.

"I think we need to talk, son."

"Sounds good, dad. Have I done something wrong?" Then I blurted out, "Anyway, I have some things on my mind too that I need to ask about.'

"No nothing is wrong. But I figured that you did want to talk." He paused, "I'm not blind you know."

What did that mean? The changes washing over me had not been exactly subtle, but did he think I was acting weird?

"When a boy reaches a certain age, he starts to become a man. That is what is happening to you. It is normal and natural. It is nothing to worry about or get stressed or upset over."

This opened the flood gates and I started peppering him with questions. I was relieved that he didn't seem shocked. Instead, he thoughtfully and calmly answered them. I had never felt closer to dad. He was the wisest man in the world. I was sure of it.

This went on for quite some time before he said, "Well, son, you need to get some rest. We can talk more later. Remember, I am always there for you."

"Thanks, dad. I feel better."

"There is one thing, though, that is important that I want to leave you with. You are going to have certain impulses and urges when you are close to girls in social settings."

Oh great, we were going to end up with a real birds and bees or biology lesson, I thought.

Sensing my apprehension, he smiled. "Kissing is normal, and you might even be tempted to go further. Touching is well . . . touchy . . . " and his voice trailed off before he added, "But remember, you are much too young to fully explore these feelings. So, go slow. Sometimes you have to stop and let your impulses cool off. Do you understand?"

"I think so. Kissing is fine but nothing else. And, I should be cautious about touching girls."

"Essentially, yes. It is basic biology mixed in with human instincts and emotions. You don't have to understand all the details right now, but you have to learn self-discipline. Agreed? You control your emotions and impulses, not the other way around."

"Yes, sir." As I said that, thoughts of guilt and shame flooded my mind. We hadn't discussed touching oneself and I wasn't even sure if I even wanted to know if this was wrong.

In the words of my parents, "Sometimes it is best to let sleeping dogs lie." For now, this appeared to be the best course of action.

I often wonder if those types of father/son discussions still take place in today's society. Or have technology and the Internet rendered them obsolete? All the information any teenager would need is available with a keyboard and a computer. Today's kids are simply more knowledgeable about sex at an earlier age. I just don't know.

At the time there was no doubt my education was advancing in ways I could not have imagined—and not just in the classroom. Somber thoughts. Despite my newly acquired wisdom and the burden to deal with things I didn't fully understand yet, I was settling into a routine.

The town was small and the school close. I walked there with some of the other neighborhood kids. When I came in from playing after school dad would be in his easy chair, his reading glasses perched on the tip of his nose, a newspaper in his lap, watching the evening news. He would thoughtfully puff his pipe and talk about the news as though I understood. Much of it was about worrying world news and civil rights here in the U.S. Was he talking to me or just expressing his thoughts aloud to get them more firmly set in his mind?

I wasn't sure, but I was mesmerized by it. At some point, he would ask me about my day. My main focus was that I was trying out for the grammar school basketball team. There was room on the squad for ten boys. I was nervous because there were twice that number of kids doing the same thing. I spent afternoons on the school grounds practicing my game, both alone and playing pickup games. Usually, the two best players present would act as captains for the two opposing teams. The rest of us would stand in a group and wait to be chosen to play on one of their teams. I was proud that I was usually one of the first to be chosen. I think this was more a function of the fact that I was tall rather than because of my skills. These games were taken seriously for bragging rights, but they were also fun and a chance to bond with my new buddies.

Often a group of girls would shyly watch, and their presence wasn't lost on us. By this time, it was known by the others that Angela was my girl. I no longer mentioned this to mom because I didn't want to get into more awkward conversations about things that didn't make sense to me.

That Angela and I were going steady didn't mean much. We did steal a kiss when we could, and my body ached in ways I still didn't understand at the time. But dad's words were always in the back of my mind. I was much too young to drive and I had no money to go on real dates anyway. I was able to collect some funds to put in my old cigar box, which served as my piggy bank, from doing chores around the house and collecting pop bottles. The closest we came to a real date were the times after school when some of us would gather a few times a week at a small burger joint on main street or the ice cream parlor. We would sit next to each other in a booth along with a group of school chums.

If I was flush, we would share a malted milkshake and an order of French fries. This extravagant order cost much less than a dollar. The shake itself was an addicting blended masterpiece of ice cream, milk, and the addition of malted milk powder, which enhanced the already sweet concoction. Just thick, foamy, and delicious.

These occasions were a chance to hone my social skills. I listened carefully to my peers and tried to figure out how to be cool. Sometimes I would say something and from the reaction of the group, I could tell what I said was not cool. With time, though, I started to get the hang of this give and take.

During that autumn I was still on my quest to make the basketball team. My first concern was that I get the right shoes. The overwhelmingly popular choice was the Converse brand. They were fairly expensive. I started to lobby dad. Finally, before the coach announced the team, he took me to the local shoe store, and I was the proud owner of a pair of Converse. They were, of course, two sizes too big but I found that with double-thick athletic socks I didn't feel overly clumsy.

I made the team! It was probably the highlight of my young life. What a relief. After a few practices, Coach Navarro assigned us positions and named me the center. Again, I suppose it was more a function of height than skill. Nonetheless, I did my best to learn the position. Right before our first game with a neighboring town, I remember him entering the locker room where he passed out the coveted uniforms. They weren't new and I didn't know how many seasons wear they had seen, but they were beautiful to me. Green with gold lettering. I was now number 11. We were responsible for them and I couldn't wait to get home and show mine off to my parents. I was living the dream.

Our gym was small. When you did a layup on one end of it you would often end up flopped on a stage. At the other end, you would run smack into a brick wall if you weren't careful.

The season passed. We were in the middle of the pack in the rankings, but it was exciting. In one of our last games of the season, we made the big bus trip to Tucson to play. The gym and the crowd were bigger than we were used to, and it was thrilling. We had one Black kid on the team. He was a late transfer when his dad, a soldier, was posted to nearby Fort Huachuca. We all liked Ellison. He was a great player and had an easy manner with us. It was no wonder he was popular.

It was well past dark when we got back on the road for the trip home. Our driver was Mr. Carlucci. He was powerfully built with curly hair, a real Rocky Marciano type. Although he looked like a tough boxer, I had never seen him mad. He was a dapper dresser and had a smooth personality to match. He walked with a slight limp as the result of a wound during World War II, but you could just tell he was no one to be trifled with.

Once we cleared the city and suburbs, he stopped at a roadside diner. The coach and Mr. Carlucci got off the bus and we lined up behind them to file into the restaurant. Ellison was in front of me. As soon as we passed through the door a heavy-set man with a greasy apron scurried around the counter and blocked our way. I didn't understand what was happening until he informed us that the team was welcome but not Ellison. He pointed to a sign that said that they reserved the right to refuse service to anyone and they didn't serve Blacks. You could have heard a pin drop at that moment. The whole diner got eerily quiet. In an instant, Mr. Carlucci was in the man's face. His look of anger scared me, but it didn't seem to have much impact on the cook.

Before things could escalate, the coach took Mr. Carlucci's arm and started to turn him around. As he did so he informed the man that we no longer had any interest in eating in such a place. We then unceremoniously marched out.

Once back on the bus the coach stood next to Mr. Carlucci and explained what had happened. To be honest we were shocked and confused since this level of discrimination was unknown to us. We found another restaurant and spent the rest of the ride home discussing what had happened, much to the embarrassment of Ellison.

To his credit, though, he said it was no big deal. Then surprisingly he proceeded to tell us some of his experiences. It was his reality of the world. When he paused to reflect, we were silent and still. This was groundbreaking to us. A real eye-opener guaranteed to make one think and wonder how we would have responded to such indignity and rudeness.

His voice was soft and thoughtful but carried throughout the bus.

"You guys know my dad is in the army. Well, many of his postings have been to bases in the South of our country. Living here in Arizona you guys haven't seen how that place is. There are two of everything. Two drinking fountains—one for whites and one for Blacks. There are often two doors to public buildings. We have to use the one for Blacks. People treat us sort of like animals. We learn to live with it. Just like the schools, many of which are segregated. We have to learn to live and work within the space they give us."

He looked around the bus. "I like it here because we all go to the same school and play on the same teams. That is nice."

When he went on to describe some of the names people called him and his family, I was shocked. I was also surprised how he could describe all of this in such a matter-of-fact calm manner. There were no wisecracks. We just sat there in stunned thoughtful silence.

After that, I started to take a renewed interest in news about race relations in the country. I felt knowing since I had seen discrimination firsthand and had heard some of Ellison's personal stories. I couldn't imagine what he had endured.

He was the first Black friend I ever invited home. We had a connection. We stayed in touch over the years with the regular but often infrequent letter. I would meet up with him years later in Washington, DC. During that period, we marched and protested together. He was a stand-up and solid guy. Someone to be admired. He had a certain wisdom and at the same time an aura of sadness about him.

Despite all that, life went on. When we were first settling into our new house—looking back, boy was it small—just a three-bedroom ranch style, in which I shared a room with Paul, and Molly had her own space. I had worked with my dad to install a shiny silver TV antenna on the side of the house. We were over 50 miles from the nearest TV station in Tucson and reception was weak at best. We got two channels, but it was the source of wonderful entertainment. In the evening during the week, I was allowed to watch TV until 8:30 if I finished my homework. On the weekends I could stay up until 10. What a treat. Mom didn't buy any snack foods, like potato chips, but we made lots of popcorn—cheap, delicious, and easy to make.

On those rare occasions when I was allowed to stay up as long as I wanted, things would go dark at midnight. A test pattern would be displayed on the screen and a patriotic song would play. That was it. If you switched on the TV after midnight that is all you would see. No one ever imagined that one day there would be 24-hour programming and the availability of hundreds of channels.

Although there were no movies yet on TV, there were plenty of entertaining shows—shows like *The Adventures of Ozzie and Harriet, Bonanza, Dragnet, Father Knows Best, Gunsmoke, Have Gun Will Travel, The Honeymooners,* and *I Love Lucy.*

One of my favorites was Ricky Nelson, one of the sons on the Ozzie and Harriet show. He was the epitome of cool. We imitated not only the way he wore his hair but his mannerisms as well. He was also a top pop singer with hits like *Traveling Man.* I tried not to miss even one episode.

They were our electronic role models. We didn't know it was Hollywood and that no matter how cool we were, we were probably never going to be like them. Nonetheless, it set our idealized standard.

From factory towns to sunny California, our characters were all acting different parts on the same stage. We were coming of age. None of us could imagine where our paths would lead later in life. If ignorance was bliss, then we were very blissful.

My parents made a big deal about me turning 13. They reasoned, "It's not every day you become a teenager." They let me have a party at home and I invited a bunch of my friends. We played music and danced. Mom made us snacks, like potato chips and dip, Vienna sausages, little sandwiches, and soda pop. I didn't want it to end. I was grateful, and secretly proud, that my parents made themselves scarce and we could act like kids. Well, teenagers, actually.

At that time, though, we listened to our parents, even if we didn't always understand. They had thoughts on everything.

Their thoughts were wide-ranging. We heard things like:

Dad would muse, "I never dreamed gas would cost 27 cents a gallon. I guess they don't want us to drive much." Or. "I would like to think about getting us a new car for the family, but if they think I'm going to pay more than two thousand dollars for it, they are crazy."

Mom would say, "Did you hear that the post office is going to raise a stamp to ten cents. Geez, imagine that."

A classic was, "Things are getting so expensive that some married women are getting jobs just to make ends meet. My how things have changed."

"If these clueless politicians raise the minimum wage to a dollar, nobody is going to hire young people to work."

Morals often topped the list of parental concerns of the day. Getting a divorce was not common at all. No matter the circumstances, a divorcee was usually seen as scandalous in some way and often the object of scorn. When mom talked about a divorced woman the way she said "divorcee" even sounded scandalous.

It was all part of our brainwashing and indoctrination. Some things, though, were just wholesome fun. A family tradition was trips to the iconic Dairy Queen. Indeed, Dairy Queen was king. Once every week or so my parents would take us there and it was such a treat. Dad would set the rules. If he was close to payday, we were allowed to get whatever we wanted. The overwhelming favorite was a banana split. If it was between paydays, we were allowed to have a ten-cent cone. No matter, it was pure fun.

While trips to Dairy Queen were a constant, new rituals were emerging. A milestone for me came one day while dad was shaving. After he finished, he looked at me and asked if I wanted to try. I was trembling with excitement as he watched me lather up and proceed to scrape the peach fuzz off my face, then he handed me his bottle of Old Spice and I slapped it on and felt the tingle from the small nicks on my face. Damn, did I feel like I had arrived. I was clean-shaven and smelling fresh. I wondered if Angela would notice. I was sure she would.

Then he proceeded to give me a lecture. "You can use my shaving gear when you want, Jimmy, but you must always clean the razor after and put it away where you found it after."

He was serious. Once I failed to do this and I was sleeping when he went to shave. He came into my room and roused me awake. He had gone to shave, and his gear wasn't where it was supposed to be, and he was not amused in the least. Worse was that I must have been in a hurry to go someplace and had failed to properly rinse his razor. It left an impression on me and I never let it happen again.

Paul's health had been steadily improving to the point that my folks had started discussing going East. Dad started getting letters. I noticed that the return addresses were schools. One day after an extended phone call he sat all of us down and informed us he had accepted a teaching job in Ohio, just south of Cleveland.

We peppered him with questions and wanted to know the timing. Dad had to be there in the fall for the start of the school year, so the timing was tight. Dad seemed to fret about this, but mom was calm and confidant. For our part, we kids were just excited. That was tempered by my feeling of sadness to be leaving Angela and my friends. Perhaps we could stay in touch with letters.

This all led to the next crises in my life. It was an identity crisis. My several years in the Southwest had brought out the cowboy in me. I had long sideburns and even wore a cowboy hat much of the time. When I moved East, was I going to maintain my cowboy persona or transition to 'botta boom'? Was it going to be denim jackets or leather jackets with the collar turned up for me? I didn't know. My time in Arizona had taught me that I could easily adapt the accent of where I was. Would my next transition be to a Midwest accent? I didn't know. Such thoughts seem random to me now, but at that age, self-image seemed awfully important.

I suppose it's not surprising that to this day, based on my accent, people have a hard time guessing where I was born or grew up.

The trip back was just reversing what had brought us West in the first place. There were fewer two-lane roads as more interstates emerged. It meant I didn't get to enjoy many small towns, making it less interesting. mom and dad tried to invent games to break the boredom caused by long hours on long stretches of roads. We played along but in the back of our mind was the burning question of, "Are we there yet?"

## Chapter 3

I was going into eighth grade, just a step from high school. It was a milestone I never thought I would achieve. My mood swung wildly, alternating between doubtful and confidant.

But there were comforting routines that helped me through those times. I always read the iconic Saturday Post magazine cover to cover. I also had the Boy's Life magazine. The stories were great and made me feel connected to what others were doing.

Molly and mom were more concerned about her crinolines. These stiff petticoats were all the rage for girls at the time. They were designed to hold out a woman's skirt much like a hoop.

When I played baseball in the Babe Ruth League, I was a catcher and as such felt important that I always had a lot of people looking at me. My favorite bat was the Eddie Matthews model. He was a star for the old Milwaukee Braves. Bats at that time were named after such stars. When our manager handed it to me and I went to bat, I felt like I could hit a home run every time. My first summer back we were the league champs and it was heady stuff.

Likewise, I enjoyed trips to my mom's dad's farm in Michigan. My grandfather was a wonderful guy to hang out with. He lived in a rambling old unpainted two-story farmhouse. After my grandmother passed away, the old man never went upstairs again. He put an old couch in the large country kitchen and slept there. Daily my aunts would bring his meals. The house had electricity but no plumbing. There was a hand pump on the kitchen sink. It also didn't have any central heat. There was a large cast-iron pot-bellied stove in the kitchen.

I loved going there. We slept upstairs. During visits over the winter holidays, I slept with flannel pajamas that came complete with a stocking hat. Mom would heat bricks and wrap them in quilts to put by our feet. Boy was it cold, but we survived just fine. No bathrooms mean you either had to use a chamber pot[45] or the outhouse.

I remember the times I had to venture out of the house to the wooden outhouse at night. It was scary. The trees all cast shadows in the form of monsters. When you were finished with your business, there was no toilet paper, just the ubiquitous Sears catalog. You would tear off a page to wipe yourself. It was

---
[45] A chamber pot was a large ceramic metal pot used as a porta potty that was then emptied the next day. Crude but effective.

a character-building experience I would recommend to anyone if they ever have the chance. It was unique and something most folks will never know.

I would soon be off to high school and couldn't imagine what that would be like, but I felt ready for the challenge. By this time, I was a six-footer and shaved most days. I suppose my folks still saw me as a boy, but I felt like a man.

In the spring we all marched onto the school auditorium stage and receive our grammar school diplomas. It was magical. I had made it to high school.

# Chapter 4

# High School Days (1961 -1963)

Even living in a world full of uncertainty, our parents kept telling us how lucky we were. After all, they reasoned, when they were kids during the depression when money, food, and opportunity were scarce. They had to walk to the now-famous one-room little schoolhouse in the snow. They reminded us of this regularly. We weren't allowed to forget. We, of course, had it better. What they wanted was for us to be grateful and appreciate what we had and not waste it.

It went beyond grateful, though. They wanted something better for us and they raised our expectations to new levels. The seeds for disappointment were sown because we would eventually come to expect unlimited personal freedom and self-fulfillment. It would be as though we were entitled to such a life. As it turned out, we weren't, and this would eventually contribute to a high divorce rate and a lack of self-discipline manifested as such things as drug abuse and a preoccupation with material goods. Perhaps we were too spoiled for own good and wanted more than we were willing to work for or deserved.

We took things to the extreme. Many of our parents even referred to us as the "me" generation. Self-fulfillment would eventually be seen in our divorce rate. It would become the highest for all generations with over half of our marriages ending in divorce. Our parents were shocked.

As we entered high school though our self-centered attitude was just starting to manifest itself. We still lived with fear and optimism that were at odds.

Truly TV and the atomic bomb separated the experience of our youth from that of our parents. We were the first generation to live in real fear of no tomorrow. We were reminded of this every time we had to hide under our desks at school during air raid drills. This impending doom haunted us throughout the 1950s and 60s. What made it strange was that it was tempered by all the high hopes our parents had for us. We were filled with contradictory feelings.

Like me, scattered around the country Brian, Kathy, Joe, and Sally watched as JFK debated Richard Nixon on the first event of its kind ever televised. As a group, we found a great deal of optimism when the young charismatic JFK won the election. But we were becoming increasingly aware that not only was the world broken, but our own country had some real problems.

We started to climb onto our moral high horses. Massive sit-ins protesting the plight of Blacks become commonplace—often involving thousands, including students. Those of us not in the South or other so-called "hot spots" saw it on TV and our collective consciousness began to be stirred. At the same time, we were becoming even more aware of our sexuality. Ironically, the first oral contraceptive, called Enovid, known as "the pill," was licensed and went on sale. It was the start of a sexual revolution. Along with college students, we were the vanguard for it.

Before that those of us who were beginning to have intimate relations with members of the opposite sex knew we could go to the restroom of any gas station and find a condom machine. We could pop a quarter into it and get a package of Trojans. We didn't have to suffer the embarrassment of going to the corner drugstore to purchase them in person. Not to mention the very real possibility that the druggist was probably an acquaintance of our parents and would no doubt mention the purchase to them. That, of course, would result in all manner of fallout, including embarrassing questions and lectures.

We were constantly reminded of the red menace. Khrushchev banged his shoe on a desk at the United Nations and said he would bury us. We laughed, but it was nervous laughter. Russia shot down a U2 spy plane piloted by Gary Powers. Before he left office, Ike warned us about the power and danger of the "military-industrial complex." Maybe our parents understood, we sure didn't know what he was talking about even though Eisenhower would turn out to be right.

Our music remained a great escape. *Itsy Bitsy Teenie Weenie Yellow Polka Do Bikini*, *Are you Lonesome Tonight?*, *Green Fields* and the Everly Brothers' *Cathy's Clown* were hot. The Drifters sang *Save the Last Dance for Me*. Ben E. King's *Spanish Harlem* was released. The U.S. had 85 million TVs by this time, and we watched *Dobie Gillis* and *My Three Sons*. On the big screen, Hitchcock's *Psycho*[46] made all of us reluctant to take showers. *Never on a Sunday* and *Exodus* also appeared on the big screen. *Black Like Me* was published. Long before *The Simpsons* and *Hank Hill*, *The Flintstones* became the first adult cartoon to air in prime time.

This was also the beginning of my lifelong love of the Duprees musical group. Their first smash hit was in 1962 when they recorded *You Belong to Me*. The words and the music just resounded within me as they sang about romantic faraway places, belonging, longing, and love. It perfectly matched my feelings and the ache in my heart as I experienced young love on a level I never knew before. These were feelings that were so intense and real to me. Later they would go on to create more classics like *Gone With the Wind* and *Why Don't You Believe Me* which all spoke directly to me and intensified my feelings of young love.

JFK's inaugural speech urged Americans to, "Ask not what your country can do for you; ask what you can do for your country."

---

[46] Anthony Perkins' played Norman Bates, a subtle, creepy, and unsettling psycho. He ends up killing a female guest in his creepy motel Bates Motel, while she takes a shower, in a scene that the viewer won't soon forget. It is still remembered as one of the pinnacles of the horror genre. Over 60 years later, when we see a spooky and seedy motel, we say it's a Bates Motel.

We thought he was talking to us and it struck a chord. We were captivated by his relative youth. Later we would find out that our knight in shining armor was just a man with character flaws like all of us as we learned about his various sexual trysts.

Our parents were building bomb shelters. The year 1961 also marked the beginning of large anti-nuke demonstrations. JFK created the Peace Corps and gave us hope with his commitment to putting a man on the moon, but we wondered as the USSR's Yuri Gagarin become the first man in space. Nationally we suffered something unfamiliar to us—defeat—at the Bay of Pigs as U.S. trained Cubans tried to invade the island. Additionally, under Russian supervision, East German border guards began construction of the Berlin Wall to reinforce the Iron Curtain.

The first two U.S. Army helicopter units landed in South Vietnam in 1961. That year we listened to The *Watusi, Hully Gully, Mashed Potatoes, Michael Rowed the Boat Ashore, Moon River, Big Bad John, Hit the Road Jack, The Wanderer,* and *Run-around Sue*. Connie Francis sang *Where the Boys Are* as the theme song to a teenage flick that romanticized our young love. Others would follow. Rick Nelson sang *Travelin' Man* the Dovells did *The Bristol Stomp* and Pete Seeger asked the musical question: *Where Have All the Flowers Gone?*. Judy Collins recorded her first album. Bittersweet love stories like *Breakfast at Tiffany's* and *Splendor in the Grass* dominated the big screen.

American soldiers became 'advisors' in Vietnam. Migrant Latino farmworkers in California began to organize under Caesar Chavez. As students, we criticized our parents for buying produce picked under what we saw as slave conditions. It was easy for us to criticize. We were just students supported by our parents with no jobs or real responsibilities in the world.

Nonetheless, slowly our voices grew louder. In 1962, the first open land commune started in California's Big Sur area—this marked the beginning of what would be for many of a flirtation with peace and love. Women began to flex their muscles and went on strike to "End the Arms Race, Not the Human Race." Marilyn Monroe, every boy's fantasy, died at age 36. The world went to the edge of annihilation as JFK's Cuban missile blockade forced Russia's hand and almost resulted in a nuclear war.[47]

The first Berkeley sit-in against racial discrimination occurred at Mel's Drive-in in San Francisco. That year we listened to *He's a Rebel* and it seemed to fit our emerging rebellious disposition. Little Eva's *Loco Motion*, The Tokens' *The Lion Sleeps Tonight*, and Shelly Fabares' *Johnny Angel* were big. We also heard *Lonely Tear Drops, Girl From Ipanema*, and the Everly Brothers' *Crying in the Rain*. The Beach Boys took us on a *Surfin' Safari*. Even though many of us never surfed, the California sound touched us and conjured up images of independence and cool danger as we imagined ourselves shooting the curl of a killer wave.

Bob Dylan's *Blowin' In the Wind* added to our feelings that change was in the air. On TV we spent time with *The Beverly Hillbillies*, and at the movies, *Lolita* titillated us and made our parents uncomfortable. John Glenn rocketed into space. It was a patriotic event, but by 1963 Joan Baez and Peter, Paul, and Mary were singing songs of protest.

That era also saw the continued push in the rise of feminism. During this period, 'Josephine the Plumber' started to appear in TV ads. It showed a cheery likable lady dressed like a plumber getting those tough dirty jobs done or advertising scouring powder. It was a less than subtle effort to let society know that we had stereotyped women for too long. If a guy could do it, so could a woman. In all honesty, though, that never registered with me, it should have but it just wasn't the reality in my world. My mom certainly never fixed a leaky pipe or faucet. Looking back Josephine was just a takeoff of Rosie the Riveter[48] in the 1940s.

No matter what happened, we escaped into our music, which was a mixed bag: *If I Had a Hammer, The Singing Nun, Puff the Magic Dragon,* and *Charlie on the MTA* competed with the

---

[47] When the US found out that Russia was putting nuclear capable missiles in Cuba, 90 miles from our shore, JFK ordered a naval blockade of the island. If Russia had tried to break that blockade it would have meant war and nuclear bombs would have been flying around. Fortunately, JFK didn't waver, or break and the Russians blinked first, taking us back from the brink of World War III.

[48] Rosie was the star of a campaign aimed at recruiting female workers for defense industries during World War II. She became iconic image of working women as they entered the industrial workforce in unprecedented numbers during the war to fill the gap left by so many young men away fighting the war.

Beach Boys' *Surfer Girl* and *The Little Deuce* Coupe and Jan & Dean's *Surf City*.

Although not readily apparent to many of us at the time, the violent end of JFK stirred something even more rebellious in us. It ignited the counterculture roiling beneath the surface. With race, war, political, and cultural issues all bubbling up to the surface, it turned into the perfect storm.

For me, like other BBs, there were times when I felt like a rebel without a cause or a rebel without a clue. I could see and sense issues like racial inequality and wanted to be heard, but perhaps had not fully formed my thoughts or found my voice yet. This caused dueling feelings of excitement and frustration. Regardless of these inner conflicts, we were moving back east.

In 1963, many of us started driving cars and we tried to imitate the sleek Southern California custom machines. Usually, though, we ended up with ten-year-old Dodges, Chevys, and Fords. The only improvements were things like crude flames painted on the fenders and a pair of fuzzy dice hanging from the rear-view mirror.

The movie *Dr. Strangelove* reflected our growing concern that the world wouldn't give us a chance to see 30 years of age. The war seemed endless. LBJ signed a memorandum that stated the U.S. goal was to help the Saigon government to a military victory. This sealed our fate in Vietnam. For the moment, though, we cruised burger heaven and dined in drive-in eateries served by carhops. For our cast of young characters, it was a magical time—even if the future seemed out of focus.

In retrospect, the Cuban missile crisis of 1962 was probably the most dangerous moment in human history. Never before did nations locked in mortal rivalry possess the technical capacity to destroy the earth. Fortunately, wise—or perhaps lucky—statesmanship averted disaster, and the superpowers never called forth their dreaded and deadly arsenals. Yet, the Cold War continued to cast grim shadows over our planet for nearly half a century.

As noted later, the outcome of the Cold War did at least register the conditional triumph of democracy over communism. But as BBs, we knew in our hearts that this victory was not a total vindication of democracy as the country still faced poverty, racism, inequality, and a spiritual weakness from within.

New words, or the use of words, included artificial intelligence, pattern recognition, and other aspects of human reasoning performed by computers. Nanotechnology or the research into the infinitesimally small and the construction of materials atom by atom were being developed in massive research and development efforts. Nano, or one-billionth of a unit, astounded us. It was hard for us to imagine that the devices of the future, such as Nano computers and nanobots, would be invisible to the human eye. The idea of robotics and the investigation and development of computerized machines that perform human tasks blew our minds—as did the idea of virtual reality or an environment that doesn't physically exist but is computer-generated so that a person can interact with it, move about in it, hear, and see things, touch and move things, even smell them, would become a reality at some point.

\*

After the family's move East, we all quickly fell into familiar patterns. It was almost like we had never left. True, I had come back a changed person having entered puberty and starting to come of age. The detour to Arizona also had given me insights into my other feelings, as well as nagging suspicions that uneasy relationships between different people ran deep. Often hidden from others. Often biased. Usually arbitrary and based on culture and skin color. I had learned from Ellison that being in the North had spared me the rampant and overt discrimination of the deep south at the time. I didn't dwell on it but there were enough signs that I somehow knew it simmered below the surface of a life that through my eyes seemed ideal and so stereotypical of the 50s and 60s. That images of the ever-present Norman Rockwell paintings seemed to capture the time. Wholesome, innocent, hopeful.

*Typical 1950s-60s main street.*

That would all explode with the 1960s as BBs found their voice and ushered in a decade of protest against the establishment. This was disturbing to our parents. It was also at odds with our indoctrinated upbringing. I was not alone in a deluge of feelings that would overwhelm me. Chief among them was guilt and a sense that somehow, I was not grateful enough for the life I had enjoyed up to that stage. So not only was the country polarized and torn apart by culture, lifestyles, and politics, but we BBs were likewise conflicted as we struggled to deal with new emotions and challenges.

The Pill brought forth a sexual revolution that altered our values forever. Vietnam would test the country's limits and threaten the establishment. Also, lifestyles, personified by hippies, would change not only the political landscape but the very essence of American life. Since my whole life up until this point was pretty much based on 'ignorance is bliss' and 'what you don't know can't hurt you,' undaunted I continued to sail on into the perfect storm along with my fellow BBs.

Sunday was the loneliest day of the week. I hated it. After church there was nothing. Like many parents of the day, mine forbid TV to be watched on Sundays. It was a dead zone day. The stores were all closed, the streets quiet, and my buddies were seldom seen. I knew better than to tell my folks that I was bored because they would simply tell me to read a book or failing that, assign me some chores to do. My way to deal with it was to find a quiet corner of the house and snuggle up with a couple of Readers Digests. These paperback-sized magazines featured stories on everything. I found them fascinating and read them cover to cover. They arrived in the post every month and dad had them arranged on a bookshelf in the living room. Some I read more than once out of sheer boredom.

My school year promised to be exciting. I had already met some of the kids in the neighborhood I would be going to school with and they seemed to accept and like me. Our bike jaunts were getting longer and more daring. Some days we even road five miles to the next town to enjoy a cone at the Dairy Queen without our folks.

For the first month or two, I dutifully wrote letters to Angela, informing her of what was happening in my life and tell her I loved her and how much I missed her. I even put several Xs in my return address, which in the teenage language of the day represented kisses. Stamps were a dime and I put them on upside down which also meant I loved her.

I badly wanted to hear her voice but calling her was totally out of the question. Long-distance calls with AT&T were expensive and limited to the occasional brief call to grandparents and other relatives.

School started and I went out for the football and basketball teams. These guys were bigger and better than my teammates in Arizona and I was pleasantly surprised when I made the team. As a freshman, I wasn't a starter but did see a lot of action. I was, however, a starter on the junior varsity team. We had real cheerleaders and boy were they perky and cute.

My letters to Angela and her replies became more infrequent. At some point, we just stopped trying to stay in touch. I often wonder if calls had been more affordable, or if cell phones had been around, our relationship would somehow have survived or at least been prolonged.

I started asking girls for dates again, especially to school dances. We were getting more adventurous. Sometimes I would go to a friend's house after school and we danced to American Bandstand music or pair off and have make-out parties. It was real progress to use a baseball analogy of the day. If kissing was first base and touching a girl's breast was second base, I made it to third base when I slid my hand under my partner's dress. Very few of us ever hit a home run. I certainly didn't, but there was no doubt we were on our way.

Over mom's objections, dad got me a new model Red Ryder BB gun to replace my old one. It was bigger and more powerful, and I loved it. We would set up tin cans against the solid wooden fence in our backyard

*The author on prom night with a skinny tie and a white sport coat and red carnation (1963).*

and plunk them. It was hours of great fun. When I found some old canvas in the garage and started to make a rifle holder I could carry on my bike, though, dad drew the line. I guess having me roam town armed with my rifle was a bit more than he was prepared to tolerate. He rejected my logic that all the cowboys had rifle holders on their saddles. And, my bike, being like my horse, entitled me to the same.

By this time, I noticed my beard was heavier and I was more physically mature than most of my peers and girls seemed to like that. I was entering the mysterious world of high school. Looking back, I suppose I was a bit of a jerk in that I largely ignored Paul and Molly. They looked up to me, but I traveled in different circles and didn't want them tagging along.

Basketball season ended when we were invited to the first tournament I had ever been to. Mom and dad were proud of me and they attended most of my games, further adding to my unwarranted sense of importance.

We were still being shaped by what we saw on TV. It was indelibly entrenched as the country's new universally shared addiction. Just like days of old when the family would gather around the fireplace as the focal point of companionship. Except this electronic hearth did not foster conversation.

The idealistic, naïve, and sappy situation comedies of the 1950s were giving way to slightly more realistic situations, like the Dick van Dyke show, although they still featured similar idealized versions of humanity and the typical American lifestyle. One change was that shows shot from the perspective of kids were emerging. These included our old favorite *Leave it to Beaver* and later the *Wonder Years*. We BBs could relate to this as it brought to life universal embarrassing moments that we were certain we would never overcome, such as approaching the object of one's affection and having to deal with the reaction of friends and family.

Instead of today's reality shows, we had variety shows. It fed us song, dance, and comedy. Shows like Ed Sullivan, Dean Martin, and Danny Thomas were just a few. Indeed, at one point during the 60s there were 18 variety shows being aired on the country's three networks!

Besides showcasing singers and comedians, they also shined a light on our chauvinistic society. It was truly a man's game. But things were starting to change. Entertainment pioneers like Carol Burnett were emerging when this funny lady headlined her own variety show. It was a precursor to the breaking down of barriers in the workplace and society in general. It even impacted race when shows like *I Spy* starred white actor Robert Culp and Black actor Bill Cosby as equals. It was a long way from the stereotypes like Amos and Andy with their over-the-top exaggerated and insulting ethnic accents and roles.

All of this was shaping our view towards others and the way we both acted and interacted. It also impacted our parents as TV became a political force. This was especially driven home by the first televised presidential debate between Richard Nixon and John F. Kennedy.

When I entered high school and started to make friends, I noticed the kids were more opinionated and even militant. They seemed to take their cue from college kids, the next rung up in our education hierarchy, and our new heroes. Many BBs had older siblings or cousins who were college students. We wanted to be rebels, too.

I was the oldest in our family but was no different and found myself arguing with my parents about events, politics, and social issues. At times I would see bewildered expressions as I expressed my new radical views. It made me uncomfortable, but it didn't stop me. There were times when I felt like Benedict Arnold.[49] A real traitor. At times dad seemed confused like I was attacking the world that he and his generation had created and supported. I suppose I was.

I remember we were sitting in the kitchen and at first, my Dad just stared at me. Then, shaking his head, he said, "Where are you getting this nonsense, Jimmy?"

"The government needs to do more to eliminate poverty. That's all I'm saying."

"It did during the Great Depression, but that was a special case. FDR and his New Deal set some dangerous precedents. If

---

[49] He was an American military officer during the Revolutionary War. He became a traitor when he defected to the British side in 1780. His name is synonymous wtth traitor.

someone wants to work today, they can find a job. They don't need some government make-work scheme."

"If you are poor and don't have a car or any training or education, what kind of job are they going to get? And, how about if they are Black?"

"If I didn't know better you are starting to sound like a communist. What are they teaching you in school?"

These became typical conversations. I felt guilty about having them with my parents, but this was offset by my feeling of solidarity with my friends. The older brother of one of my school buddies had been drafted into the Army, which prompted another thread of disagreement with my dad. Undaunted I spouted the standard line of my school chums.

"Aw come on, dad. Why should someone be drafted at 18, but not be able to vote until he is 21? And, why aren't girls drafted like us boys?"

"Would you want Molly to go off to war?"

That took me aback as I considered what he said. "Well, girls could serve in some other way."

"Maybe but before the country goes down that road it should be thought through. Jimmy, when you get older you will see that most young folks are not ready to make an informed vote until they are of legal age."

It was classic. As my folks got older, they were becoming more conservative, and I was the youthful idealist liberal. I suppose subconsciously I was aware of this but didn't dwell on it. I was pretty much convinced I knew everything.

Yeah, right. In hindsight, my hubris was astounding but typical of my generation. I hadn't gone through a world depression or fought in a war. Nor had I worked and raised a family. We knew little of the world, but we were convinced we were worldly.

In a way, it reflected the world affairs of the time. Everything was about the world's two superpower titans. Russia and America. When a Russian satellite first orbited the earth, it marked the official beginning of an arms race. Newspaper headlines declared that the U.S. didn't have enough missiles to defend itself and we didn't have enough engineers to design and build the missiles.

Accordingly, schools were pressured to re-emphasize math and science to catch up with the Soviets.

Beyond education and capabilities, this competition was both a political and moral crusade to convince people around the world that our Western-style democracy was superior to Communism. The news was full of stories as this rivalry unfolded and both countries injected themselves into the affairs of nations around the globe.

While the U.S. was acting as the world's policeman, we went to classes, played sports, attended parties and school dances, and probably had more social and political discussions than the U.S. Congress. We also went to pep rallies and hung out in burger joints.

I got my learner's permit. Dad had been letting me drive the family sedan on every possible occasion. I pestered him incessantly.

"Dad, I finished my homework. Can we go out for a drive so I can practice?"

"Sure, Jimmy. Take the trash out for your mom, first, then we can go."

Once in the car, it was a familiar routine. "Adjust all of your mirrors and the seat before you start the car."

I dutifully complied. There was no mention of seat belts at the time.

I put the clutch in and moved the column shifter up to reverse.

"Now give her a little gas and ease off on the clutch." And so it went.

On my sixteenth birthday, he took me to the motor vehicle department and I passed with flying colors, although my parallel parking left a little to be desired. Boy was I proud.

Despite these outings, my relationship with my dad had become somewhat strained. The closeness of the earlier years was gone. My militant liberal attitude seemed to confuse him and hurt his feelings. I felt bad, even ungrateful at times. I know he thought that I thought I knew it all. One day in a dry caustic observation, he suggested that I get a job. After all, he reasoned that since I knew everything it might be a perfect time since I would be highly employable. His sarcasm was lost of me.

The 60s were a time when owning a car in high school made you a god. Talk about the haves and have nots. There were two distinct groups—those who had a car and those who didn't. It was a big deal. Over 75 percent of American households of the 60s only had one car. Despite my haughty and youthful political views, I became obsessed with making money.

It was triggered when I mused, "Dad, I need a car. Do you think you and mom could help me achieve this?"

He looked thoughtfully at me and lit his pipe. "Jimmy, that is not happening. If you want a car you are going to have to work for it. Even if mom and I could give you a car, it wouldn't mean anything."

"What do you mean by that? Of course, it would."

"No son. When you get something for nothing, it has no value." As an afterthought, he couldn't seem to resist adding, "That is what you young people don't understand about pushing this nonsense that the government should be your mommy and daddy. You have parents. And, if they gave you all kinds of crazy things, they would have no value."

I just looked at him. Gosh, where did that come from? Was he right? I would have to think about it. For the moment, though, I was a boy possessed. I wanted the prestige, independence, and popularity having a car would bring. It would make my life perfect. Of that I was sure. I was able to borrow dad's car occasionally for dates, but this only intensified my feelings for that which would bring me what I craved. So, I pressed on.

"If I was able to save up the money, it would okay if I did buy a car, wouldn't it dad?"

"Yes, Jimmy. If you do that your mom and I will allow it."

There it was. I had permission and this made me all the more determined.

Dad added, "But working better not interfere with your studies."

I knew at that moment I would have to be careful. And how about playing sports? There were football and basketball to consider. If I dropped off the team, it would greatly change my stature in school. This might be offset by having a car, but it sounded like a lousy trade. I was going to have to work it out. The good news was that I already had earned varsity letters as a jock.

Later that day I rode my bike down to High street where the used car lots were strung along it like giant magnets. It looked like whatever I could get would be seven or eight years old and cost 150 to 200 dollars. I stopped by our hometown newspaper office. From church I knew the man responsible for circulation. I left the proud new paperboy of our extended neighborhood.

The following day I set my alarm for 5:30 am. Not fun but I dragged myself out of bed. Just as planned a stack of newspapers sat neatly on our front porch. I got dressed and spent the next half hour rolling them up and popping a rubber band around each. Then I slid them into the canvas saddle bags they had given me which fit neatly over my rear bicycle fender. Just as I was about to mount my bike and do my route, dad came out on the porch in his bathrobe and slippers carrying a cup of coffee.

"Looks like you're off," I nodded and he added, "Don't be late for school."

"I won't, dad." And, off I went. After about 10 houses I was perfecting my technique of reaching back, grabbing a paper, and slinging them as I rode on. I mostly hit the front porches or at least the front sidewalk and just kept getting better. I chuckled to myself and thought, maybe I should try out for pitcher on the baseball team.

*The paperboy (Norman Rockwell Saturday Evening Post magazine cover).*

I barely made it to school on time. I would have to step it up on my next run. I did the calculations in my mind and knew I had my work cut out for me. At less than a dollar a house every two weeks it was going to be challenging to get cash for my new used dream machine.

The following day it rained, and I had to spend extra time not only rolling the papers but wrapping them in wax paper, too. Dad helped at the end, but it was a slow, soggy, dispirited ride. Maybe I had overestimated this making money business.

After a month I was ready to throw in the towel. Not because I couldn't handle the work, but I had been overly optimistic about the money I would collect. That's when my next brainstorm hit me. Dad had just grunted when I told him I was quitting and going to plan B. The next day after school I put it into action.

I was dressed in slacks and a clean, freshly pressed shirt. I started at the far end of Main street and looked down it and took a deep breath. I had no resume, of course, but I was armed with a smile and can-do attitude. The first shop was Woolworths, the 5 and 10 cents store. I walked in and found Mr. Garber behind the cash register. I plastered on my best smile.

"Hi, Jimmy. What can I do you for?"

"Good afternoon, Mr. Garber."

"How are the folks?"

"Just fine, sir."

"I saw your mom over at the bakery the other day. Gosh, are Paul and Molly are getting big."

I approached the counter and stood as straight as I could. "I was wondering if you might have any work I could do?"

"So, you want a job?"

"Yes sir."

He stroked his chin. "Well, if the truth be told, things have been a little slow lately."

"I'm willing to do anything. I could sweep up. Help stock the shelves, Whatever."

"I'm sorry, son." He must have seen the disappointed look on my face because he added, "Might could use you for the upcoming Christmas season if you want to check back with me."

I thanked him and quietly left the store as I promised to say hi to my folks for him.

Next door was Wright's shoe store where the same theme was repeated. My confidence was waning. Maybe working to get my dream machine was not going to be as easy as I thought.

But I wasn't going to give up. I entered the small grocery and market run by a kindly Italian man named Santini. When I approached him, he adjusted his green apron over his rotund midsection and eyed me curiously.

"I maybe could use some help after school and on Saturdays. You look like you could handle the produce boxes."

"That would be great, sir. I would work hard."

"I know you would. When could you start?"

"Right now if you want."

"I can only pay you 50 cents an hour. Would that work for you?"

It was music to my ears. "Yes sir."

And just like that, I had a job of sorts. I couldn't help but start doing the numbers in my head. Three hours after school would give me $1.50 a day times 5 would add up to $7.50 then add in about 4 bucks on Saturday and I would be knocking down over $10 bucks a week. Not bad and if I was careful it would add up. I told myself that I was the man.

My relationship with the kindly grocer would last throughout high school and beyond. I carefully watched how he handled his customers and felt like I learned something they didn't teach in school. I was proud to be part of his business.

He eventually gave me some colored tee shirts with *Santini's Market* lettered on the back. What I wanted was a black leather jacket with the market name neatly lettered in red across the back. I had seen his brother Pauli wear one and I thought it was beyond cool. I was pleasantly surprised when he gave me one for Christmas that year. With the collar turned up I was sure I was one of the coolest guys around.

After I quit my paper route, I worked as hard as I ever had for the market. The money was great, and he even gave me a little extra, and his constant encouragement and praise made my chest swell.

Then the world turned gray and cold. It happened in a flash, the news coming across every radio station in America. It was November 23rd, 1963, a blustery leaden day with quiet streets and the late fall leaves swirling around on the sidewalks and doorways. I walked the streets with little traffic and no people and felt more alone than I ever had. It felt like the world was ending. Not since the Cuban missile crisis when John F. Kennedy stared down Russian leader Nikita Khrushchev, demanding he remove his missiles from Cuba had the national mood been more somber. During the missile crisis, all of us thought it would be the start of World War III and the end of the world as we knew it. Now he was gone. Dead. Shot by an assassin named Oswald. How could anyone as vibrant and full of life as JFK be gone in the blink of an eye?

Mr. Santini told me to take the afternoon off because he was closing early. I didn't argue. I walked the streets but didn't want to be alone. I wanted to be in the comforting presence of my parents, knowing that they would assure me that everything would be okay. This longing made my guilt bubble to the surface. Lately, I had been such an ass towards my dad. I had hurt his feelings. I saw him as he started to age, no longer the invincible man I had worshipped. I saw the hurt and confusion in his eyes as I challenged everything he believed in with my radical ideas and know it all attitude. What was I becoming? I didn't know. But I did know that my dad's pride in me had taken a big hit.

How could I be true to my new feelings and yet support and be closer to dad? How do you challenge someone's core beliefs and not hurt them? Would it ever be the same? I hoped so because I loved him and mom unconditionally.

JFK's assassination was the final spark that ignited the fire that coalesced into a decade of protest. Today we lament the chaotic state of politics, society, and just about everything else. That may be true, but the 60s were wild beyond belief with conflict and civil unrest, and cultural shifts. It wasn't just that we were different as a result of being raised differently. Society and the world were different, too.

With time, of course, people's thinking about basic things tends to change; for example, the belief that corporal punishment works has waned with younger generations. Or, letting things run their course without overreacting or interfering when it comes to dealing with kids. We were treated differently. And the list goes on.

In doing research and gathering background material by talking to other BBs for this book, though, it seems that many of my peers don't believe that such changes or new ways of approaching things always hold up or are better. The thinking is that the old ways allowed us to express and find ourselves. This despite many studies to the contrary. To illustrate this, one leading edge BB used the following comparisons of life in the 1960s to today.

On what sets us apart, he said, "Consider these scenarios about how things were handled back in the 60s as contrasted to today. By today's standards and what we faced, none of us were supposed to ever make it or turn out normal. We were spanked and brainwashed. Imagine two boys named Bobby and Richie get into a fight after class on school property. A crowd of kids would gather. After some shoving and posturing, Bobbie gives Richie a shiner. Richie gives up. With nothing more to see the crowd disperses. The point is that the two boys might even end up shaking hands, but at the very least they end up with some workable uneasy truce. They would deal with it."

He smiled and asked, "What would happen today? The cops would be called, maybe even some sort of tactical squad like a SWAT team. Both of these young men would be arrested and charged with assault. They would be suspended from school. Would this overreaction be beneficial? And this is not even considering that one of the boys' parents would probably get a lawyer and sue the other family. We are and were different because things were different."

We also talked about disruptive kids in class. He said, "If you misbehaved, you could expect to be sent to the principal's office where you would get a swift swat on the butt with the dreaded wooden paddle. Today you would be given a huge dose of Ritalin. Then the kid becomes a zombie and tested for some type of attention deficit syndrome. And suddenly the kid is on meds and has a disability. This escalation changes a kid's life and not for the better."

"Are you advocating corporal punishment?"

"No, but we seem to have lost our sense of balance. I'm not advocating a solution, except to say that we tend to overreact today. What if your kid gets headaches? You give them aspirin, which they take to school. They end up expelled for violating the school's drug policy. I could go on, but anyone from our generation gets the idea."

At the time, though, such weighty issues didn't occur to me. I had other things, like how others saw me, to worry about.

I had my leather jacket and wore it everywhere. It was my image. We all had our 'look.' Some of the kids cultivated a preppy look with loafers and button-down shirts. Then there were the jocks with their athletic jackets, jerseys, and sweatshirts. I was going for the James Dean look.

Although he died in a fiery crash years before in 1955 at the young age of 24, he was still wildly popular and remembered as a cultural icon of teenage disillusionment and social estrangement. Even his most celebrated film, *Rebel Without a Cause*, was a reminder that he was his own man.

Image was all-important for BBs. It defined you and how your peers saw you. I often wonder what that said about me or our generation. Perhaps we were that superficial. Or, maybe we were in search of an identity, having been overshadowed all our lives by our parents, the greatest generation. Later, if we dropped out for a while, like quitting school or taking a road trip, we would tell our parents we needed time to find ourselves. They, of course, would wonder what we were talking about because they didn't know we were lost.

For the moment, though, my piggy bank was growing. I was up over a hundred bucks. I was getting closer to my dream machine. It bothered me a little that I was no longer able to swing both sports and work, but by this time I had earned varsity letters in basketball and football, which was some consolation. We even won a state football championship. Not a bad way to cap my high school sports adventures.

My folks splurged on buying me a school sweater and I was able to proudly display my sports letters. It was a big deal at the time. The sweaters were button-up and dark blue and the big letters were white. Mom stitched them on for me. There were also 4 white bands on the left sleeve, which were covered by blue. For each successive year of high school, you had to remove the strip of covering to reveal the white stripe. If you were a sophomore, you had two stripes and so on.

*Parade with author and some teammates in a vintage convertible cruising down main street celebrating our Ohio state football championship (1963).*

They were expensive and while many kids had them that was

not true of everyone. I was sympathetic for the less fortunate kids whose folks had other priorities for their hard-earned money.

My folks also sprang for a gold class ring with my target graduation year engraved on it and a blue stone. Somewhere along the years I have lost or misplaced the ring, but my sweater still fits and hangs in my closet. I get a kick out of wearing it around the house on chilly days or even out.

They were also prized processions for the girls of the day. Boys would give girls their class ring to show they were going steady. Since they were usually too big for their fingers, they would wear them on a string or chain around their neck. And, if a boy was really into a girl, he would also give her his school sweater. I did both and it turned out to be a humiliating experience for me.

One afternoon my ever-observant mom said, "Jimmy, where is your class ring? I haven't seen it for a while. You didn't lose it, did you?"

"You know I'm dating Diane Foster."

"Yes, but what does that have to do with your ring?"

"Mom, we are going steady."

"Jimmy, your dad and I didn't work and sacrifice to get you that ring so that you could give it away."

Yup, I was busted and embarrassed. "Well, I can't exactly go and ask her to give it back."

"Yes, young man that is exactly what you will do."

"Aw, mom."

"And where is your school sweater? Don't tell me she has that, too?"

Double busted. I flushed and just nodded.

She studied me for a moment then said, "You are going to march over to her house right now and get them."

Was she joking? Nope, she had that look. I had screwed up and hadn't thought it through when like a big shot I had given them to her after a particularly steamy make-out session.

"Go on now, I'm serious. You best do it before your father gets home."

I had no real options. I stood and knew I had to make the awkward trip to undo what I had done. She lived two streets over. When I explained the situation to her, she was pouting and asked if that meant we were breaking up. I assured her it didn't, but it was embarrassing for both of us. I knew her friends and others would find out and make fun of me. I would just have to deal with it and make light of it.

The result was that things were never really the same between us. We ended up breaking up a few weeks later. As silly as it sounds, going steady at this time was like a teenage version of marriage. I tried to make it as amicable as possible and got through it with minimal discomfort. The one good thing that came out of it was that it again made me one of the most eligible 'bachelors' in school. I learned something and on dad's advice sort of played the field. Unfortunately, it wasn't always advice I stuck to in my later life. In high school, though, it was fun and I enjoyed parties and social occasions where I could flirt and dance with whoever I wanted.

The day came when I rode my bike to the used car lot. I strolled along the rows of cars with Mr. Wyatt, although I already knew that my prize was a burgundy 1953 Chevy. She was a beauty. Clean and rust-free from what I could see. He let me start it up and take it for a spin around the block.

We went to his small office and I carefully counted out $175.00 in small bills. He smiled at me. "Jimmy, you drive carefully and treat her right and she will treat you right. You know, over the years I've sold your dad a car or two." I nodded and he added, "And, don't forget, you have a 30-day guarantee. Anything mechanical goes wrong just bring her back."

We shook hands and off I went with my heart pounding. I took one cruise down main street proud as a peacock then went home. Dad came out of the house as soon as I pulled up in the driveway. He nodded approvingly. Then he also shook my hand. "Don't forget I put your name on our insurance and you have to pay mom and me eighteen dollars on the first of every month to pay your part of the premium."

"I won't forget, dad, and thanks for helping me with that."

"I know you feel like a big shot now but take it easy. You still have to be home by nine during weekdays. And, if your grades go down, I'll take your keys away from you."

That was it. I was mobile without having to pedal. That

evening I got permission to skip dinner and picked up Sheila, a girl I had been recently dating. Her dad sternly warned me to be careful and have her back by 8:30.

She sat next to me on the bench seat in the front and I was in heaven. I took her to the A&W Root Beer stand and pulled up in an empty slot. We ordered over the speaker and within minutes a cute girl in shorts and skates rolled up next to us with a tray. I rolled down the window and she hung it on the side. It was only two Coney Island cheese dogs topped with a chili hamburger meat sauce and cheese and two small baskets of fries. There were also two large megaphone-shaped containers of frothy root beer. The cool thing was that you could remove the bottom and use them as megaphones at football and basketball games to cheer your home team.

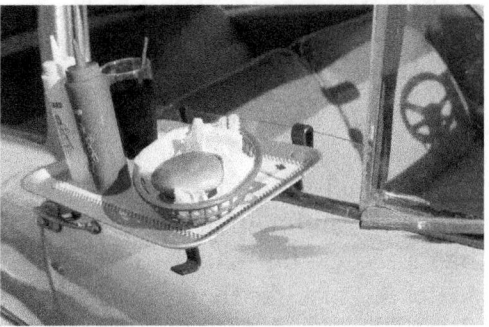
*Drive-in burgers on the side of a vintage car.*

After we had devoured our gourmet teenage meal we drove around for a while. Sheila put her arm around me, and I just smiled and turned up the radio. At that moment I was sure life couldn't get any better. We passed other couples cruising the streets and drive-in burger joints in their jalopies and waved. We were part of an exclusive club.

At school, there was a lot of talk about the push in Washington, DC for civil rights legislation. I started to become increasingly aware that some of my friends were becoming more hostile to the Black kids in school as they got older. Dad said it was a reflection of what they heard at home from their

*Typical teen fare with mini jukebox.*

parents. Others seemed neutral. Some, like me, felt equality was long overdue. My mom seemed unusually quiet on the subject, but dad was vocal that racism needed to be addressed.

There was a protest that had been organized at a community college the next county over. I asked dad if I could go and march in my first protest. His answer surprised me.

"No, son. I'm afraid not. It is too dangerous to be at such an event. There are rallies for other things, but this is just too highly charged and too dangerous."

"But it is a peaceful event."

"It is supposed to be a peaceful event. But there is a lot of suppressed anger over race in this country and like most things, there are two sides. On one side you have the minorities. They are frustrated and angry over many decades of being treated as less than human... more like property. Then you have some whites who think that is just fine. Put the two together and it's explosive."

I just looked at him. It was certainly a lot to think about. Then I thought of my friend, Ellison, and knew I had to do what I could to help change things. It seemed important and I knew my actions would help define the man I was becoming. I didn't feel like a radical but had a strong feeling that it was the right thing to do. So, just like that, I made the command decision to willfully disobey my dad.

The next day was Saturday. I made an excuse to be out most of the day and arranged to meet others at a fast-food drive-in at the end of Main street. There I loaded up the Chevy with a crowd of my friends and off we went.

When we arrived at the campus there was a crowd of several hundred people milling around outside the school administration building. I had never seen so many people gather like that outside of going to a major league baseball game with my dad. They were holding signs and chanting slogans like "equality now."

It was exhilarating. The crowd was mostly Black kids and adults. As we started mingling with them no one said anything to us, but we did get some smiles. You could feel the comradery. I felt like a real rebel. I wished Ellison was there. Minutes later a large crowd of white kids and adults marched into the area and they weren't smiling. Although the two groups were separated by a narrow grassy park, things got ugly in a hurry.

Taunts turned into pushing and shoving. Punches were thrown. It was bedlam. My heart was racing. This was a playground fight on steroids. It was as if a miniature version of my dad was perched on my shoulder whispering in my ear as he kept repeating, "I told you so."

Someone grabbed my shirt and roughly pulled me back. It was a friend. "We need to get out of here before we get hurt or worse, get arrested. We heard sirens in the distance. We managed to get everyone together and move towards the area where I had parked the car. As we approached, I just stared.

Someone had broken the back window. Two concerns flooded my mind. One was that someone had damaged my baby. The other was dad was going to find out I disobeyed him. I didn't know which was worse.

We hastily brushed the broken glass off the backseat and all piled in. By this time police with batons had arrived on the scene. From the distance, I couldn't tell who was gaining the upper hand and, to be honest, just wanted to get out of there.

I got back to town and in somber moods my friends scattered. I drove home without any more unexpected events and parked next to the family sedan in the driveway. When I woke the following morning, I went outside and found dad standing next to my car with his hands on his hips. He heard me when the door closed but didn't even turn around.

"Do you want to tell me what happened?"

I couldn't deceive him any longer. "I went to the rally, dad. I'm really sorry but I just felt strongly about it."

"I'm not proud you deliberately disobeyed and deceived me." He hesitated for a moment. "I am proud that you felt the need to support what you believe in." And, almost as an afterthought, "Were you or any of your friends hurt?"

"No sir."

"Good."

Was I hearing right? No rage? No lecture?

"Let's get something to cover the window if it rains. We are not reporting this to the insurance company. You will be responsible for getting the window replaced with your money. Is that clear?"

"Yes, sir."

"Now go and get me your keys. No car for two weeks. You had better get your bike out of the garage. A little exercise will do you good."

In a softer tone, he added, "I will help you find a used window over at Pete's junkyard. Save you a few bucks."

With that, he turned and started back inside. Over his shoulder, he said, "We will not speak to your mom about this because I don't want to upset her, but you and I will find a quiet moment and you can tell me all about it, and you can tell me if you learned anything from this experience."

The raging storm I had imagined never happened. Except for the rather mild fallout, it was over. No matter how savvy I thought I was, parental behavior was hard to figure and predict. Dad and I did have a quiet chat later as we puttered around the garage. What I had learned was debatable, but it brought dad and me closer again. Not in total accord but closer.

Later I played my actions many times in my mind, wondering what they said about me. Had they been cowardly? No, I wasn't afraid to get physical and fight. I was more afraid of getting arrested, but not of the police. I realized what it would have done to my parents. Having to bail me out of jail would mean I had truly insulted them and sullied our name big time. It would have cut them deep. Something they didn't deserve.

Did it mean I wasn't committed to my youthful ideal of equality? I didn't think so. Ellison always sprang to mind. He was a friend and deserved my support. So, to keep my self-image and teenage sanity intact, internally I rationalized that my withdrawal from that particular conflict was a strategic retreat—not running away. Things might change later, but those thoughts were all I could process at the time. I told myself that my real life was about to start. I was excited and scared at the same time. About half of us would enroll in college as we started the next phase of our lives.

# Chapter 5

# Off to College (1964 – 1966)

Lyndon Baines Johnson, or LBJ as he was known, beat Barry Goldwater, an Arizona senator, after painting him as a dangerous warmonger with his finger on the nuclear button. Little did we know that it would be LBJ who dragged us deeper into Vietnam, the most controversial conflict in American history up to that point in time. Before he did that, though, he declared an unconditional war on poverty.

Depending on where you are on your political spectrum, it was either a catastrophe that made people more dependent on the government by robbing them of their self-respect and initiative or it lifted the value, dignity, and potential of the poorest segments of American society. I wasn't worldly enough yet to figure out how I felt about it.

Regardless, one thing it did do was help usher in the era of big government. It created Medicare and Medicaid and expanded Social Security benefits. It also established food stamps as a permanent program to help the poor. Additionally, it helped create programs to fund school districts with predominantly impoverished students, including school lunches. Trillions of dollars later liberals and conservatives continue to argue the value of so-called government social engineering, entitlement, or welfare programs.

LBJ did follow through on Kennedy's push for civil rights action when the landmark 1964 Civil Rights Act was signed. I always found it incredible that it took 99 years from the end of the Civil War to finally codify equality. Unfortunately, the battle against discrimination is still being fought today.

The surgeon general warned about cigarette smoking. Those of us who smoked didn't worry because we were convinced that by the time it became a problem, they would have cured cancer. Besides, our parents smoked. They wouldn't do it if was unhealthy—would they?

Bob Dylan whined that *The Times They Are A-Changin'*. We ate it up. The full impact was just starting to hit us. We started to not only feel more like rebels but embrace that image as well. The Beatles appeared on Ed Sullivan and in our hearts, we knew that things were changing. There was no doubt that "doo-wop" was giving way to other sounds we had never heard. Teenage girls swooned, the boys were jealous and saw the Fab 4 as a collection of long-haired flashes in the pan. They sang *Can't Buy Me Love* and *I Love Her* and filmed *Hard Day's Night.* They went on a 25-city tour. Cassius Clay became Mohammed Ali and "whupped" the seemingly invincible Sonny Liston[50].

Many of us were confused and angry when Cassias Clay became a Muslim. At the time, it seemed a slap in the face to what it meant to be an American. "How dare he refuse to be drafted to embrace a religion that seemed to be at odds with our self-image?" Most white guys my age shared this self-perceived outrage. This was not shared by our Black classmates. It was the beginning of "Black is Beautiful" as they struggled to reverse over a century of negative stereotypes. Our parents seemed uncomfortable and confused and this impacted our feelings, too, causing us to be conflicted.

The oldest BBs graduated from high school and some, like Kathy, entered college. Others stayed home and found work.

---

[50] We followed these heavyweight boxing matches with interest. Although some of us were mad that Ali joined the Nation of Islam, not necessarily that he became a Muslim but that he refused to join the military and fight in Vietnam.

Those left behind started to be drafted into the Army or joined other branches of the military. The Warren Commission Report on the JFK assassination said Oswald acted alone. We had our doubts and immediately bought into the conspiracy theories floating around at the time.

Mick Jagger and the Rolling Stones swaggered onto the Ed Sullivan Show. We listened to Petula Clark's *Downtown*, Gerry and the Pacemakers, and Herman's Hermits. *Walk on By, We'll Sing in the Sunshine, Baby Love*, and Roger Miller's *King of the Road* were all popular. *Gomer Pyle, Gilligan's Island*, and *U.N.C.L.E* were TV hits. *Zorba the Greek* and *It's A Mad Mad World* hit the big screen.

In 1965, Volkswagen started its American sales campaign 'Think Small' when they introduced their Beetle to America. We were listening to the Beatles and driving Beetles. Ironically, we were on the verge of being the most rebellious generation ever and yet *Time* magazine said we were "a generation of conformists." The Byrds released *Mr. Tambourine Man*. Bob Dylan sang *Like a Rolling Stone* and that's how many of us began to feel—just being dragged along by events out of our control. The release of the song *Eve of Destruction* hit the top of the charts and summed up the feelings of many of us that we were still doomed. I'm still not sure how we were able to simultaneously feel doomed and optimistic at the same time, but we did.

The first two Marine divisions arrived in Vietnam as advisors and the first psychedelic light shows were seen. Simon and Garfunkel became our singing poets with their haunting songs like *The Sounds of Silence*. At the same time, the Beatles told us *We Can Work It Out*. Miniskirts were in. Not surprisingly, young guys loved them. Some of us started burning draft cards, for those of us serving it was the beginning of a generation split by an unpopular war. The term "hippie" became the name for a whole counterculture.

Sonny and Cher were hip and sang *I Got You Babe*. But the Yardbirds told us *We Gotta Get Out of This Place* and the Byrds sang *Turn Turn Turn*. Young men fantasized about scantily clad *I Love Jeannie* on TV. Hare Krishnas[51] were part of doing your own

---

[51] They dressed in robes like monks. They were groups of young people who were members of the cult. We all saw them in places like airports and bus stations asking for money to support their cause.

thing. Malcolm X[52] was assassinated. Suburban sprawl continued to take its toll and the core of U.S. cities were rotting away with the rise of strip malls.

How things had changed. It had only been about 20 years since the end of World War II when absolute patriotism had gripped America. Yet here we were with thousands of draft dodgers fleeing to Canada to escape military service. Those of us uniform resented it bitterly. The U.S. draft was calling up about 50,000 young men every month.

Head shops started to open in San Francisco's Haight Ashbury district, and they were imitated around the country. They sold things like pot pipes and love beads. Make love, not war was the message. The hippie invasion had begun.

Inflation drove prices up. The war in Vietnam kept heating up and heavy bombing was inflicted on the North. Bobby Seale and Huey Newton formed the Black Panthers in Oakland. War hero song *The Ballet of the Green Berets* topped the charts along with Donovan's *Sunshine Superman*, showing how our generation was being split.

The Mamas & Papas were *California Dreaming* and sang *Monday Monday*. The Beach Boys harmonized about *Good Vibrations*. We hummed *Parsley, Sage, Rosemary & Thyme* by Simon and Garfunkel. The Monkees added their voices to the charts. There were almost 400,000 American troops in Nam as it had come to be known. John Lennon met Yoko. Although the pill was the thing, some of us started to become parents.

I graduated from high school. It was a proud moment for me and my folks. There were several other boys and girls from our neighborhood who walked across the stage with me. In their take-charge way, our dads all got together and decided to have a block party. I don't think they even asked permission from the town government or if they did it was an informal conversation.

---

[52] He was an African American leader in the civil rights movement, minister, and supporter of Black nationalism. He urged his fellow black Americans to protect themselves against white aggression "by any means necessary," a stance that often put him at odds with the nonviolent teachings of Martin Luther King, Jr.

They simply blocked off both ends of the street with homemade wooden sawhorses.

The moms all got together and coordinated the food they would provide. It turned out to be tables laden with all the typical fare of the day, stuff like potato salad, baked beans, green jello, meatloaf. Some Italian families added pasta salad and tasty spaghetti with marinara sauce. It was a feast.

BBQ grills were set up and our dads cooked everything from burgers and sausages to hot dogs. It was a blast. The street was full of mouthwatering smells, music, and people. There was a comradery and neighborly closeness about it I'm not sure I ever saw repeated again on such a scale in my life.

We danced old and young, each with our own style from 40s swing to jitterbug and rock and roll. There was no one to complain about the noise because everyone was part of the festivities. We new high school grads were the celebrities for the night. The adults all congratulated us. Even better they slipped $5s, $10s, and even $20s into our pocket. No checks, just cash. Later when I straightened out and counted the bills in my shirt pockets it would total a whopping $200. They were giving us the support we needed to start our lives.

Boys—but not girls—were expected to leave their parents' home when they left high school and turned 18. There was no choice. We had to move out. We also had to register for the draft. Girls did not have the responsibility of military service hanging over their heads. If ever called, we were obligated to serve. This is something that would be severely tested during the Vietnam era.

I had applied to a small state university in Ohio and been accepted. My parents beamed and bragged to family and friends. I was lucky because high school would be as far as many of us would go educationally when only about half of us would get to enroll in college. The rest of us would stay back in the old hometown and do things like pump gas, become tradesmen, work as secretaries or as salesclerks in retail shops, stock shelves, and bag groceries.

My dad had been the first in his family to graduate from college, but that was due to the GI Bill. If I made it, I would join him. It was a source of pride and I hoped I could pull it off.

I was still in my teens, but in the eyes of society, I was every bit a man fit to take my place in the military or the community. No pressure there.

Tuition and living expenses were modest by today's standards—a few hundred dollars a semester. Not the thousands it costs today but looking back it was all relative. The average worker only made $75 to $100 a week.

Mom and dad had agreed to give me a few hundred bucks, but it was understood that the rest was on me. I had to work and figure it out. There were no student loans or free rides, and I didn't have a scholarship. I knew I would have to support myself in this endeavor, but I was cocky and didn't show the worry I felt inside.

My Chevy was starting to have some mechanical issues, so I sold it, and with that money and some of my graduation loot, I bought a 1956 Ford Crown Victoria. It was two-tone. With the red on the bottom and the white on the top separated by a chrome strip. It wasn't new by any means, but in my eyes, it was a beauty.

Not long after our graduation party, I found a large hard-sided suitcase at a church bazaar sale and bought it for a couple of dollars. Mom helped me pack my clothes and the big moment arrived. Molly, Paul, mom, and dad all stood in the driveway and watched me tuck my suitcase into the trunk of my car.

I was flush with cash but knew I would have to be careful. I had no credit card. The thought never crossed my mind. Credit just wasn't something people like us used. I had withdrawn my money from my savings account and had it stacked, folded, and slipped it into the front pocket of my slacks.

"Call when you get settled," dad said. "You can call collect.[53] And, don't forget that mom and I will meet you on campus that first weekend for fall registration," dad added. "Do you have the map I gave you?"

I assured them I was set and wouldn't forget any plans we had made. I gave hugs all around and I told Paul he was now the big brother of the house and could have my bike. I slid behind the wheel and rolled down the window. Mom had tears in her eyes. Dad just puffed on his pipe and looked stoic. I was off.

---

[53] Since it took so much change to make a long-distance call during that time, collect calls were popular. The operator would ask the receiving party if they would accept the charges and it would get billed to the receiver's phone bill.

In my rear-view mirror, I could see the little group waving and growing smaller.

I stopped by the market on my way out of town. In bidding me goodbye, Mr. Santini had slipped me a couple of $20s and kissed me on both cheeks. I was touched and his eyes were moist. He seemed as proud of me as my folks were. His parting words were, "I know you will make us all proud, son."

Once I cleared the town neighborhoods and suburbs it was an open road. My destination was an area west of Cleveland. An old army buddy of dad's had promised me a summer job at a sawmill. I probably could have kept working more hours at the market, but I wanted to leave home and find my own way. I heard dad inform mom that this was a good thing and would help me become a man. Mom was reluctant, but it was a done deal. I was leaving. This parting was a ritual repeated thousands of times across the country for BB boys.

I had no idea what the new job entailed but was confident I could handle it. His buddy had told dad that there were plenty of boarding houses in the area for me to find a room. It would be up to me to find one and settle in.

*The author off to college, skinny ties and white socks were the uniform of the day (1964).*

These relics left over from the Great Depression would turn out to be my salvation for living arrangements as I came of age. The idea was simple. When times were tough in the 1930s, families would often rent out rooms to single male workers to help make ends meet. There were still lots of big old houses where this was done, especially around areas where there was industrial or manufacturing activity.

My destination was about a two-hour drive on a two-lane road. After about an hour I stopped at a roadside diner to eat. I ordered the all-day breakfast special for an early dinner. The waitress was a friendly middle age lady who called everyone honey. When she brought my food, she pointed out that I wasn't a regular or a local.

*Typical diner.*

I told her I was just passing through. I told her my destination, and that I had a job for the summer. She smiled knowingly and said so you are off to college in the fall. It drove home that I was now on my own. It made me feel excited, important, and nervous at the same time.

By late afternoon I arrived and slowly cruised the streets checking out my new surroundings. Then I drove to the mill. It was an impressive sprawling complex with train tracks behind it. The rail cars were loaded with logs.

From there I cruised back towards town. I saw a sign that said Mrs. Landry's rooms for rent and decided to visit her. It was a big old house of indeterminate age, much like the lady herself. She was friendly and informed me she had rooms to let.

"The fee is $5 per day or if you prefer to rent by the week it is $20. You have your private quarters but have to share a bath with another lodger. I provide three clean bath towels a week unless you prefer your own."

She gave me the tour. The rooms were clean and airy with a view of the graveled area used for parking. The bathroom was ancient with a tub and pedestal sink, but spotless and well maintained.

As an afterthought, she said, "For another dollar a day I serve breakfast from six to seven am. Eggs, sausage or bacon, home fries, and two slices of toast. Pancakes on Sunday."

"May I ask who stays here?"

"Well, we have a couple of fellas from Kentucky who are here most of the year. They come up to work in the mill. A couple of other men are from deeper south, Georgia, I think. You at the mill? You look kinda young."

"Yes ma'am."

"You pay in advance and are not allowed any visitors upstairs, especially ladies. You can entertain your visitors downstairs in the living room, but absolutely no parties and no alcohol outside your room."

Although she had given me the tour and we had talked for a while, I hadn't introduced myself, an oversight I wanted to correct. I stuck out my hand. "I'm Jimmy Bennett."

"Pleased to meet you, young man. So, what will it be? Have you decided to stay with us for a while?"

I dug into my pocket and pulled out my wad of cash and started counting out bills. "Yes ma'am. I'll pay for a week and hopefully will stay longer. I'll take the food, too. Breakfast sounds good."

She accepted the bills and stuffed them into her apron pocket and smiled. "Well Jimmy, I think we are going to get along just fine. Then the smile vanished, "Remember what I said about female visitors upstairs. And I don't cotton to tardiness. If you want to start the day with a proper breakfast, you have to be there when I serve."

I assured her that would be no problem and thanked her. I went to the car for my suitcase and settled in, putting my underwear and socks in the old dresser and hanging my few shirts and pants in a closet that smelled like cedar. At that moment I felt an unexpected pang of homesickness but quickly brushed it off. I had my dreams, not the ones that come in sleep, but the ones we hold close day after day, and I wanted to live them as they beckoned me into an uncertain future.

The following day I went at six to the dining room. There I met most of the other men. They were comfortable to eat with, but most of them were old enough to be my dad or lease an older brother. With their easy banter, they started calling me the kid. I took no offense and sort of liked it.

By seven that morning I was at the mill. I found the foreman and he took me to his small orderly office. The whole place smelled great, like freshly cut wood. I remember thinking that this wasn't going to be so bad. I filled out a few forms and he imparted some basic information.

He informed me that starting pay was $1.50 an hour. It was all I could do to keep from getting giddy. I had just tripled my salary from my market days. I was going to make a whopping $60 a week. My mind was like a calculator. That meant if I was careful, I could save over a hundred bucks a month for school. With tuition and registration fees of about $500 per semester, it was going to work. Dad had been right.

Next, we went down on the busy floor. There was a light sawdust fog hanging over the place as big power saws whined everywhere. I could understand why they had no smoking signs everywhere. One ember and the air would ignite with a big woosh.

We started where the logs came into the building, rumbling down metal rollers. Big blades cut the sides off and once the piece was square it rolled to another station. By the time it reached the assembly area the wood had been cut into thin boards and small blocks. We were making wooden pallets for the automobile makers in Detroit. There were stacks and stacks of them everywhere. Fascinated, I watched as forklifts moved the six-foot squares towards the flat rail cars. There were trainloads of wood coming and trainloads of pallets going out to the motor city.

Later over a beer one of the guys explained that the pallets were used for shipping parts to automobile assembly plants around the country. He laughed when he said, "So I tell my friends that I work making cars." That idea appealed to me and I felt like part of the mighty automobile manufacturing machine.

I was taken to a station where the cut wood came down the rollers and my job was to cut the wooden spacer blocks. Dozens and hundreds of them hour after hour. As I cut them, they fell into large canvas carts with wheels. It wasn't rocket science and my training lasted less than 10 minutes.

After a few weeks on the line, I became an industrial statistic. I suppose it was inevitable that it should happen. The saw was mounted on rails and was retracted by a spring into a nook inside the wall. It moved with little resistance. As the wood rolled through my job was to pull out the big saw and cut the blocks. Then I released it and gave a light push where it went back and was cushioned by rubber bumpers. If I pushed too hard it would bounce back out. You had to have the right technique and touch.

That day I heard a ping. I felt nothing but then saw a rooster tail of blood hit the wall like someone had slung a brush full of red paint. I had pushed too hard and as I reached down to pull the wood into position the saw had bounced out from its resting place. I was afraid to look at my hand.

I wrapped it with my handkerchief and walked over to the foreman. He calmly removed the blood-soaked material. I had lost the tip of my index finger. I knew I was lucky that I hadn't lost all my fingers. He drove me to the emergency room where they stitched me up.

He gave me the rest of the week off and told me when to check back in. It hurt like hell and I only got paid a dollar an hour for those days I lounged around Mrs. Landry's recovering, but I felt lucky.

As a sign of the times, it never occurred to me to take any other action, nor did the company offer anything. I didn't go find a lawyer and sue or anything else. That never crossed my mind. Even when I let dad know, it apparently never crossed his mind either.

After a few days of boredom, I returned to work a slightly wiser veteran and found I was accepted by the guys as one of them. My bandaged hand didn't prevent me from doing my job, albeit with more care.

My first weeks of work, though, was a time of learning some restraint. This level of self-discipline was new to me and it took me a while to figure it out.

Some of the guys invited me out for a beer from the first day. I was only 18 but was physically mature and the bartender didn't look twice as we gathered at a gin mill down the road. It was a raucous place full of guys with work clothes and boots like us. Music blared from the jukebox. I loved it and had never experienced anything like it. We were loud, too, and poured down round after round of frosty mugs of tap beer. And, for the first time in my life, I was tipsy.

Fortunately, my system rebelled, and I made it to the men's room just in time to vomit most of it up. I washed up and rejoined my new crowd in a more somber mood. I switched to Coca-Cola to the good-natured ribbing of the guys. This was repeated throughout the first week. There were times when I was sure I looked green, at least I felt like it. I wondered if any of them noticed.

Everyone smoked cigarettes and I puffed up on my first real smoke. This compounded my unsteadiness. Unfortunately, it would be the beginning of a lifelong battle with nicotine addiction for me. I even dropped a couple of dimes in the cigarette machine and bought my first pack, which I rolled up in my tee-shirt sleeve like one of the cool guys.

One night when I calculated my finances, I realized that despite working full time, with my drinking I had lost money the first week. It was a sobering thought, and I would have to be more frugal. The rest of the summer I did go out with the guys on occasion and learned to pace myself. I was back on track moneywise and didn't feel as miserable. I decided hangovers were not fun. As one of the guys joked, "In the morning you feel like every one of your teeth has a small sweater on it and your mouth is stuffed with cotton." That pretty much summed it up.

I enjoyed the camaraderie but working on a factory floor was not my life. At least not the life I wanted. I wanted the suit and tie and the salary that came with it. By September, I said my warm goodbyes to the crew. They slapped my back and told me to go and make them proud. Mrs. Landry surprised me when she got misty-eyed and hugged me. "Don't be a stranger, young man. You know where to find us."

I was touched but it was time for me to go and head down the road to school. As planned, I met up with the whole family at a motel off-campus and related some of my less embarrassing summer moments with them.

The following day mom and the kids wandered around the campus while dad and I registered. I was set for the semester but knew I would have to work part-time to make living expenses. As promised dad put up a few hundred bucks and it all came out even with some spending money to spare. It wasn't much, but with a dorm and meal plan, I wouldn't starve. He didn't seem to have any doubt that I would make it academically or financially. This in turn gave me confidence.

Before they left and I started my classes, I got my final surprise was when dad opened the trunk of his sedan and presented me with a used manual Smith and Corona typewriter in a case. Since most of the professors required typewritten papers it would turn out to be a lifesaver. In high school, mom had made me take typing. I hated that I was the only boy in the class, but she told me I would thank her later. I am still thankful that she didn't make me take home economics classes where the girls had to learn life skills like cooking and running a home kitchen.

But learning to touch type, albeit slowly, gave me an advantage. It would turn out that most of the other guys were at the mercy of their girlfriends to prepare their assignments for them. Not me. I was Mr. Independent.

The dorm rooms were small, tidy, and comfortable. My roommate turned out to be a guy named Brian. I told him he didn't sound like an Ohio guy with his Jersey accent. He explained that his family had moved from New Jersey to Ohio the year before. Almost instantly we became like brothers. Nights were spent with our room door open and us guys talking everything from childhood to politics and girls. We not only exchanged stories but good-naturedly argued about a lot of things. Like our neighborhoods before, you were loyal to your dorm, like a band of brothers.

One bit of disturbing news we argued about was the founding of the Black Panther Party for Self Defense. The newspapers were full of stories about them. According to the news, it was started in 1966 in Oakland, California by community organizer Bobby Seale and an ex-convict turned law student, named Huey Newton.

It was billed as a revolutionary political organization. But it was more. They were armed, menacing, and militant. In your face. I wanted change but not in the manner of the many shootouts these guys had with the police. I thought this was more of an armed military group than a political organization. They even had a defense minister.

They weren't the only ones. On the other side of the spectrum were the Ku Klux Klan or KKK. A more subtle version of conservative white supremacy were those in the John Birch Society.[54]

I found it unsettling. This was America, not some developing country. Maybe I wasn't the rebel I thought I was. Some buddies sided with me but many of my friends found such organizations exciting and with merit. Our informal debates were spirited. I wondered what Ellison would say about it.

---

[54] The Society was founded in the late 1950s by businessman Robert Welch to combat what he saw as the growing communist threat to American democracy, but the radical right-wing group didn't support the civil rights movement and had definite racial discrimination tendencies.

No matter, it continued to bother me as my parents' indoctrination echoed in my mind. Whatever happened to change via the ballot box? The term "community organizer" also bothered me. What did that even mean? At the time I wondered why communities needed organizing anyway. In dad's words, it smacked of communism. Despite my liberal views, I had grown up in this anti-communist environment. It was ingrained in me.

Along with our dorm discussion free for alls, we were there to learn new things. The classes were large, and the instructors didn't seem to care if you went to class or not as long as you showed up and took your exams. It was a freedom we weren't used to and many of my friends paid the price with failing or mediocre grades. I wasn't one of them. Working in the mill had planted the seeds for self-restraint. My guilt was reinforced by the little imaginary figures of my parents perched on my shoulders like an ever-present conscience. I seldom skipped classes.

I kept monitoring my dwindling stash and midway through the first semester, I knew it was time to find some part-time work. When I would talk to dad, he always inquired about my state of financial affairs but never offered to help. I wasn't sure if it was because he couldn't, or it was an extension of his lessons for me on how to be a man. It didn't matter. It was obvious it was up to me.

To save money I canceled my school meal plan and started to live on burgers, hot dogs, fried chicken, pizza, and other junk food and taking advantage of the daily specials. I considered dropping out for a semester and working full time then returning. Instinctively I knew this didn't seem like a good idea, but things were critical. Besides, if I did drop out, I would lose my student deferment and would most likely be drafted into the military and send off to Vietnam.

I was sitting in the cafeteria in the student union building with Brian one day and he was watching me stir a dollop of ketchup into a tall glass of water to make my version of tomato juice.

He eyed me skeptically and said, "That looks disgusting."
"Yeah, it is, but it sort of works."
"Why don't you get a job bussing the tables here. I'll join you. My dad says he can't afford to give me much more. It's not much money but if we do, we can make some cash and eat free."

And that was it. We became busboys. We clowned around a lot and flirted with female students, but got the job done.

The dorms were not coed. If you visited a girl in her dorm you were not allowed to go past the lobby. This was strictly enforced by the dreaded 'dorm mothers.'

We found time to go to the occasional keg party, but not many. After a few long months of lugging heavy bins loaded with dirty trays to the dishwashing station, it was getting old fast. I started scouring the classified help wanted ads in the local newspaper.

I ended up being the night clerk at a downtown hotel. I went to work at 9 pm and got off at 7 am. I would go back to the dorm and sleep and then have afternoon classes. My money troubles were over and I could study on the job. Despite the bright side, though, it was not perfect as it did wreak havoc on my sleep and social life but hey . . . I was getting it done. Grades weren't a problem, and my credits were stacking up.

Brian was also forced to take even more extreme measures and went to work on the night shift at the local Ford assembly plant. We suddenly had money again because we had little chance to spend it. During that time, I seldom had the opportunity to see or talk to him, but it didn't matter. We shared an unbreakable bond.

The university policy was that you had to live at least one semester on campus in a dorm then you could move off-campus. Brian and I and another friend eventually ended up renting rooms above a beauty parlor. It was great having our own place.

I sold the Ford and bought a used 1961 Volkswagen Beetle. It was jet black. It had no gauges, just a speedometer. Not even a gas gauge. If you ran out of gas you just flipped a lever under the dashboard and could go another 40 miles or so. I got it cheap because it had a bad cylinder. The VW engines of the time, though, were bolted together, the cylinders stacked together like a pile of baloney. With my friends, we unbolted the bad cylinder and replaced it.

It ran great. The only problem was that with the engine in the rear it only produced a thin stream of warm air in the front and winters in Ohio were frigid. I rode around with a blanket on my lap to keep from freezing. I even kept a small stack of covers in the small back seat for my passengers.

By this time my folks were complaining that I didn't stay in touch enough. It was a fair criticism, but I had my hands full, and I seldom went home, except on holidays. To solve the problem, I went to the post office and bought a stack of generic postcards that included postage. For a nickel, I could dash a few lines and it kept them happy. Then, when time permitted, I would pen the occasional long letter to fill in the gaps.

In addition to a lack of parties, I missed a lot of campus protests that I wanted to be part of, but my diligence eventually paid off. I finally cobbled together both credits and money and found myself on the list to graduate in the spring. I was going to make it and it hadn't even taken me four years. My folks were proud. I was even prouder.

With my dad's help, I put together my first resume. I had a lot of menial experience to fill up a page. I started calling and mailing them out. I wasn't at all sure what my degree in business qualified me for, but surely, I could do something. Nothing came in immediately and that gave me time to think more about the future.

On the rare occasion when I had time over beers with Brian, he made something come alive in the back of my mind that I tried to ignore. Namely, I should take some time and do a road trip. When I talked about it with my folks, mom was mortified. She pointed out that I should get set up with a real job before goofing off, as he called it. Dad was more supportive and seemed to get it.

It didn't matter. I was my own man, and it was my choice. I started planning my trip. I couldn't see myself cruising Route 66 in a VW bug, so I found a 1965 forest green Chevy Belair. It was owned by an elderly lady who had crumpled the front end. Her son informed me since he was strongly recommending that his mom give up her driver's license and he didn't want the bother of fixing it, I could have it at a bargain.

I cruised the local junkyards and found the right radiator, fenders, and grill. I enlisted the help of my friends one Saturday and we unbolted and bolted until she looked great. A couple of cans of green spray paint and she was ready. It was big. You could lay down in the back seat like a twin bed and take a nap. This was great because when I took road trips, I often slept in my car in parking lots or along the road.

I bought an Atlas from the local auto club and began mapping out my trip. I planned to drive to Chicago and take Route 66 to Santa Monica, California. I even did some library research on the iconic and historic road. It had been the primary route for those who migrated west during tough times, like the Dust Bowl[55] of the 1930s.

This was captured in author John Steinbeck's powerful novel, *The Grapes of Wrath*, which had been made into a powerful symbol of loss and escape. Later it was turned into a classic movie with legendary actors like Henry Fonda and John Carradine.

Many a family had used it. In my mind, it conjured up images of a Model T Ford top-heavy with every personal belonging imaginable tied down with ropes as these brave souls sought to find a new life from the one nature and the economy had taken away from them.

I couldn't imagine the hardships they had to face, but I didn't dwell on that long because my trip was going to be a pure lark. Just cruising, looking, and enjoying. I swung home before starting and spent a few days with the family. Mom was a bit morose and dad was thoughtful. I tried to be upbeat and assured them I would see them before summer ended when I would settle down.

I made it to Chicago and started. I drove through Missouri and stopped in a few interesting bars in the Ozark mountains to drink cold beer. I saw one bar fight and almost managed to avoid the fracas until a big guy almost my dad's age broke a beer bottle on the bar and looked menacingly at me. It seemed to be over a pretty lady in her 20s, but I wasn't sure. By this time half the bar was swinging. I remember my heart hammering in my chest.,

The large man seemed intent on doing me bodily harm, so I stood on the rungs of my stool, placed one hand flat on the bar, and executed a neat vault over it. I landed behind the bar temporarily out of harm's way. That was about the time the local cops burst through the door swinging their batons.

I avoided being clubbed and I tried to insist that none of this had anything to do with me. They weren't interested in my story.

---

[55] During the dust bowl in the 1930s, while in the midst of the Great Depression, thousands of 'okies' from Oklahoma piled their families and meager belongings into their jalopies and headed for a better life in California. With no crops they simply couldn't survive any longer on their poor farms.

They didn't handcuff me—I supposed they ran out of them—but I was grabbed by the back of my shirt and dumped unceremoniously in the back of an ancient Studebaker police car with a large, faded star on the door. For the first time in my life, I found myself locked in a cell with others. The men who milled around uneasily seemed to have cooled off enough that it didn't flare up again. I was grateful for that.

After a few hours, I was hauled before a justice of the peace. The elderly man peered down from his perch through thick glasses and asked who I was. I told him the short version of my story. He told me I was free to go and that I might want to keep on moving down the road. I took his advice and left town.

As I did, I realized what was missing. This should have been a buddy trip, not a solo journey. I had asked Brian to go with me but knew his folks were having a hard time and he had to go home and help his dad take care of the family. He said that a diagnosis of cancer in his mom had left her devastated and weak. His dad was struggling.

Kansas was tabletop flat and I saw nothing but fields and a few guys plowing on big tractors off in the distance. Without much to see I kept moving and swung down into Oklahoma. Oil wells were everywhere pumping the black stuff out of the ground. I thought about spending the night in Oklahoma City but decided against it. Cities were more expensive for lodging and drinking and I was better to stick to roadside diners, bars, and motels.

As I left the red dirt of Oklahoma behind it was a welcome sight to see a young guy in an army uniform hitchhiking. He wasn't much older than me and we chatted easily. He told me he was heading to an army post in Texas and from there they were shipping him to Vietnam. We chatted about current events and rode together into Texas where I left him at a truck stop after wishing him well and safe travels.

I often wonder if he was one of the lucky ones or his name, along with 57,000 others, is on the wall of the Vietnam Memorial in Washington, DC. Since he never mentioned his last name this remains a mystery to me.

Once again, the only sound to fill my Chevy was music. The Beatles continued to reign supreme with the release of Sgt.

Pepper's Lonely Heart Club Band album. The music of The Grateful Dead. Jefferson Airplane and The Byrds also filled the airways. Once in a while, I would catch a radio station that featured talk as I rolled through West Texas. I listened to the callers as my parent's generation lamented things like pot smoking among BBs.

A man named Timothy Leary took mind-altering drugs to new heights by advocating the use of LSD.[56] A lot of people were dropping "acid" as it was known and hallucinating. The hippies I met called it "trippin." I stayed away from it having seen people flip out on it. Getting high and banging my head against the wall didn't appeal to me at all.

This was a time when drugs like marijuana, LDS, and others moved from the back alley to main street and became recreational for many BBs. The 1960s era of rock festivals helped spread both drugs and the counterculture across the country. Not surprisingly, all of this turmoil was not without its critics—especially those who were more conservative who tended to characterize the counterculture movement as self-indulgent, irrational, and narcissistic. Yet both liberals and conservatives agreed it had a significant impact on American culture and politics.

I would see more guys in uniform thumbing rides. I suppose that wasn't surprising because by 1967 LBJ had poured almost half a million troops into the country. The military was on the move. Not everyone was for the war, including the boxer formally known as Cassius Clay. After he joined the Nation of Islam and became Muhammad Ali, he was stripped of his world heavyweight boxing crown for refusing to be inducted into the US Army. The number of antiwar protesters seemed to multiply by the day.

Nonetheless, war seemed to be the order of the day. In the middle east, Israel went to war with Syria, Egypt, and Jordan in the six-day war. When it was over Israel controlled and occupied a lot more territory than before the war.

On the home front, cities throughout America exploded in rioting and looting. They were on fire. One of the worst was Detroit where 7000 National Guard troops were ordered in to restore order in the streets.

---

[56] LSD was and is a synthetic compound used recreationally for its mood altering and psychedelic effects.

Culture, especially styles, was also changing. In the United Kingdom, a new stick-thin model became a sensation. Her name was Twiggy and she inspired and was responsible for miniskirts becoming shorter and shorter and more popular.

Although war and radicalism were the themes of the day, it is ironic that historians would dub that summer as "The Summer of Love." The ubiquitous hippie chant was "make love, not war." They were on the rise as hundreds of thousands of young people started to gather in US cities. The center of the hippie universe, though, was San Francisco's Haight-Ashbury neighborhood. They were known as flower children. They were distrustful of government and consumerism and immersed themselves in art, music, poetry, and mystical and spiritual meditative practices.

They not only wanted to be at peace with other people but nature as well. They started to form communes and collective farms to create what they needed to live. They sprang up everywhere, especially in California.

I reflected on these things as I cruised down the road. Songs on the radio would sometimes send my thoughts off into new directions. No matter, I drove on.

New Mexico and Arizona were beautiful and like driving through a picture postcard. By the time I reached Santa Monica, I started to see the news reports about hippies come to life. The coastal area was filled with young people in jeans, flowery shirts, and sandals. Many of them with beards and long hair. They sported colorful headbands and beads around their necks. They were super friendly and seemed to be overly fond of using terms like "dude," "that's really cool," and "far out."

As the attendant filled my gasoline tank at a station in Santa Monica, he said the car was leaking water. I stood alongside him as he lifted the hood and informed me my water pump had broken. It wasn't terribly expensive or serious, but I knew it had to be fixed or the car would overheat. I left it for their mechanic and headed toward the beach. After walking out on the long pier and taking in the magnificent view of the Pacific, I silently congratulated myself that I had made it. It was a travel milestone for me.

From there I walked along the beach area and stopped in a coffee shop. It was crowded with young people and boisterous.

The tables were full but as I stood there balancing my cup, hesitant and unsure where to sit, a group of hippies motioned for me to join them. I smiled and walked over.

I introduced myself and they went around the table each saying their names. I was

Hippies.

struck by their open friendliness, and I was fascinated by some of the unusual names, obviously made up and adopted, but still cool. I met a "Moonbeam, Indigo, and Marley."

After telling them I was just bumming around, they urged me to explore Northern California and named some places to visit, including a commune. I told them my car was in the shop and I had to get home and find a job. This seemed to amuse them.

Then out of the blue, they invited me to go up the coast with them. Their ultimate destination was the Big Sur area but said I could ride as long as I wanted. They assured me my return trip could easily be accomplished by hitching rides down California highway 101, pointing out there would be no shortage of rides.

I was a bit speechless but at their urging, I agreed. I told them I had to go back to the gas station get my gear and let them know I wouldn't be coming back for the Chevy for a few days. They said that was no problem. Then I found a payphone, got the operator, and placed a collect call home.

Such calls were expensive, and I knew I couldn't talk long. Mom accepted the call and then dad came on the line. Like all parents, their first thought was that something was wrong. I assured them it wasn't and let them know I would be spending a few days in California before my return trip. They sounded concerned and told me to be careful. After the call disconnected, I felt sorry that I was causing them so much angst but told myself that I had to live my life.

I met up again with my new best friends and we piled into a classic VW bus with a peace sign painted on the side. We cruised up highway 101 and chatted easily getting to know one another. I thought I was a rebel but in talking to them it became clear I wasn't even close. Their counterculture views were so different from the way I saw the world. For me, it was enlightening and educational.

For two straight nights at dusk, we set up camp on the beach and built a fire. Those nights were spent sitting around it preparing food then sharing stories as it grew late. They all smoked pot and offered me a joint. I took a puff and found it mildly intoxicating, but visions of my drunkenness when I first went to work at the sawmill kept me in check. I didn't want to lose self-control. I also wanted to remember these magic moments.

Sleeping arrangements were fluid. There didn't seem to be any couples or jealousies involved, just however it happened. One of the girls seem to like me a lot and even said I should consider joining them and their plans to settle in a commune. I told her I would think about it, but in reality, I knew that was not a long-term plan that fit with who I thought I was or wanted to be. I wanted financial independence and a modicum of order, not necessarily total lifestyle freedom. I knew I wanted to get back soon and get on with my life.

They let me off one morning on the side of the highway. We promised to stay in touch and they scribbled the name and box number of a commune. I stuffed it into my pocket then crossed the road and stuck out my thumb. Their prediction came true and I was transported back to Santa Monic in an almost continual series of rides, many of them with hippies in VW buses.

I paid my service bill and decided to spend the night in Santa Monica. That evening I was eating alone in a diner and noticed an attractive girl in a nearby booth. She was with an older woman who I assumed was her mom. They were engaged in conversation, but I started to have eye contact and flirt with the girl. She stared coolly back at me—almost like a challenge.

When her mom got up to use the restroom, I summoned the nerve to saunter over to her booth. "You look so familiar," I lied. "Do we know each other?"

## Chapter 5

She rolled her eyes and said, "Not very original."

I flushed a little and decided to cut my losses, shrugged, and turned the leave.

"Wait, don't be so sensitive."

At that moment her mom returned. The girl said, "Mom, meet Mr . . . " as her voice trailed off, I stuck out my hand.

"Hi, I'm Jimmy Bennett."

"I'm Gladys Foster. This is my daughter Kathy."

Kathy smiled at me. "Saved by the bell."

I grinned back.

"Won't you join us," said Mrs. Foster? "We were thinking of ordering some pie."

"Sounds good."

We chatted easily for a while. Then Mrs. Foster said, "Well I've got to get back to the shop."

"I was hoping we could chat some more," I said.

Kathy's mom eyed us with a measure of amusement in her eyes.

"My car is in the shop right down the street. I would be happy to give Kathy a ride home when I pick it up."

Kathy pushed her dishes away from her. "Sure. Why not? Is that okay with you, mom?"

Her mom picked up the check and rose. "Well, I guess I'll see you later then . . . "

Kathy and I ordered coffee and continued to talk like we were old friends. I was smitten by her and she seemed to be interested in me, too. It was a whirlwind but there was definitely chemistry between us.

"I was planning to head back east, but there is no reason I have to hurry. If I stayed a day or two, would you go out with me?"

She gave me that look that was at once cool and standoffish and shy at the same time. "I think I would like that."

We walked on the pier for the better part of an hour and watched several old men fishing. Then we headed down the street and got the Chevy.

She gave me directions and I drove her home. I walked her to the door and was hoping for a kiss. Instead, I got a peck on the cheek.

"So, lunch tomorrow? I'll pick you up at noon?"

"I'll look forward to it."

And with that, she ducked into the house. I felt giddy like I was back in high school.

The following day was a wonderful blur. We ate at a beach joint and flirted and talked. The time passed altogether too quickly.

We exchanged addresses. I told her that I wanted to get on with finding my first real job. She suggested that maybe I should consider relocating to the West coast. The thought was enticing.

But with her contact info carefully tucked in my pocket, I got back on the road. I considered an alternative route, but the lure of Rt. 66 was just too great. At one time it was billed as the main street of America. Sadly, most of it no longer exists, having been absorbed into the interstate highway system. Proving that some changes are for the better and others are not. I wish it had been somehow maintained and better preserved. It was a national treasure.

I got home and went back to work looking for work, but with a lot more on my mind. I wasn't even working, yet and my Ohio life seemed mundane, and I longed for a change. California and Kathy seemed always on my mind.

We exchanged a flurry of letters as things heated up. When I mentioned to my folks that I had met someone they didn't seem enthusiastic about my moving across the country.

I seemed destined to be conflicted by guilt and wanting to just do what I wanted and the hell with everything and everyone else. One thing I didn't want to happen was to lose the uplifting feeling my trip and meeting Kathy had given me, but my old life started to suck me in again.

As I thought about it, though, I couldn't see myself starting all over again in California. If I was honest with myself, it just wasn't my scene. I was a mid-west guy and despite any doubts I had, I was comfortable here. To soften my guilt, I told myself that maybe later I would try it. For the moment I just wanted to find a job and start my life as a young professional.

## Chapter 6

# Protests of a Generation Divided & the Man on the Moon (1968 – 1969)

By 1968, many BBs had blossomed into hippies, yuppies, and flower children. I wasn't among them even though I had come into intimate contact with the counterculture. I still fancied myself the all-American boy. I had slicked-back hair and wore pegged pants and white tee shirts with my cigarettes rolled up in the sleeve. I liked my beer, but that was the only mind-altering thing I indulged in.

The line was drawn for drugs. Timothy Leary's LSD Celebration arrived in San Francisco. For many users of the drug it caused them to freak out to the point of screaming and banging their heads on the wall. They went nuts and just the idea of trying it seemed nuts to me. I wouldn't have ingested it if someone had paid me.

Communes continued to spring up daily throughout the country. This whole scene further alarmed and confused our parents. We started to try and find ourselves. Transcendental meditation became the 'in' way for discovery. Long hair and flower power were the order for many of us. Hippies were fond of telling everyone they encountered to "Make love, not war." It became even more of a cliché of the day.

The Beatles released *Strawberry Fields Forever*. The Doors sang *Come On Baby Light My Fire*. As the pill gained popularity free love started to be the norm. Even if you didn't do drugs, like me, it was a mind-blowing experience.

Liberal Democrat Eugene McCarthy ran for the presidency on an anti-war platform. A lot of BBs worked for his election. Otis Redding recorded *Dock of the Bay*. Sadly, he was killed weeks later in a plane crash. Some of us continued to smoke pot and started dropping even more acid. Donovan sang *Mello Yellow*. Jimi Hendrix wailed his music. A young Dustin Hoffman lived out every boy's fears and fantasies of adulthood on the big screen in *The Graduate. The Planet of the Apes* movie also debuted.

By 1968, feminism was on the rise and bra-burning became commonplace as a symbol of women's liberation. We debated the feminist protest about the Miss America contest. The question being why women were objectified and not men? The role of women as full-time homemakers had especially been under fierce attack since the beginning of the 1960s, but things were heating up even more. And, in defense of BBs, most of us felt it was long overdue.

Tens of thousands of BBs protested the war on campuses across the country. In many ways, we had become the show. Events in Nam reminded us we were not winning the war, despite what the Pentagon said. Every day the news would report the body count of enemy soldiers who were killed. It was a grisly measurement and I'm not sure we believed that day after day hundreds or thousands of Viet Cong were killed while we only lost a few soldiers.

Sensing the intensity of the anti-war mood in the country, LBJ decided not to seek another term. When Martin Luther King was assassinated it set off another round of race riots. The King assassination riots, also known as the Holy Week Uprising, was a wave of civil disturbance that swept the United States following his death in April 1968. Many believe it was the greatest wave of social unrest the United States had experienced since the Civil War. Some of the biggest riots took place in Washington, D.C.,

Baltimore, Chicago, Detroit, and Kansas City, but they erupted in over 100 cities nationwide.

In Washington, DC, for instance, the 14th Street corridor was gutted and burned. It was a war zone. The reports from places like Detroit were equally grim as the National Guard was called out to try and restore order. Most Americans, including me, were shocked and started to become numb from such events.

The BBs who went to school on student deferments started to graduate from college. When Russian tanks crushed the Czechs[57] we were reminded that the Cold War was still hot.

For some BBs, protest had become ingrained as a way of life by this time. We started to adopt many causes, including those of Native Americans. Nixon defeated Hubert Humphrey in the presidential election.

By 1968, Simon & Garfunkel were singing about a *Bridge Over Troubled Water*. Fleetwood Mac, Steve Miller, and Sly and the Family Stone also made an impact. We also had *A Yellow Submarine*; Tiny Tim, Blood, Sweat & Tears; and an Iron Butterfly.

The rock musical *Hair* shocked our parents and delighted us. It was a musical that focused on the lives of two young men in the Vietnam era against the backdrop of the hippie culture. Even those of us who didn't see it identified with the fun, free-loving, rebellious spirit the show represented. That American Tribal Love-Rock Musical reflected the hippie counterculture and sexual revolution of the late 1960s, and several of its songs became anthems of the anti-Vietnam War peace movement.

We listened to *The Age of Aquarius* and *Raindrops Keep Falling on My Head*. Airplane hijackings reached their peak as they were diverted to Cuba. It was as though everybody was a rebel.

Tennis player Arthur Ashe won the U.S. Open, becoming the first Black man to win a Grand Slam event. Boeing rolled out the first jumbo jet with its 747.

The Apollo 7 spacecraft made history as its three astronauts got launched into orbit, with a live telecast. The Apollo 8 astronauts, the first humans to orbit the moon,

---

[57] Approximately 200,00 troops and 5,000 tanks invaded Czechoslovakia to crush the "Prague Spring," which was a brief period of liberalization in the Communist country. Despite demonstrations and resistance, the Czechs were no match for Soviet tanks, and they imposed their iron will once again.

read from Genesis from the Old Testament Bible to millions of Americans, including how *In the beginning God created heaven and earth. And the earth was without form and void, and darkness was upon the face of the deep. And the Spirit of God moved upon the face of the waters. And God said, Let there be light: and there was light. And God saw the light, that it was good: and God divided the light from the darkness.* Could that happen today? I doubt it because the words would no doubt offend someone.

Our kids and grandkids may think that the US was all about sex, drugs, and rock and roll during this time, but it was much more than that. For those who were at Woodstock on a farm in upstate New York, it was the chance to rebel against their uptight parents. It was counter-culturalism on drugs that clashed with prevailing moral standards and censorship.

We seemed to revel in endless conflict and change. Rowan & Martin's *Laugh-in* changed comedy on TV and *The Smothers Brothers Show* was canceled for being too controversial. Senator Ted Kennedy drove Mary Jo Kopechne into a watery grave on Chappaquiddick[58] and dashed the hopes of many BBs for a Camelot revival in the White House.

Amid all the craziness, astronaut Neil Armstrong walked on the moon and took "a small step for man and a giant leap for mankind." The country paused for a fleeting moment of national unity and pride. Everywhere you went it was the talk of the town. People kept saying, "Imagine, we put a man on the moon!" Images of our venture into space

*Man on the moon.*

---
[58] Known as Chappaquiddick, it was a single vehicle care crash that occurred on Chappaquiddick Island. It was caused by Senator Edward (Ted) Kennedy and resulted in the death of 28-yeard old Mary Jo Kopechne, who was trapped inside the car. Kennedy fled the scene and was severely criticized for his actions, but no charges were ever filed. It effectively ended any chance Kennedy had of winning the presidency.

were broadcast continually.

Here on planet earth, *the Midnight Cowboy* disturbed us with its grimy depiction of greed, shallow character, and casual sex on the big screen. And the movie *Bob & Carol and Ted & Alice* seemed to capture the openness with sex that many of us felt.

Barbershops stopped existing and unisex salons pushed the notion that we were all the same. There were no men and women, It was the start of gender neutrality. Our parents thought such notions bordered on lunacy. As my dad said at the time, "Good grief, it's biology, there are men and there are women, period. They are biologically different in case these nuts haven't noticed that they have different parts."

I listened to these rants and said nothing. I didn't know what to say because such notions were so new to me.

North Vietnam dictator Ho Chi Minh died, but the war simply wouldn't go away. Shadowy domestic terrorist groups like the Black Panthers and the Weathermen Underground continued to keep the FBI busy chasing subversives here at home. Surprisingly, many BBs admired these groups for challenging authority in such a radical way. Others thought we may have crossed the line.

The expression "burn baby burn" came from the 1960's exhortations of the Black Panther Party to set city ghettos on fire as urban decay disproportionately affected minority communities.

Now, in an odd twist in the 21st century, the Black Panthers market a BBQ Sauce with their trademark "Burn Baby Burn" phrase. My, how things change. Billed as revolutionary hot sauce, it is distributed by the Dr. Huey P. Newton Foundation, which was created by former Black Panther Party members.

Today, as this is being written, and I talk to my grandchildren and others in their generation, they fear that the country is on the verge of a nervous breakdown. But I point out that we have been here before. After all, 1968 was the pivotal turning point in an era in which all established norms were either under siege or outright attack. It was when idealism clashed with fear. When our collective national psyche went from hopeful to fearful. We fell into despair in such a freefall that many wondered whether the America they knew could even endure.

The drama was endless from Vietnam and the Tet offensive[59] and the tumultuous Democratic convention in Chicago to Nixon, riots, student rebellion, Black Power, Sisterhood, and turmoil in Poland and Eastern Europe as the Iron Curtain was under assault.

All of this coursed through our national veins against a backdrop of music that screamed of cultural expression. The Beatles, Jimi Hendrix, Aretha Franklin, and the Rolling Stones all brazenly challenged musical norms. Men were orbiting the moon and here on earth people took other trips with LSD. Still, others were transported with free love. We had Broadway nudity and yippies tested the limits. We were grieving, rebelling, and demanding change all simultaneously. We could no longer shut the world out as advances in communications bombarded us with waves of change and cultural clashes.

Many of us BBs were angry but didn't always understand the disquieting nature of our discontent. When declaring his presidential candidacy, Senator Robert F. Kennedy said, "I have traveled, and I have listened to the young people of our nation and felt their anger about the war that they are sent to fight and about the world they are about to inherit."

The first wave of protest had been aimed at civil rights, poverty, and liberating college students. But by the mid to late 1960s, the tide of protest changed for students and young adults as they shifted their attention to the Vietnam war.

The nation continued to be gripped by protest fever about everything. In a 1969 moratorium, more than 600,000 gathered to demonstrate against the Vietnam War. The march and all-day rally on the Mall in Washington, DC culminated a week of protests throughout the city, including a "March Against Death" from Arlington National Cemetery past the White House to the U.S. Capitol led by pediatrician Dr. Benjamin Spock and the Rev. William Sloane Coffin of Yale.

In 1968, the Orangeburg Massacre occurred when a civil rights protest at South Carolina State University turned deadly after highway patrolmen opened fire on about 200 unarmed

---

[59] The Tet Offensive was one of the bloodiest military campaigns of the Vietnam War when the Northern Communist regime launched an all-out assault on the South and its cities. It marked a sharp turn in the war and reminded us that despite the rosy body counts we weren't really winning the effort at all.

Black student protestors. Three young men were shot and killed, and dozens injured as students rallied against the segregation of a local bowling alley.

Activists Jerry Ruin and Abby Hoffman established the Youth International Party—the YIPPIES, who were radicalized hippies.

Figure skater Peggy Fleming won the only U.S. gold medal at the Winter Olympics in France. The International Olympic Committee voted to invite apartheid[60] South Africa to participate in the Summer Games, but withdrew the invitation months later after dozens of countries threatened to boycott the event.

A police station in Haley, Alabama, was the first to officially use 911, the nation's universal emergency number. They, of course, could never have imagined that 33 years later, on September 11, 2001—911would come to represent the day true terror came to America.

Janis Joplin made the cover of Rolling Stone.[61] Standards and our very morality kept changing. Linda LeClair, a sophomore at Barnard College in New, made scandalous national headlines when she defied school rules by moving off campus to live with her boyfriend. Our parents' generation were indignant—how dare she do such a thing? The school expelled her. Us BB boys wished we could be lucky enough that some women would shack up with us.

We had long-haired hippies, the pill, and counterculture protest, but oddly, deep down, the country was still fairly conservative. Imagine an unmarried woman like LeClair living with a man out of wedlock? She was severely criticized for her lack of morals, which all fed into feminist activism and double standards for women. Perhaps not surprisingly, the pantsuit gained in popularity as women said, "we can wear pants, too."

That was the world we lived in before coed dorms and universal cohabitation. It was the prevailing attitude we had to deal with as we came of age. If a man had sex out of marriage, he was just being a man and "sowing his wild oats." If a woman did it, she was seen as lacking with low morals.

---

[60] Apartheid was a political and social system in South Africa during the era of white minority rule. It enforced racial discrimination against non-Whites.
[61] Joplin was a singer-songwriter who sang rock, soul, and blues music. She was an iconic symbol of the times and one of the most successful and widely known rock stars of the era.

Many of our parents didn't see the hypocrisy and lack of equality in any of this. We did. It was another cause to protest.

The slogan "You've Come a Long Way Baby" market testing for a Virginia Slims cigarette ad began in California. It was a vivid reminder that the empowerment of women was gaining ground.

As more cracks appeared in our culture, cracks also started to appear in the Iron Curtain as it began to crumble as witnessed by the Prague Spring, even though it was eventually crushed by Russian troops and tanks.

The Bureau of Narcotics and Dangerous Drugs was formed to curb the surge of illegal drug use.

Hair, the American Tribal Love-Rock Musical was still breaking taboos on Broadway with its antiwar, counterculture messages and nude scenes. There was pressure for the government and the entertainment industry to control this breakdown of decency and morality. The Motion Picture Association rolled out the first rating system: G, M, R, and X to indicate the intended audience as General, Mature, Restricted, and X for strictly adult.

Shirley Chisholm became the first black woman elected to Congress. It was a welcome milestone and no laughing matter.

Politics, though, were increasingly becoming fodder for comedians. "I think I'm a pretty good candidate because I've been consistently vague on all the issues and I'm continuing to make promises that I'll be unable to fulfill," said comedian Pat Paulson, in his mock run for president, which he announced on the controversial Smothers' Brothers comedy hour.

Julie Nixon, daughter of the president-elect, Richard Nixon, married David Eisenhower, the grandson of former President Dwight Eisenhower.

Millions of viewers tuned in to NBC to watch Elvis Presley's first television special. Mrs. Robinson, the soundtrack from the movie *The Graduate* by Simon and Garfunkel reached number one on the pop charts. In a more earthy setting, singer Johnny Cash performed live at California's Folsom Prison and the concert became a hit album.

RFK was fatally wounded within minutes of giving a victory speech celebrating his win in the California Democratic primary.

## Chapter 6

The first modern automated teller machine—the ATM—was invented in Dallas. Before that, if you needed cash after bank hours or on the weekends, you no longer had to go to a grocery store and buy something. Credit cards were just coming into being but not commonly used so you had to plan your expenditures and activities carefully. ATM cards continued to emerge as more ATMs began to pop up. It signaled the being of the end of the 'cash was king' reign.

※

Upon my return from my road trip, I mailed a letter a day to Kathy. I was smitten but still torn by the pull of California. That didn't stop me from sending out my resume in earnest. I made phone calls. My dad tried to help me network, but most of his connections were in the education field.

I dressed in my Sunday best and went on several interviews. Based on their body language and words I could see the interviewer's reaction. It was like looking at an image in a mirror.

A couple of weeks into my search I got a letter from a medium-sized industrial chemical plant close to Cleveland. I wasn't a chemist, but they needed front office staff. People to order material and do things like taking care of billing, receiving, and accounting. I wanted it. It was my first opportunity to get some real business experience. I told myself it would only be temporary and I would eventually head to California with a better resume.

They offered me a starting annual salary of almost $12,000. I kept a straight face and secretly wondered how I could even spend a thousand dollars a month! My mental calculator was in overdrive—$500 every two-week payday. I wasn't sure of taxes and deductions, but it seemed like a sweet deal.

I told my first outright real lie to Kathy when I said I had accepted a temporary position while I tried to line something up in California. She didn't know that something was holding me back from moving to the West Coast. I wasn't even sure why I was reluctant myself.

I pushed that problem to the back of my mind and plunged right into my new job from the beginning. The office staff was mostly guys and what women there were worked as secretaries. There seemed to be a big filing cabinet on every corner. No computerized files meant that we had to keep a paper system for everything from invoices to deliveries and consumables, but it worked. I learned to put my hands on any file I needed. I liked the work and felt like I was doing something important.

Despite it all, there was still that nagging in the back of my mind that I was selling out and not just Kathy but myself as well. Was this going to be my life? Dad was happy when he learned that they had a pension plan and insurance.

I was still several hours away from home but got there every month or so. My parents seemed proud and relieved that I had joined the civilized establishment that was their world. Since I had to wear a coat and tie every day mom advised me on building up my wardrobe. For the first time in my life, I took my dress shirts to a laundry. What a great service. No more looking for my cleanest dirty shirt or looking like I needed a good press.

I tried to stay in contact with Molly and Paul, but our telephone calls became more infrequent. This nagged at me, but I shrugged it off. I did try to get them to visit the folks when I did so I could kill two birds with one stone.

I didn't want to spend a lot of money right away on a proper apartment. And it didn't seem worth it to rent a tiny crappy unit. Maybe I would get my own apartment when I got a little ahead and could buy furniture and all the things that entailed. So, I fell back on something I knew. I found what I thought was an upscale boarding house and took up residence. My landlady let me have kitchen privileges and I stocked up on a few food essentials. I got my first telephone and kept in contact with my chums from college. There were still no cell phones, but my landline also enabled me to call Kathy more frequently, but long-distance was expensive so the calls were only several minutes in duration.

I spent weekends having a few drinks with office mates and friends and ate most of my meals in drive-ins and diners. My school network kept me apprised of protests that were happening at the time. I had learned my lesson and took the bus to rallies and avoided putting my car in danger. I usually didn't have to travel far because a lot was going on around Cleveland.

In 1968, for instance, in what became known as the "Glenville Shootout," police officers and a group of Black men confronted each other in Cleveland's Glenville neighborhood on the city's east side. After more than an hour of violence, four Blacks and three police officers had been killed. This incident set off a two-day riot when looting, arson fires, fights, and beatings occurred until order was restored.

Such events almost always spurred even more protests. I couldn't participate in all of them, but I did march with groups of whites and Blacks on many occasions. Sometimes these were peaceful and other times violence broke out as we skirmished with the police or people smashed store windows and looted. I managed to not get arrested or get my head bashed in. It was a balancing act, but I knew I was more lucky than prudent.

We moan about the insanity of our country and the world today and the surreal quality caused by what happens in Washington, DC among our political leaders. We lament outrageous behavior, cultural tension, political scandal after scandal, and investigation after investigation. Unsettling and chaotic to be sure, but most of it is just talk. In 1968 and 69 the country was burning. I'm talking about flames. Not only were people at odds and upset but it was being manifested as fire bombing and rock-throwing. It was violent and physical.

In the early fall of 1968, Brian called me and said we needed to go to Chicago. He went on to explain that we should be part of the protests at the Democratic National Convention. We decided to bus it. When we arrived, we melted into the large gathering at Grant Park. A lot of different groups were involved with different agendas, but in our naivety, we didn't realize it at the time that they all had different motives and tactics in mind.

As we poured out of the park and our numbers grew, we entered a war zone. It was a sea of tear gas and billy clubs. We were chanting "The whole world is watching. The whole world is watching." Those in the front of our crowd taunted the police. They responded by wading into the crowd and swinging their clubs. Brian and I managed to stay close and avoid getting bashed by what we thought of as bullies in blue. But it was hard to see and our eyes stung from the tear gas. It was pandemonium.

*Riots at the 1968 Democratic Convention in Chicago.*

We were crushed up against the façade of the Hilton hotel where the Democrats ended up nominating Hubert Humphrey over Senator Eugene McCarthy. The delegates had adopted Humphrey's platform which continued President Lyndon Johnson's unpopular Vietnam policies and rejected McCarthy's antiwar plank.

It was an extraordinary protest. We were thousands united against the establishment, but still, everyone had their unique agenda. There were the yippies who wanted to protest by getting high and having sex outdoors to thumb their noses at what they saw as a corseted and uptight society, Black and Latinos, including the Puerto Rican Young Lords, a leftist group who wanted to challenge police brutality, McCarthy supporters who wanted to change the system including ending the war, Students for a Democratic Society or SDS who wanted to shred it, and young men and women like Brian and me who just wanted change to a fairer and more just system.

Everyone wanted to be heard and knew their way was the right way. People were being arrested and loaded into vans. Rocks and bottles were flying. Rumors swirled. It was mind-blowing and beyond comprehension.

I remember jeeps coming down Michigan Avenue with iron cages mounted in front with a tangle of barbed wire as the National Guard joined the Chicago cops. That got everyone's attention. They had bayonets fixed to their rifles. What was striking was that these kids in uniform were mostly our age.

## Chapter 6

We could see the fear in their eyes just as I'm sure they could see it on our faces.

The event turned into a blur I would later reflect on and question and attempt to put it into perspective. How had the system failed me? What did I have to complain about? Did I feel entitled to something society had failed to provide? Or, was I really in search of a fairer and more just society? Young men were being drafted and used as cannon fodder for some political agenda. It hadn't happened to me but that didn't make it right. Some young lads were draft dodgers hiding in their parent's basements or fleeing to Canada and burning their draft cards.

Thoughts were flying and colliding in my head at an alarming rate. One thing was certain. I felt uncomfortable and depressed. I tried to put my finger on why. Was it disrespect to my folks? Dad had served and his country and played by the rules. Was I being an unreasonable jerk?

After the event, Brian and I talked about such issues for hours but didn't reach any earth-shattering conclusions, except that I was saddled with the guilt my parents had instilled in me when I was young. Brian expressed similar sentiments and we tried to shrug it all off.

Things were stretching out. I tried to take preventative action and invited Kathy to come to Ohio to visit me. She agreed. Even though I was only in my early 20s I desperately wanted some stability in my life and a sense of normalcy from our crazy world.

It was magical after she arrived. My boarding house rules had caused me to move into a small apartment. I scrambled in the weeks before she arrived to furnish it from the local Salvation Army thrift store.

She helped me set up the place which made it feel like we were married. Like the astronauts, I was on the moon. We shared many happy hours walking and enjoying dinners. I was in love or at the very least a deep infatuation. My heavenly feeling, though, was not destined to last as I came crashing down to earth.

One night she quietly informed me she was pregnant. I remember My folks' words echoing in my mind. They were repeated often as I came of age and started seriously dating. "If you get a girl pregnant you have to marry her." So, I swallowed hard, expressed my joy, and promptly proposed. She accepted but looking back I don't remember seeing a glow of happiness in her eyes. She was always cool and practical.

"We can make this work, honey."

"I'll try but you know I'm a California girl."

"I know but we can visit as often as you want."

"I plan to find a job doing arrangements in a local flower shop."

"What about the baby?"

"We will have to arrange for a nanny and daycare until he or she is old enough to go to school."

I thought of my own life and how my mom had sacrificed to be there for us. "Yes, we can do that, but you might also consider taking a year or two off and staying home."

I saw the flash of frustration—or was it anger—in her eyes at the suggestion? "Why don't you stay home then."

"I would but I think my salary would bring in more to support us."

"Perhaps, but not necessarily."

We looked at each other and I forced a smile. "I'm sure we will find a way to work it all out."

It wasn't settled but we had reached a plateau. I wanted to just let it drop for the moment. In the back of my mind, though, I could hear my mom being critical of my soon-to-be wife for not doing what her generation had done. I had heard her talking before about how the women of my generation didn't understand the important role of homemaker and sensed this was going to become a significant issue. According to mom, they were being selfish and not conforming to the norms of her world.

We had a small civil ceremony in front of a justice of the peace. Both our parents were relieved, but mine were not happy. They wanted a big church wedding with all the trappings.

I could see my mom's coolness when she and Kathy talked about the baby. I could tell mom was put off by Kathy's approach to daycare and her working. She pointed out that she would be happy to care for the baby but that was not practical because they lived too far from us.

I was unsure how it would all play out as we started to make plans. We wanted to buy a house and the whole nine yards. With her experience and skills in the floral world, Kathy easily found a job and worked almost until the baby was born. Then life, of course, threw me another curveball.

It happened after our daughter, Abbie, was born that I got my next shock. The health of Kathy's mom started to deteriorate, and she wanted us to move back to California where Kathy could help more with the family's business.

I thought a lot about what I wanted and chaffed when Kathy told me we would either move or she would go without me. I had never seen her act like she did that day. I could tell there would be no compromise on the matter.

Her pretty face was set in a classic pout. "Can't you see how important this is to me?"

"Yes, but you could go out and spend some time with her until she gets better."

"Jimmy, she has cancer. I don't think she is going to get better and besides how will my dad cope with the business and all?"

"I'm sorry, Kathy. I just don't see me starting over on the West Coast."

Her next words stung. "It's not like you have a big job here."

Then I blurted out words I would regret for years, "Maybe we should just separate and let things cool off and see how it works out." Immediately, I wondered where that came from. I guess I hadn't learned my lesson from my playground years when my mouth worked faster than my brain.

"No, if you aren't going to support my decision, I want a clean break. Running the business that my mom built has always been my dream. I would think you could understand and support that."

As enlightened as I thought I was, this rubbed me the wrong way. Were we a partnership or was she the boss dictating that it was her way or the highway? Somehow, I felt that if I gave in at that moment that the dynamics of our relationship would be forever changed.

"If that is how you feel you know I will support you and our child."

"I don't need your support. I will, however, expect child support."

The implication was clear. She could probably make more money than me. This further assaulted my self-esteem and added to my feeling that things were out of control.

Our divorce was somber but amicable. My folks were horrified. I had disappointed them. Or at the very least I'm sure they wondered if I had lost my mind. We had long talks and I kept insisting that what I wanted was important, too. Dad said it wasn't about my feelings but rather about my responsibility. Kathy left and I was left to ponder my future.

When Kennedy's dream of the man on the moon had become reality, we all shared the pride even if we didn't work for NASA. Despite all the turmoil in the country it seemed to validate American exceptionalism. Like the rest of the country, I was completely distracted from my personal issues, at least temporarily, when our astronauts continued to reach for the heavens. Collectively we were proud and giddy with excitement as we became the men on the moon.

Against my dad's advice that I move slowly, I started seriously dating again. I think what he secretly meant was that I had screwed up my personal life for the time being and I should cool it. I met an attractive lady lawyer named Emma and pushed thoughts of Kathy and our daughter to the back of my mind. After a whirlwind romance of three months, I proposed. It was a spur of the moment and I just sort of blurted it out in a moment of passion. Dad and mom were sure I had lost my mind and reached new heights of lunacy and immaturity and told me so.

Within weeks of our ceremony, which my folks refused to attend, I faced another ultimatum. Emma informed me she had taken a position with an association in Washington, DC, and we were moving. It was Deja Vu. I didn't relish the idea of another divorce or further scorn from my family, so I agreed to resign from my job with the hopes I could find another one in the nation's capital.

At the time, I failed to see the inconsistency of not moving for Kathy but doing it for Emma.

Dad lectured me about career management. I was supposed to gratefully work at the same place for 40 years and get my meager pension and the gold watch. That was the way things worked in his world. He simply could not understand that I would throw away that security for the unknown. I expressed my confidence it would work out and he just shook his head like I was from Mars.

## Chapter 6

Undaunted I followed my path. Ellison was still in DC and I called him and instinctively started to work my network.

With our combined income, we were able to hire movers to pack and do the heavy lifting and things went smoothly. It was a new experience for me where I packed my belongings and rented a U-Haul truck or piled into my car. We were off the nation's capital and despite the feeling of being swept along with little control over events, I was excited.

We had the moving company temporarily store our belongings until we found a place. Living in a hotel with all the trappings was a new experience for me. Emma had countless meetings as she settled into her new job as counsel for her association.

I polished up my resume and started my search. Each afternoon for several weeks I met Ellison in a pub on Capitol Hill. We drank beer and renewed our friendship.

"I never dreamed we would end up here together," he said.

"Yeah, it's a long way from Arizona. Remember those days?"

"Oh yes. Great times."

How are your folks?"

My dad passed. He was killed in Vietnam where he was serving as an advisor to government troops."

"I'm so sorry to hear that."

He shrugged. "He was a soldier."

I broke the silence that had settled over us. "Any thoughts where I might look for a job?"

"Did you bring me copies of your resume?"

I handed him a folder.

I know a guy at an association in Alexandria, Virginia who is hiring. I will pass it along to him."

"Emma wants to live on the Hill, is it far?"

"No, it's just across the Potomac. It's an easy commute."

"Thanks. It sounds good."

Then he smiled. "You know I'm getting married?"

"Congratulations. Who is the lucky girl?"

Her name is Rosa. We've been dating for a while. We are having a small ceremony at her church in Takoma Park, Maryland. I was thinking, would you want to stand for me as my best man?"

"I would be honored."

Others were also pursuing their chosen paths or those that were set by fate or nature for them. In 1969, at the Stonewall Inn, a gay bar in Greenwich Village, in New York City, there was a spontaneous and violent demonstration against a police raid on the establishment. This was one of the first times that the gay community fought back against laws and policies that persecuted sexual minorities, making it a defining moment in the gay rights movement.

Despite all the exciting changes and events in my life, I ended the decade a much more cynical person than when it started. I had alienated my folks and was twice married. I had a daughter I barely knew thousands of miles away. I wasn't necessarily wiser and suspected that I was becoming a poster boy for the "me" generation.

The sacrifices my folks had made and the stability they had provided wasn't lost on me. They married, respected their vows, and did it all by the book. It all made me feel selfish.

# Chapter 7

# We Prevail—The War Ends (1970 – 1975)

In 1970, the Beatles broke up. *Monday Night Football* and *The Mary Tyler Moore Show* became television hits. We were still trying to find ourselves through such things as Arthur Janov's Primal Scream Therapy.[62] As the 1960s protest spilled over into the next decade, we bombed ROTC[63] buildings (well, not me personally) and the National Guard was on 21 campuses in 16 states. Demonstrations on campuses were the order of the day and many schools closed.

We were not, of course, without our losses. Jimmy Hendrix and Janice Joplin, both 27, were casualties of our indulgence with drugs. Chilean president Allende became the first Marxist

---

[62] Primal scream therapy is a method for stress therapy developed by Arthur Janov. This therapy was aimed at healing our stresses, mainly dedicated to release a childhood trauma. The patient often ends up screaming out loud or sobbing to release stress through this activity.

[63] The Reserve Officers' Training Corps is a group of college and university-based officer training programs for training commissioned officers of the United States Armed Forces.

to win an election in our backyard. This shook the establishment. Castro doesn't count—he did it with a gun. It was a mix of music with singers like Eric Clapton, James Taylor, Rita Coolidge, Elton John, and Black Sabbath. *The Dick Cavett Show* started. *Little Big Man* and *M\*A\*S\*H* hit the big screen.

Perhaps it was fitting that Alvin Toffler's book *Future Shock*[64] was printed as the news and events became more bizarre and disturbing. In 1974, Patty Hearst, the 19-year-old granddaughter of newspaper publishing mogul, William Hearst, was kidnapped in Berkeley, California by two armed Black men and a white woman. Several days later a small leftist group called the Symbionese Liberation Army, or SLA, announced that they were holding her as a prisoner of war. This was disturbing news for America. Were we at war with ourselves? I suppose in a way we were.

But it wasn't just about money and power. The SLA demanded that the Hearst family give $70 million in foodstuffs to every needy person from Santa Rosa to Los Angeles. Hearst reluctantly gave away $2 million worth of food. The SLA demanded $6 million more.

Later, the story changed surprisingly and dramatically when CCTV footage showed Patty Hearst participating in an armed robbery of a San Francisco bank. In a subsequent tape, she declared that she had joined the SLA of her own free will.

The police eventually raided their headquarters and killed 6 of the 9 known members, including Donald Defreeze, an ex-convict who called himself General Field Marshall Cinque. (Hearst was not there but was arrested in 1976 and sentenced to 7 years in prison. After 21 months her sentence was commuted by then-President Carter.)

If all of this left us BBs scratching our heads, you can imagine what it did to our parents. During the early part of the 1970s, there were more than 1000 politically inspired bombings in the US. In the words of my dad, "Shocking." As a country, we seem to be on the verge of some type of nervous fit. If the country was a person, we would have been committed to an insane asylum."

---

[64] The book explores change and what happens to people as they either do or don't adapt. Massive changes result in stress and disorientation, especially if the changes happen quickly.

Cult leader Charles Manson[65] and his crowd were convicted, but even behind bars we had a morbid fascination with them, and they gave us the creeps. We gained political muscle when Congress lowered the voting age to 18. Peace marches were still the order of the day.

The Supersonic Transport Program was canceled and some of us wondered if we were losing our technological edge to other countries. This was a U.S. federal government program that selected Boeing to build the prototype for the country's first supersonic transport (SST).

Government funding was withdrawn in 1971 before the prototype was finished. The Boeing SST, however, fostered advances in supersonic transportation and led to the High-Speed Civil Transport project as part of the NASA High-Speed Research program.

The Concorde would later fly at twice the speed of sound for a period and cut air travel time between London and New York to about 3 hours. Although it was discontinued because of cost, it was a sign of what air travel would eventually become. That the world was shrinking was not lost on us BBs.

I continued participating in protests, but my zeal was waning. Emma never joined me. She was too focused on money and promotions. Slowly but surely, I was starting to be drawn into the material side of life, too. More troubling was the way she rolled her eyes when I did go out in the streets. I could sense she wished I would grow up in her eyes.

In 1970, a week after the Kent State shootings, Ellison and I joined 100,000 others who converged on Washington to protest the shootings and President Nixon's incursion into Cambodia.[66]

On May Day in 1971, there was a mass rally by Vietnam antiwar militants to shut down the federal government. The slogan was "If the government doesn't stop the war, we'll stop the government." The official protest button featured Gandhi with a raised fist. It was primarily a non-violent mass civil disobedience

---

[65] Manson was a criminal and cult leader. He formed what became known as the "Manson Family", a quasi-commune based in California. His followers committed a series of nine murders before they were arrested and brought to trial.

[66] In an expansion of the war, President Nixon authorized the use of US combat troops to engage Viet Cong communist troop sanctuaries in Cambodia, which set off massive demonstrations.

*Vietnam anti-war protest in Washington, DC.*

campaign of blocking traffic, but it led to the single largest mass arrest in the history of the United States: some 10,000 people, many of them temporarily held behind fences at the then Washington Redskins football practice field, surrounded by National Guard troops. I was one of them. We didn't just march on DC, we shut it down. It was chaotic and ugly.

My arrest and overnight detention would be my last real protest. I was weary and continued to question my motives and actions. Did I do all of that for the excitement and to feel like a rebel? Or was I just a phony rebel wannabe? When it came down to it, had I ever really believed? I told myself I did, but doubts lingered in the back of my mind. No matter if I was a true zealot or just caught up in things, like many other BBs my focus was shifting from changing the world to achieving success and making money. It was becoming all about me, me, me.

No matter my internalizing, the country was still gripped by discontent and chaos that ranged from the women's and gay liberation movements to radical ecology, and militant Native American, Chicano, Puerto Rican, and Asian-American movements. Most BBs still naively dreamed of a world free of war and oppression. In 1971. there was a march to end apartheid in South Africa.

In 1974 there was a large rally to impeach President Richard M. Nixon. If there was a real or perceived injustice, people took to the streets in Washington and other cities.

The Pentagon Papers[67] documenting the secret Pentagon history of the Vietnam War appeared in The New York Times, revealing lies and more lies. For those of us who were still trying to be at least a little traditional like our parents, our trust in the government was further eroded.

American vets started to admit to U.S. atrocities in Nam. It wasn't many, but shocking nonetheless. Those of us who served or supported the government felt betrayed at how we were used. It had become increasingly clear that it was a Vietnamese civil war and purely about politics. On both sides of the issue, those feelings would impact all our lives.

The economy started to fall apart, and we wondered what happened to the golden age our parents—and us—thought we would be enjoying. Nixon declared a 90-day wage and price freeze, which further added to our fears. At the time, strife and disturbing news were even common in unlikely places. There was a 5-day prison revolt in Attica, New York, that ended when 1000 cops stormed the place.

The Kerner Commission report said that by 1980 most of our cities would be Black and Brown and bankrupt. The stock market crashed in 1973-74 as a result of inflation and a collapsing monetary system. Those of us with jobs were nervous. Those without jobs wondered if the sky was falling, thinking, "Whatever happened to the good times we thought would never end?"

To add to the chaos and uncertainty, the Organization of Petroleum Exporting Countries (OPEC) began to flex its muscles and it was the end of cheap gas and the beginning of us standing in long gas lines. Egypt and Syria attacked Israel, marking the start of the 1973 Arab-Israeli war. Today, the Middle East is still fighting over some of the boundaries established because of that conflict.

---

[67] This was one of the most important cases involving freedom of the press. When Robert McNamara was secretary of defense he became disenchanted with U.S. involvement in the Vietnam War and ordered a secret study of all Defense Department documents relating to how the United States had gotten involved in the war. They were kept secret and even detailed lies the Pentagon told to Congress about our entrance into the war. They were finally leaked to the New York Times by military analyst Daniel Ellsberg, who had worked on the study. and eventually came to oppose the war. This led to a Supreme Court legal battle between the Times and the US government in which the newspaper prevailed.

A lot of us were in our late 20s and we kept wondering whatever happened to the "good old days" of the 1950s? Were they gone forever? It seemed that way. Detective Frank Serpico told the Knapp Commission of widespread police corruption in New York City and we wondered if anything was sacred. Actor Al Pacino would go on to star in a hit movie about the fearless cop.

Greenpeace was formed reflecting our concern that we were killing the planet. *All in the Family*, starring Carroll O'Conner as a blue color bigot, Archie Bunker, reflected the bigotry of many of our parents (and us) and the gap that existed with BBs. Archie was always in conflict with his onscreen son-in-law, who was a baby boomer. The relationship was characterized by the fact that he called him "meathead." That probably summed up what many of our parents thought of us during those times.

The *Jesus Christ Superstar* rock opera[68] delighted many BBs and angered religious groups. Hot pants were in for women and men's shoes with heels and platform soles were popular. Bell-bottom pants were the thing for most men and women BBs.

In a preview of horrors to come Arab terrorists attacked the Munich Olympics. This was the worst tragedy in Olympic history when Arab terrorists stormed into the Olympic village and raided the apartment building that housed the Israeli contingent. Two Israeli athletes were killed and nine more were seized as hostages. They demanded the release of over 200 Palestinians serving time in Israeli jails, along with two renowned German terrorists.

After a day of unsuccessful negotiations, the terrorists collected the hostages and headed for the military airport in Munich for a flight back to the Middle East. At the airport, German sharpshooters opened fire, killing three of the Palestinians. A fierce gun battle then claimed the lives of all nine of the hostages, along with one policeman and two terrorists. We were outraged and shocked, asking ourselves, "Was nothing sacred? Not even sporting events?"

Nixon visited China. They had been isolated from the world since the communist revolution in 1949. Can you imagine a world without inexpensive Chinese goods? Unlike today they weren't even players on the world stage. They were hermits walled off

---

[68] The rock opera was a contemporary version of the final days of Jesus' life, shocking our parents, but not us.

from the community of nations. At the time, though, the most cynical among us realized it was because it represented a great new market for American products. What company doesn't dream of a billion potential new customers?

J. Edgar Hoover died after 48 years at the helm of the FBI and rumors and conspiracy theories swirled about secret files, which added to our distrust of Washington. In what seemed like a minor burglary, five men were caught breaking into the National Democratic Campaign Headquarters at the Watergate, which led to the downfall of a president.

The last U.S. military unit was withdrawn from Nam and there was a frantic scramble to get out. The images captured that day show helicopters on the top of buildings and South Vietnamese swimming for boats as hordes of evacuees desperately looked for a way out. There were also crowds of Americans and other foreigners lined up in installations around Saigon waiting for buses to take them out. This all happened to the soundtrack of gunfire in the background as the Viet Cong closed in.

Some Americans who pushed towards the buses tried to pull their Vietnamese wives and children along with them in desperate scenes of families separated and crying out for help, pleading not to be left behind, clutching at the last straw of hope. It was hardly the exit of a country victorious in war.

Musical groups like the Blue Oyster Cult, Alice Cooper, and the Eagles topped the charts. They were joined by others, including Steely Dan, Curtis Mayfield, and David Bowie.

We were more than a little nostalgic listening to Don McLean's *American Pie*, although we argued about the meaning of the lyrics. What did words like "*Bye, bye Miss American Pie. Drove my Chevy to the levee but the levee was dry*" mean anyway? I surely didn't know.

As radical changes in music continued, many of us were already yearning for the "good old days" when songs and lyrics weren't so disturbing. *The Godfather* was a hit, as were *Deliverance* and *Last Tango in Paris*. *Ms. Magazine* reflected the solid move towards feminism. LBJ died.[69]

---

[69] The man who had replaced an assassinated JFK and then led us deeper into war in Vietnam; and who also declared war on poverty which led us to deeper national debt that seemed to mark the end of fiscal responsibility at the federal level.

The military draft ended. Young men still had to register with the draft board, but it was no longer mandatory that they had to serve in the military. It was a huge victory for the more liberal among us as our military transitioned to an all-volunteer force. This had a significant impact on the young men of America, especially BBs.

When I planned to go on to college, it wasn't to avoid getting drafted and most likely sent to Vietnam, I just wanted to further my education and be successful. Later, though, I would feel guilty because many of my friends didn't have that option due to money or family situations. I had dodged a bullet, literally.

Reality and logic seemed to be slipping from our collective grip. We were becoming immune to alarming news, When Nixon announced that all American troops would be out of Nam within 60 days, our government simply declared victory and came home, but the US didn't win. It was just a word game. We BBs had won. The country had lost. Watergate heated up and we were talking about Nixon's secret recording system. His vice president, Spiro Agnew, resigned in disgrace.

The former Maryland governor's downfall began when he was investigated in connection with accusations of extortion, bribery, and income-tax violations during his tenure as governor. Faced with federal indictments, Agnew fought the charges, arguing that the allegations were false, that a sitting vice president could not be indicted, and that the only way he could be removed from office was by impeachment. After the solicitor general released a brief asserting that sitting vice presidents could be indicted, Agnew launched an attack on the administration and vowed not to resign.

With Nixon in danger of impeachment for his role in Watergate cover-up, the administration sought to remove Agnew from the presidential line of succession, and a secret plea bargaining took place between Agnew's lawyers and a federal judge. The result was that Agnew resigned from the vice presidency and ended up in court. Acknowledging that the plea was a felony conviction, Agnew declared that he had resigned in the national interest. He was fined $10,000 and sentenced to three years of unsupervised probation.

We BBs scratched our heads and all this fueled conspiracy theories. If it had been one of us, we would have ended up in jail. So much for accountability and no one being above the law.

The economy was still in the toilet. Those of us working were worried as the government seemed to unravel and we wondered about our jobs. Suddenly our wellbeing rose to the top of the list of our concerns and the end of the war seemed less important.

On the verge of impeachment, Nixon made history by resigning the presidency in 1974. He had technically ended the Vietnam war, but it actually ended in the spring of 1975 when Gerald Ford was president. His resignation was fueled in apart when Senator Barry Goldwater and other senior Congressional leaders visited him, and Nixon realized it was over and he tendered his official resignation.

We BBs again were outraged. People in positions of power were just allowed to walk away with no real consequences. In the end, though, we shrugged it off.

Ex-Beatles John Lennon sang *Mind Games* while George Harrison recorded *Living in the Material World.* (Boy was he right.) We were increasingly looking back to the past with movies like *American Graffiti* and *The Sting* with Paul Newman. We lightened up a little when pet rocks and CB (citizen band) radios became fads. Even though we weren't truck drivers, expressions like "breaker, breaker" became popular and we ran around saying them. The term was used by truckers to get a response from other drivers as they drove America's roads. CBs were the primary way they communicated while heading down the road and across America.

Maria Muldaur and Eric Clapton were on the music charts. TV had soft-hearted tough guy *Kojak* and *Chinatown* with Jack Nicholson was on the big screen. On the airways, Barbara Streisand haunted us with the song *The Way We Were.* To a large extent, we were self-absorbed. The "do your own thing" way of life continued as we struggled "to find ourselves." Our parents were still puzzled because they didn't understand when we said we were lost.

I interviewed and got a job as a senior financial analyst at the non-profit organization Ellison had referred me to. I was grateful to him and told him so. Emma and I found a small but stylish townhouse on Capitol Hill and quickly settled in. It was heady stuff. I was sending child support to Kathy for Abbie, but between Emma and I, we were able to live a lifestyle level that was new for me.

I had no delusions. Even though it was private and not technically a government position, everything in the nation's capital revolved around the government. The overall economy in the country was rocky, but for those of us living in DC we were in a bubble and all drinking from the government trough on taxpayer money as the Midwest became the rust belt.[70] A whole segment of BBs found it impossible to follow in their parents' footsteps and work in our industrial heartland. I was getting mine and prospering and didn't see anything wrong with that. Later, upon reflection looking back, I would.

Just as our parent's greatest generation bore the brunt of World War II, we BBs paid the price for our war. By the end of the Vietnam war, we flooded our veteran's clinics and hospitals with many vets who suffered from PTSD, drug addiction, and dim employment prospects. Unlike their fathers and uncles, they were not warmly received or respected by the public when they came home from the unpopular war. Even though it was a political war, our vets were the ones who paid the price for their patriotism. Worse, most were drafted into compulsory service and had little choice whether to fight or not.

As Joe would later point out to us, when they first came home you could spot them with their military haircuts and black military dress shoes even though they might be wearing civilian clothes. They stood out and were looked down upon.

I settled into my job and at Emma's urging enrolled in graduate school to earn my MBA. My job was laid back and it was fairly easy to juggle work and study. Emma and I entered into our "let's celebrate to show off how successful we are" phase. We hosted fondue[71] dinner parties and patted ourselves on the back at how sophisticated we were. We weren't alone. Many of

---

[70] The Rust Belt stretches from New York state through the Midwest. This region was once dominated by steel mills and manufacturing companies that made everything. It is now characterized by abandoned factories as the US experiences industrial decline.

[71] Fondue was all the rage at the time. It was a melted cheese dish served in a communal pot over a portable stove heated with a candle and eaten by dipping bread into the cheese.

us BBs congratulated ourselves for having arrived and gone from humble meatloaf culinary beginnings to fare our parents didn't indulge in, so I suppose in a way we had.

We played the latest hits on our turntables and had endless discussions about politics, world affairs, and the state of America. We tried to keep pace as technology took us from vinyl records to reel to reel tape decks to 8 track cartridges to cassette tapes and beyond.

I got my MBA and was promoted to head of the financial department at work. Heady stuff and I wanted to go even higher and make even more money. I even got a secretary. She was an attractive young woman named Sally from McKeesport, Pennsylvania. She told me during her interview that she had come to Washington after a nasty divorce to start a new chapter in her life.

She certainly was a head-turner, but I had already divorced once and remarried and reminded myself to have some self-control, in the words of my dad. It helped that rattling around in my brain were mom's words, "Jimmy, just pretend dad and I are standing on your shoulder watching and don't do anything that you wouldn't be proud of." The old brainwashing and sayings were still very much a part of my psyche.

Not long after my promotion, my boss called Sally and me into his office. "The board thinks it would be good press for us to hire some vets. And, I agree. Sally, I want you to reach out to some veteran's organization and set up some interviews for James." (I was Jimmy to everyone but my boss.) We were dismissed after he told us to keep him informed of our progress.

Two weeks later Sally told me that she had scheduled a candidate for an interview. When he arrived, Sally introduced us, and I suggested we go to the conference room. I noticed he walked with a slight limp, but he was a trim athletic guy a few years younger than me.

He seemed to have a certain haunted look in his eyes. No wonder. The man had just helped fight a war. After we had taken our seats, I plunged right in.

"Tell me a little about your background, Joe."

"I grew up in Arizona but to be honest there aren't a lot of jobs in that area so I thought I would try my luck here. I visited Washington on a class trip in high school and liked it. And, I wanted a fresh start after my service."

"Really? Small world. I spent some time in Benson in my younger years. I liked Arizona, but my family moved back East again."

"I was further north in Tucson."

"Yes, I know it well. From your resume, it looks like you went into the military after school."

"Yes. Before I could register for some college courses I was drafted. I went into the army in 1969 after high school. It wasn't long before I found myself in Vietnam. I managed not to get shot too badly. When I got back, I went to community college on the G.I. Bill and got my associate degree and I plan to enroll in some sort of night program and earn my bachelor's degree. It might take a while, but I will get there."

"The position requires a bachelor's or the equivalent, but with your AA and years of experience you would qualify." I glanced at his resume. "It says here that you earned a purple heart for wounds received."

He just nodded and didn't say anything. I could tell I was making him uncomfortable and shifted back to safer ground. "Well, with your experience and background, you certainly would fit in here."

He smiled his easy smile, and I knew at that instant I wanted to give him a break. After a quick word with my boss, I made Joe an offer. I liked the quiet dark-haired guy. He had a confident, but unassuming demeanor.

He started within a few days and from day one I could tell there was definite chemistry between him and Sally. We discouraged interoffice romance, but there was no written policy and I just watched it happen. If there was ever a young man who deserved a break it was Joe. He was both likable and a hard worker.

After six months, and for the second time in my life, I was asked to be the best man at a wedding. I was pleased to do it. It was a beautiful ceremony.

Things settled down. A few weeks later Brian was in town and staying with us and we invited Ellison and Rosa and Joe and Sally for dinner. Like most of our dinner parties, the conversation was always lively but could quickly become heated. And, like most groups of young professionals of the day, we spent many hours around the table solving the world's problems. At least in our minds. These often involved hot button issues of the day, like the busing of school kids[72]. Each of us was sure we had the answers. We were smug know-it-alls.

Brian said, "If I work hard and buy a house in a nice neighborhood so my kids have good schools, how is it fair that they should be bussed to a crappy school district? Especially since the liberal idiots who mandate this send their kids to fancy private schools. They are telling us what to do, but it has absolutely no effect on them."

In his calm and quiet way, Ellison replied, "I hear what you are saying, Brian, but then how would you suggest that kids from poor and disadvantaged neighborhoods ever get the education needed to break the cycle?" He paused. "The school standards are just not the same. I remember a few years ago that a valedictorian who graduated from an inner-city high school sued the school district when he got to college and found out that no matter how hard he tried he was not prepared for the courses. Can you imagine doing everything they ask and finishing at the top of your class and then realizing you weren't adequately trained for college-level courses?"

He shook his head and the table got quiet as we all briefly reflected on that.

But Brian wouldn't let it go. "I'm not saying that I have all the answers and that something shouldn't be done, but why should they screw up my kids' lives to do it. Hell, why not fix the inner-city schools?"

Emma piped in, "LBJ's war on poverty has only succeeded in making minorities more dependent on the system. It hasn't improved anyone's life. It's just another form of slavery."

---

[72] School busing, also known as desegregation busing was the practice of transporting students to schools within or outside their local school districts as a means of rectifying racial segregation. Even though American schools were technically desegregated in 1954 by a landmark U.S. Supreme Court decision, in practice they remained largely segregated owing to trends in housing and neighborhood segregation. Busing came to be the main remedy by which the courts sought to end racial segregation in the U.S. schools. It was one of the biggest controversies for American education at the end of the 20th century.

She paused a moment then said, "I'm not sure of the solution either. One thing for sure is that our SATs were a lot higher. I know they were. Standards have been dumbed down. Hell, we had to diagram sentences. We studied Latin. Who does that any more? We memorized Lincoln's Gettysburg Address. Some of my classmates even had to repeat a grade in school. We endured the pressure of real tests and real grades and managed to escape with our self-esteem intact."

She took a sip of wine, "Today we have social promotion. You are deemed worthy and successful for just showing up. Heaven forbid we should have accountability and hurt any student's self-image. Where is the pride today? Hell, having a baby is now a social status symbol. Some schools even have daycare centers, and the government is supposed to foot the bill and take care of them. Everyone is a victim of something. Self-reliance and being an individual are dying."

Wow, where did that come from, I wondered?

We all just stared at her as she ended her critical outburst.

I glanced at Ellison and chimed in, "I know what we were protesting when we were younger, but I wonder if we made a difference? Seems like things aren't really better but more screwed up."

"I think in some ways we did," said Ellison. "We've come a long way with a long way to go. We baby boomers challenged our parent's world and wisdom. I'm not saying they were bad but there was limited awareness during their times. And, make no mistake, they were different times. It took a man like Martin Luther King to raise that awareness. His 'I Have a Dream speech' did just that. Regardless of your politics, people have died trying to make a difference—Malcolm X, King, Kennedy, and Lincoln were all assassinated in the quest for economic and civil rights."

We all just sat there lost in our own thoughts for a long moment. It dawned on me at that moment that we baby boomers all started as idealists and liberals and now some of us were becoming conservative like our parents and others still wanted the dream. I suppose that was inevitable.

Joe and Sally had just listened as the exchange between Brian and Ellison had progressed. He cleared his throat and we all looked at him. "I can tell you if there is one place where minorities have achieved the most equality, it's in the military."

Ellison smiled, "I'm happy to hear that."

"I'm not saying there was no racism in the ranks, but it is hard for anyone to deny a man his due as an equal when he proves himself in a firefight."

In a self-deprecating way, he went on to regale us with some fascinating war stories, even admitting that he suffered from PTSD when he got back. In his humble and modest way, he glossed over the wound he had received when he took a bullet in his leg. Even though he was the only one at the table who had served, he managed to convey some of the horrors of the war. He ended by saying the best medicine ever was Sally as she beamed at him.

At one point he must have realized he was doing all the talking. He sheepishly said, "Sorry, I don't normally talk about the war. In fact, I don't like to waltz down that memory lane." With that, he looked down studied his hands.

Then Emma asked, "I'm guessing you are not too fond of those guys who avoided the draft and went to Canada?"

"I guess they were following their conscience, but yes it pisses me off that they chickened out. Of course, those that were smart enough to go on to college and stay there were also able to get out of service too with student deferments."

Maybe it was just my guilty conscience, but I felt my face flush a little since I fit into the latter category but I said nothing.

With all that talk about the military, it was ironic that little later we would learn that Joe, who had been exposed to Agent Orange in Vietnam, had cancer. Hell, he was only in his early 20s. Sally and I were devastated. He had survived the jungle war only to now face the fight of his life.

That night, though, it was a typical dinner gathering for us. Our conversation transitioned into other matters and we laughed, drank, and pontificated.

The draft ending in 1973 was just the beginning of more momentous changes. Like his vice president, Nixon was forced to resign in 1974. With both the president and vice president disgraced into exile, nice guy Congressman Gerald Ford was installed as president by the US Congress in what could have spelled a political and constitutional disaster for the country. That same year he granted conditional amnesty to some draft dodgers. Later in 1977, President Jimmy Carter would pardon all draft dodgers. Over 100,000 had fled to Canada to avoid military service. We joked that Nixon had brought the boys home from Vietnam and Carter brought the rest of the boys home from Canada.

I could tell it was a sore subject for Joe and could only imagine how he felt. Some months later after the discussion at our dinner party, we were sharing a few beers at a bar on the Hill after work.

"I can't believe those guys were just allowed to come home with no consequences," Joe said. "Can you imagine if they had refused to serve in World War II? They would have been rightly shot for treason my dad says."

I listened sympathetically.

"My life may be over and there they were gleefully burning their draft cards and just skipping the country."

I assured him he could fight the disease, but his words were to prove prophetic because even though his cancer had gone into remission for almost a year, it came raging back and took him with startling swiftness. Emma and I flew to Tucson with Sally for the funeral at a veteran's cemetery in his hometown. It was touching with a group of young fresh-scrubbed soldiers in uniform in attendance as an honor guard. Some of them didn't even look old enough to shave yet. I had been to funerals before, but they were mostly old relatives, this was one of ours. It was sobering.

Almost immediately upon our return to Washington from the funeral, Sally said she was resigning to go home and spend some time with her folks. I tried to talk her out of it but in a bittersweet turn of events, she said she was pregnant. It brought both of us little comfort that Joe would live on as the next generation was on the way.

More and more I was starting to realize that we BBs were becoming divided like the rest of the country. Some of us, like me, were becoming a firm part of the establishment. Not necessarily conservative but definitely not rebels or radicals. Others of our generation seemed to never have left the campus. Oh, sure they physically left and took jobs and started their careers, but their heads were still in the clouds. We were polarizing into political camps of liberals and conservatives. I had protested but rightly or wrongly had seemingly outgrown it. It was a little disconcerting that I now wanted success and money while many of my brothers and sisters were still fighting the good fight to right what they perceived was wrong, unfair, or unjust.

So much for never trusting anyone over 30. We were fast heading towards the big three-oh and that was us now.

My wallowing in self-examination was cut short the following week when mom called. Dad had suffered a mild heart attack. I let the office know I would be gone for a few days and drove to Ohio.

Dad had been released from the hospital. Mom heard me pull into the driveway and met me at the door. She looked red-eyed, tired, and nervous.

"Thank goodness you are here. He won't listen to me."

I hugged her. "Don't worry mom I'm sure he will be okay. I talked to the doctor and he told me if he changes his diet a little and walks a little more, he will be around for years."

I put my bag in the hall and found dad sitting in his recliner. "Son, I'm glad you are here, but you didn't need to rush home and put your important work on hold for me."

It struck me how old he looked. The confident look in his eyes had been replaced by a trace of bewilderment and uncertainty. "It was time for a visit and I just wanted to make sure you are okay."

"Well, pull up a chair, and let's catch up then."

He went on to describe how he had felt pain in his arm and chest. "I was changing the oil in the sedan and it was a helluva shock to me, I can tell you."

"Well, you know you are going to have to cut down on bacon for breakfast every day."

"Yes, the doctor already gave me that lecture. And, your mom has already taken draconian measures. Whatever happened to the simple pleasures of life? I told your mom and I'll tell you, I'm not giving up my pipe. I've agreed to only a couple bowlfuls a day, but that's as far as I'm willing to go."

"It's a start. Let's just take it one step at a time."

"But enough about me, what's going on in your life? I hope you are building a future and making sure you get a good pension.

Believe me, it's important."

"We've had this conversation many times before, Things are changing, dad. Pensions are becoming a thing of the past. My friends in the government tell me they will be gone by the time I'm ready to step aside."

"I don't understand. How can anyone retire without a pension?"

"They say that eventually, people of my generation will have to contribute and save for retirement."

He shook his head. "What in the hell is the world coming to?"

"Don't worry, dad. I'll be fine.

He didn't seem to want our conversation to end, even when I suggested he might want to take a nap. So, I regaled him with exaggerated stories about how important I was. The nagging thought in the back of my mind, though, was that much of what I said was just bullshit. I knew I was going through the motions for what I perceived as prestige and money with no real commitment.

He inquired about Emma and wondered aloud if there might be any kids in the future. I dismissed the thought and told him about her career path.

He looked hard at me. "Are you happy, son?"

That took me back a little and I stumbled to answer him. "Well, sure, dad. What else could I want?"

"Well money and status are nice but having a good relationship with your spouse is more important."

This uncomfortable conversation went on for a while and ended with his asking if I was keeping in touch with Paul and Molly. I hedged a bit, but the honest answer was I was not making the effort. I was caught up in my own little world. Not since our shaving conversations had we spent so much time talking.

After a few days, I headed back to DC. He had made me think. And, on the drive back I wondered how things like job-hopping for more money would affect my future. It was something to think carefully about. For the moment I told myself that my life was exciting and full. Besides, living in Washington seemed to insulate me from the ups and downs of a changing economy. Did I feel entitled, special, and a little smug? You bet.

As I pushed 30 life seemed a blur of going out to trendy cafes and restaurants and dinner parties. We had disposable income and credit and we enjoyed every penny of it. All I had to do was just whip out my magic credit card then roll my eyes when the bill came at the end of the month. The expression "fly now, pay later" became a lifestyle for most of us BBs. It did for me.

I called Paul and then Molly and told them about my visit with the folks. Yet, despite the occasional call, I felt somewhat of a failure as a big brother. Sure, I wrote the infrequent short letter or generic post office postcard to them, but I could have been more supportive and engaged in their lives. I vowed to do better, but at that time my own life and interests dominated my time.

Our generation was starting families, but many young professionals like Emma and me were too caught up in our newfound positions in life to be inconvenienced by children. We BBs became split between young professional couples like Emma and me who demanded total lifestyle freedom with a focus on career and living what we deemed the good life; and, those couples who started families and forsake the constant partying, dinners, and drinking.

I didn't think much about it because Emma made it very clear that we didn't need the muss and fuss of children in our lives. Anyway, I had Abbie even though I didn't bring her to DC very often. When I wanted to see her, I went to California. Emma seldom accompanied me on those trips unless it included some type of excursion or entertaining side trip—like the time we drove up the Pacific Coast Highway through the Big Sur and Monterey to San Francisco and on into the Napa Valley and wine country.

It was all about us. Or, to be even more honest about me. She was just as into herself. Sure, Emma and I were a couple, but our main focus was more personal. We disguised this by cloaking our selfish me me me attitude by saying we were embarked on journeys of self-discovery and getting in touch with our feelings. My dad would have said that was a crock and I would not have argued with him.

Brian decided to stay in DC after his mom had passed away and his broken-hearted dad soon followed. Brian and his siblings sold the small 1940s bungalow and divided the modest sum. He continued being barkeep at a pub on the Hill not far from where Emma and I lived. I saw him almost daily since he was now not just a bartender, but one of the owners of the pub.

He loved the whole bar scene, had the gift of gab, and was popular with the customers. He was happy that he had been able to swing a deal to buy the bar with another bartender when the current owner decided to retire. It was perfect for him and it became our favorite place to hang out after work and late hours. It was the perfect venue for our marathon gabfests. A few pitchers of beer and we could go one for hours.

When disco came along, we went through a prolonged period when we were either drinking and talking or dancing under glittering disco balls.[73]

Whether we liked it or not, time was marching on as we entered our Saturday night fever period.

---

[73] Round balls with dozens of tiny mirrors on them. The balls were mounted over the dance floor and spun slowly. The light would hit the mirrors and it looked like stars dancing over everything, including us. Sometimes clubs would use strobe lights too which enhanced the action and made the dancers look like they were gyrating in cool jerky motions.

# Chapter 8

# Financial Nightmares, Disco Days, and Saturday Night Fever (1976 – 1979)

Inflation and unemployment were the highest since the 1930s. We partied a lot and lived for the moment because for leading-edge BBs tomorrow didn't seem all that promising. We said that but didn't want to believe it. Somewhere in the back of our minds, we thought we were smart and would land on our feet. How dare life deal us such a hand? It never dawned on us that this could happen to us but then again, we had never been tested like our folks. They were bizarre times, but we danced on.

Throughout the country, disco was in full bloom. Nightclubs and bars which used to have small bands and live musicians like duos and trios or even a single guitar player/singer had seemingly changed overnight. They disappeared and if they were replaced by another human being, it was a disc jockey and recorded music.

This caused us to develop disco fever. Singers like Barry Manilow belted out hits like The *Copa Cabana*. Laura Branigan gave us *Self Control* with lyrics like "*Oh the night is my world.*

*City lights, painted girl. In the day nothing matters. It's the nighttime that flatters. You take my self-control. I live among the creatures of the night. I haven't got the will to try and fight against a new tomorrow. So, I guess I'll just believe if that tomorrow never comes."* And, Gloria Gaynor's big, catchy disco sound was *I Will Survive* with lyrics like *"Oh as long as I know how to love I know I'll stay alive. I've got all my life to live and all my love to give."*

We took to the dance floors in our flowered pirate shirts, platform shoes, and bell-bottoms. We all felt like John Travolta in the disco movie *Saturday Night Fever*. It was an exciting if troubled time.

The singing group the Bee Gees came to personify this period. The group was comprised of three BB brothers—Barry, Robin, and Maurice—and who became known as the Brothers Gibb, hence the Bee Gees. They were born on the Isle of Mann between Great Britain and Ireland. During the disco era, they recorded hit after hit. They were everywhere on the airwaves and as soundtracks for movies.

Drama was still the order of the day and could be found everywhere. American cities were going broke. New York City especially was on life support, having almost gone bankrupt the year before when banks refused to service the city's debt, which left New York unable to borrow. The federal government refused to help, and they had to resort to pressuring the teachers' pension fund to buy the city's bonds. The country's economic mood was grim and that set all working adults on edge.

Our senses were being assaulted and our space invaded as we started to worry about our personal privacy as Big Brother seemed to get bigger. We found out that the CIA had illegally spied on American citizens and plotted to assassinate foreign leaders. (Sound familiar? Yeah, I know, not much has changed on that front.)

Everybody from the Kent State University shootings walked free and we were—especially us BBs—convinced it was one more conspiracy by the government. It was the fallout from when unarmed college students were gunned down by twenty-eight Ohio National Guard troops during a mass protest against the

US government bombing of Cambodia. A time when our military tried to stop the Viet Cong from using the country as a detour as they traveled from North to South Vietnam in the slender country. The troops shot into a crowd of students, killing four and wounding nine, some of whom suffered permanent paralysis.

Not all the students were even protesting. Some had just been walking by or watching the protest from a distance. In the aftermath, eight Guardsmen were indicted by a grand jury, but they claimed to have fired in self-defense. This claim was accepted by the courts and there was no trial. Case dismissed. Since the students were not armed, we wondered how such a ruling was even possible.

When not one Guardsman was held accountable for the killings, the country went nuts. Hundreds of universities, colleges, and high schools closed throughout the US when over four million students went on strike.

I was out of step with Emma and most of our friends. I left them shaking their heads around the table at one of our gatherings when I didn't blame the young part-time warriors. I said that putting a bunch of ill-trained 18- and 19-year-olds in a tense campus situation with live ammo was crazy. What could go wrong? I reasoned it was the chain of command officers who had failed. Not to mention the politicians who put them in that situation.

The wheels of justice had ground slowly, having been several years since the actual shooting. I felt we should have been objective enough to realize where the real fault and lack of accountability should lie. I stuck to my guns, but it wasn't a popular or majority stance.

Things eventually cooled down. We had other things to worry about. OPEC still had us by the throat, and we worried about even being able to buy gas as we sat in lines to get to a gas station pump with the scarcity of oil. But since I didn't have to drive far to work, I wasn't especially troubled.

When did I become so self-centered and selfish? I wasn't sure, it troubled me, but I didn't want to dwell on it.

Cool Jamaican Bob Marley made Reggae hot. *Saturday Night Live* started on TV and we loved the way the show's comedians poked fun at everything and everybody. John Travolta was on

*Welcome Back Kotter*. On the big screen, Jack Nicholson and *One Flew Over the Cuckoo's Nest* made us squirm uncomfortably and *Alice Doesn't Live Here Anymore* became more than a movie. It became a phrase to indicate that something had changed.

In the movie, when Alice's less than ideal husband dies, she and her young son leave their small New Mexico town to find their future in California where she hopes to make it as a singer. Along the way, short of money, she takes a job in Arizona as a waitress in a small diner. This gets complicated when she becomes involved with a local rancher as her poor taste in men continues.

On some level, this resonated with us because like Alice, we were still struggling to find ourselves and create and sustain meaningful relationships.

One of the first billionaires, Howard Hughes,[74] died. John Denver was on a *Rocky Mountain High* and Paul McCartney was spreading *Wings Over America*. Peter Frampton and The Captain and Tennille with their hit *Do That To Me One More Time* were popular. The Sex Pistols became the first big punk group. Billy Joel burst on the scene with his hit *I Love You Just the Way You Are*. It was about romantic love but just like the lyrics, we also loved ourselves just the way we were.

On TV, *Happy Days* with the cool cat Fonz, *Laverne and Shirley*, and *The Little House on the Prairie* reflected our longing for simpler times of the past. *Charlie's Angels* began and Farah Fawcett's hairdos became all the rage. Sylvester Stallone and *Rocky* fought their way to our hearts on the big screen. Actor Robert Redford and *Three Days of the Condor* chillingly fascinated us. *Taxi Driver* showcased the talent of actor Robert De Niro and *All the President's Men* about Watergate and the two intrepid reporters—Woodward and Bernstein—who broke the scandal, and *The Marathon Man* entertained us in theaters. Moonies continued to accost us on the street and in airports.

The term blackout took on a new meaning when a glitch in NYC's power grid turned out the lights and freaked out Manhattan's residents. It left many in the dark or stranded in elevators. We BBs wondered what in the world our world was coming

---

[74] Hughes took over his family's tool company and went on to become a pioneer in the aviation industry. He later made his mark in Hollywood and film making. In his later years he became an eccentric recluse whose life was shrouded in mystery and legend.

to when even something so basic as lights couldn't be counted on.

The Son of Sam serial killer[75] was captured. Woody Allen's *Annie Hall* was in theaters and like the film, some female BBs started dressing like men, complete with suits and ties.

We escaped as *Close Encounters of the Third Kind*[76] and the first *Star Wars* hit the screen at warp speed. It was the first of the *Star Wars* saga that would span four decades. We walked out of theaters and pumped our fists at the heavens while pretending to hold aloft our imaginary lightsabers. Wow! We had never seen anything like it. The force was with us.

It was a new leap in special effects for Hollywood. Like every story, though, there were two sides to it. It would be years later that I would be struck by the realization that this movie might have marked the beginning of the end of films with a soul, having been replaced by flash and bang.

That is, they became all about bigger, better, louder, and more spectacular special effects. Plot and character development seemed largely lacking in more and more films as the years went by. Maybe that is why viewing old black and white films have become so appealing to my generation. It was a graphic reminder of a time when, like a good book, the actors led you down a path where you cared about the characters. It didn't just stimulate your senses, but it made you emotionally invested in their lives and what they were doing on the big screen. There was actually a plot that told a coherent story.

Later when I had such discussions with younger folks, like my daughter Abbie, they would roll their eyes and tell me I was being unnecessarily critical and unfair.

---

[75] David Berkowitz was an American serial killer who murdered six people in New York City. This panicked an entire city and unleashed one of the largest manhunts in New York history. This bogyman was eventually arrested and tried and sentenced to six consecutive 25-years-to-life terms.

[76] This film starred Richard Dreyfus and like the reality of the time begins with strange events occurring all over the world when people see strange lights and phenomena. Our hero, Roy, starts to have visions of it. The film focuses on a large alien spaceship as Americans became consumed with UFOs. Roy becomes obsessed with sculpting a monument to it. He uses mashed potatoes, potting soil, and anything he can get his hands on to recreate his vision. (I think of this scene every time that I eat mashed potatoes.) His wife and kids leave him and in the end, he is seen being willingly beamed up.

Our discovery that nothing is really what it seems continued as news came out about the side effects of birth control pills. The worst week in stock market history depressed us even though most of us didn't have a dime invested. Jim Jones' People's Temple mass suicide claimed over 900 lives and we wondered to what depths will some people go to belong. He was an American preacher, civil rights activist, and faith healer turned cult leader who conspired to direct a mass murder-suicide of his followers in his jungle commune at Jonestown, Guyana. This gave rise to the popular saying "Don't drink the Kool-Aid . . . "

The Bee Gees' *Stayin' Alive* kept us trying to look like John Travolta at our favorite clubs. *Grease* the movie and *The Buddy Holly Story* made us nostalgic and mellow and Robert DeNiro and *The Deer Hunter* stirred uneasy memories in many BB Vietnam vets. The intensity of *Apocalypse Now* by director Francis Ford Coppola nearly sent some vets over the edge.

Some of us were starting to admit that we were getting older. After all, many of us were now in our 30s. The sale of 200 million pairs of sneakers signaled the beginning of the fitness craze. Runner Jim Fixx's *The Complete Book of Running* became a bestseller.

The price of gold soared as the economy "stagflated." We kept spending every dime we made trying to live up to our expectations because many of us were starting to become convinced the whole system was going to come crashing down around us. At least we told ourselves that. Whether we believed it or not was another matter. We were never big on reality. Our lives were supposed to be charmed.

I even bought myself an investment house to fix then flip. Because of interest rates, though, that turned into a disaster. Rates were so high that nobody wanted to buy because home mortgage rates resembled credit card rates. Over 18%! That little adventure cured me thinking I could make a killing with real estate.

Even the farmers came to Washington with their tractors and went on strike. In a continuing sign of the times, the city of Cleveland defaulted on its loans.

With the fall of the Shah of Iran, the Ayatollah Khomeini returned from exile in Paris and oil became even more scarce.[77]

---

[77] This ended decades of the westernization of the country as it returned to Muslim rule under Khomeini.

The Three Mile Island nuclear plant incident chilled us and made us believe that the *China Syndrome* could become a reality where theoretically the material could melt through the earth to China. Not a reality and a bit dramatic, but the term was descriptive.

Those of us who were divorced or single joked about being careful with our girlfriends or boyfriends when actor Lee Marvin's ex-live-in won "palimony." It was like alimony only for unmarried couples who split. On the big screen, we watched Dustin Hoffman and Meryl Streep battle it out in a messy divorce in *Kramer vs. Kramer*. Although my divorce hadn't been messy, I could relate to this marital failure.

Margaret Thatcher became Prime Minister of Britain and reinforced the notion that women could do any job men could. She was formidable and earned the nickname "the Iron Maiden." At the Vatican, though, women were officially barred from the priesthood.

We continued to sit in gas lines and fume while inhaling fumes and wondering what went wrong and cursing the system our parents had created as we unfairly blamed them. Like Joe, other BB vets were finding out that the chemical Agent Orange might kill them, even though they had survived a war called a "police action" by disingenuous politicians. Because of Joe, I was already painfully aware of the dangers our vets faced.

Increasingly, stories started to appear about the rusting of the mighty American industrial belt in the Midwest. TV show Mork and Mindy had all of us try to imitate the wacky sounds of Robin Williams. We watched in frustration and fascination as Iranians held America hostage after they took over the US embassy in Teheran.

Someone forgot to tell them that Embassies are supposed to be sacred because they are considered to be the soil of the guest country. No matter the hostilities or hatred, they are not invaded. That all changed for America when in November of 1979 a group of radical Islamic Iranian students stormed the US embassy in Tehran. They then proceeded to hold fifty-two American diplomats and citizens for 444 days.

It created a new type of diplomatic crisis. One that President Jimmy Carter seemingly could not handle or resolve. This lasted until the day tough taking President Ronald Reagan was sworn in as the president, succeeding Carter.

The crisis spawned a new type of news program when *Nightline* was created, featuring newsman Ted Koppel. Night after night he reported what was going on. The unprecedented and outrageous crisis stoked the anger of many Americans, especially older folks, but many BBs as well.

With increasing competition from Japan and Europe, the big three auto companies teetered on the brink of bankruptcy and the federal government had to step in because they were deemed 'too big to fail.' The Chrysler bailout caused the United Autoworkers to accept a pay cut. On all fronts, it seemed that we were going the wrong way as a nation. US Steel closed 15 plants, putting 13,000 out of work.

More scary details about the Three Mile Island nuclear plant meltdown and the China Syndrome movie came out, giving rise to new conspiracy theories. The Soviets invaded Afghanistan.

The KKK was still active, further depressing us. This violent American white supremacist hate group targeted African Americans, as well as Jews, immigrants, leftists, homosexuals, and Catholics. The Klan today is not as powerful, active, or centralized as it once was, but it is reported that 42 different Klan groups are still active in 22 states. During their peak, their heinous crimes included midnight visits to burn crosses on the lawns of their victims to terrify them and even going so far as lynching many minorities. Like many BBs, I found it outrageous.

The price of oil continued to surge hurting everyone and making BBs wonder what other surprises the future held as we became more and more responsible as our parents retired. Astonishingly, during our peak home-buying years, the cost of mortgages and almost everything else soared with over 12% inflation and even higher loan rates.

※

Emma had gone to New York to attend a conference of lawyers and I begged off and elected to visit my folks.

The first night home I sat in the dark on the porch with my dad.

"What do you think about the hostage crisis?" I asked.

"I don't know what this country is coming to," he replied. "In the old days we would have bombed the hell out of them and that would be the end of it."

"I think it's more complicated than that, dad."

"No, it's not," he fumed. "Screw diplomacy. The only thing those Arabs understand is strength and force."

They aren't Arabs, dad. They are Persian."

Fiddlesticks Mr. know it all, they are Arabs."

"Well, we have long been meddling in their affairs and they are mad."

"Jimmy, we play a critical role as a moral beacon to the world, not to mention we are the world's policeman."

"I hear you dad, but not everyone sees things like that."

He looked at me and shrugged. I could see equal parts of stubbornness and hurt in his eyes. "Where are you getting these ideas?" Then as if talking to himself, he said, "I suppose it started in college and only got worse when you moved to Washington."

I let it drop and wondered when things had become so awkward between us. It certainly wasn't the same as when we had our talks while he shaved.

Later that day I met some friends to catch up over a few beers at the local tavern. High school chums Vinny and Eddie never left town and were good old hometown boys. Vinny managed the local supermarket and Eddie ran a tire business. One thing I loved about them, even if I didn't share all their views, was that they were the real deal—down to earth and candid. There didn't seem to be any gray in their lives, everything was black and white.

Vinny said, "So how is life in Washington?"

"We enjoy it. It is expensive as all get out. We are sitting here drinking this beer, which costs about half of what it costs there."

"You're kidding," chimed in Eddie. Then he added, "But you are making the big bucks, right?"

"Probably more than I could make here, but it's all relative, I guess."

Then we started waltzing down memory lane and telling war stories and making the inevitable comparisons.

"Kids today aren't like us," Vinny said. "They don't want to work hard. I have a difficult time finding things like stockers for the store. They seem to think it's beneath them."

"I don't think that all kids are like that," I said.

"Yeah," Eddie said. "I have the same problem. The tire business has been good to me. I may get my hands dirty, but I support my family. These kids, though, don't seem to have any drive."

"Do you remember when we used to say we would never trust anyone over 30?" I asked.

Eddie laughed. "Yeah, and now look at us. Do you ever feel like life is passing us by?" Before Vinny or I could respond, he added. "I look at my parents. Damn, they are so set in their ways. To them, everything was better in the old days. Life was less gray and more black and white."

I hesitated then said, "And you don't find any irony in that, Eddie?"

Eddie lit up a cigarette and took a long drag. "Yeah, I guess I'm starting to sound like my dad. He lectures me all the time about putting money away for the future and a rainy day. I keep telling him it is not easy. It's kinda scary because I can see things changing when people like him worked for 40 years in the same job. Then they got the gold watch and pension. I'm not sure what I will have because I chose to have my own business. Will anybody even want to buy it when I want to retire? I'm not sure. Hell, even big companies are getting rid of pensions."

He paused, but was on a roll, "I'm not going to be giving any gold watches to my employees. I have set up a modest pension system, but they contribute and help fund it. My dad doesn't seem to get it."

"When I was a cashier, I was union and my pension was sort of set," said Vinny. "Now that I'm management it's different. No union. If for some reason the company goes belly up, I'm screwed."

I nodded knowingly then said, "But even unions can mismanage or underfund their pension plans."

Vinny laughed, "Then the fat cat politicians and the government will make it right—right?"

"Maybe. I'm in Washington, but I'm not government. Besides, do you trust those bastards?"

Vinny drained his glass. "What choice do we have?"

"My dad is thinking about getting a part-time job to make ends meet," Eddie said as he lit another cigarette. "He says his pension and social security aren't enough. Do you think it would hurt his feelings if I offered him a job at the shop?"

"Vinny shook his head, "I don't know. Our folks will all probably end up living in our basements or spare bedrooms."

Then he laughed and added, "Hell our kids will probably do the same. The cost of living is off the chart. I don't think they will be able to make it without our help. This may not be what people want to hear, but in my opinion, our kids are becoming products of an American education system that is changing from a place of learning to a place of political indoctrination."

Eddie added, "Worse, it's not their fault. It's ours." I looked sharply at him as he continued. "We, baby boomers, are taking over the system from our parents and we are screwing it up. Everybody is a winner and gets rewarded."

I was fairly sure they were deliberately trying to be provocative, and I could tell they were both watching me to see what my reaction was. I just nodded thoughtfully.

We also talked about our legendary—in our minds—high school sports teams. We had been champions, but it seemed that many of our sports heroes of that day ended up pumping gas or bagging groceries. That talk made me sad and uncomfortable. I didn't know the future, but that things continued to change in unexpected ways was clear to me.

After we convinced ourselves that we had solved all the world's problems, we promised to stay in touch and parted. I went home and told my folks I had to get back.

In the morning I kissed mom and hugged her. Dad and I walked outside. I stood in the driveway and shook hands with him. Unexpectedly, he pulled me in and hugged me. His eyes were moist, and it broke my heart. My big strong childhood hero looked gray and a little stooped. With what I felt as no choice, I shrugged it off and got back on the road and back to my life.

Even though we danced a lot of disco, the good life had made all of our belt sizes go up a notch or two, but I was shocked when Brian told me he had been diagnosed with diabetes. He had gone from a fit and gifted athlete to being out of shape and overweight. Too much beer and eating too much pub food I suppose. Just like me.

I thought of Joe and it reinforced the notion that we were not invincible like we all thought. We were not supermen and women. We were just in our thirties and time and bad habits were already starting to take their toll.

Our one consistent activity was dancing and clubbing with our platform shoes and outrageous styles. Like others I let my sideburns grow long down past the lower tip of my ear. Yup, we were cool in our minds if nothing else.

Looking back, I realize we were the last generation to dance as a regular activity that was a part of our lifestyle. The thirty-somethings of today go to clubs and sit around drinking and trying to have conversations over music that is too loud to hear any talk. Not us. Several times a week Emma and I would go to clubs, order a drink every hour or so and dance most of the night.

It continued to be a time when clubs were transitioning from small live music groups to disco. We didn't like this change. but had to appreciate that disco music was lively and fun to dance to.

One sign that the times and we were different was drinking and cars. Not that we thought people should drink and drive, but cops didn't enforce driving under the influence. You had to be falling down drunk to get stopped. After clubbing, we would get on the road at two or three o'clock in the morning and drive home. Maybe it wasn't a problem because we paced our drinking and spent most of the time moving on the dance floor. It was probably a combination of that and that the cops were more lenient.

Other changes were more subtle. Indeed, quiet changes were taking place that hardly made a ripple in our lives at the time but would become tidal waves later. Things like the founding of Apple computer in Steve Jobs' basement in Mountain View, California. And, cocaine was quickly becoming even more fashionable.

When I picked up Emma at Union Station from her NY trip, she seemed excited and nervous, almost like she was on speed. Later I would find that she had gone to a party on travel and been introduced to snorting cocaine. It became the source of many heated arguments over the ensuing couple of years.

She would reason that it was harmless and it gave her vitality and energy to work even harder and bill even more hours. I would shout back that she was addicted to a dangerous drug that was not harmless.

Out of frustration she would harp on my drinking and smoking cigarettes. My only retort was that it was legal. I told her that all the extra money she would make was being used to snort the substance up her nose.

I would learn later that she was just one of the millions of young professionals who flirted with cocaine as a trendy and cool way to get high that they thought was innocent. It wasn't my thing. My dad's words always echoed in my mind. "The reason they call it dope is because it's stupid."

I was still learning about office politics and how to handle myself. We argued politics and culture—you name it and we all had opinions. As usual, some of us were sounding more and more like our parents and some of us still maintained our idealistic dreams.

Emma increasingly worked late and my stopping by Brian's bar became a given. Usually, I met friends, like Ellison, or just chatted with the other regulars. Since his wife Rosa was a nurse with all types of crazy shifts, we spent a lot of time together. As always, politics and work dominated the conversation. We didn't seem to mind that the topics of our arguments didn't vary much. We were passionate and never tired of the discussions.

It was a fluid time. Although we loved the energetic music, the disco era was gradually winding down and the city's clubs changed again as just places to drink and find pickups. British singers invaded America with a new punk sound from the Sex Pistols. The New Wave punks' toned-down cousin came after and suddenly for a brief period dancing was back. With time, though, dancing as a regular outing as we did was ultimately destined to die out.

Things like platform shoes and pirate shirts faded out of fashion and we started to dress more conventionally. Families boomed as many of our friends, acquaintances, and other young couples kept having kids. So much for thinking of ourselves as rule-defying, carefree rebels. That myth had all but been extinguished.

I felt out of step and told Emma that we should consider going down the same road. She was not interested at all and I suppose that was the beginning of the end of my second marriage. It became a sore subject, like her cocaine use it festered in the background between us.

On more than one occasion our heated arguments made me stomp out of the house, get drunk and end up sleeping on Ellison and Rosa's couch. The more Emma worked to bill an increasing number of hours, the more I hung out in the pub.

It was a typical weekday and I found Brian behind the bar. About half the stools were filled and there were several large groups scattered around the tables that surrounded the bar. He saw me come in and motioned to a vacant table. After his backup barkeep took over, he joined me with a guy who looked familiar but I didn't think I knew.

The guy was wearing a Harris tweed jacket with patches on the elbow and looked like the stereotype of a college professor, which it turned out he was. We all shook hands.

"So, Steve, how is life at George Washington University?" I inquired.

"Challenging. It's getting harder to teach than it used to be, especially grading papers."

"Really? Why is that?"

"Well, with each new class of students it changes. Many don't want to put in the work. Instead, they seem intent on doing the minimum and content to try and negotiate their grades with me at the end."

"So, what you are saying is that they aren't like us when we were in school?" I said in a sardonic tone.

He laughed. "Yeah, right, we were model students, but that is exactly what I'm saying. Our education system keeps changing. I have whole classes that I could fail if I don't grade on the curve."

I smiled and wanted to see how spun up about it he would get. "Interesting. I wonder what that says about our education system or even our culture?"

Brian rolled his eyes. "Why not just fail them and wake them up."

The professor smiled. "It's not that simple. My dean would fire me and the parents who pay their tuition would lynch me." Then the conversation took an unexpected turn as he added, "Across the board things and our youth are different; for example, they are not passionate like we were. They don't even protest. What they do is talk, but there is no action behind it."

I shook my head. "I'm not sure that is fair or true. These are just different times and things run in cycles."

He hesitated, "Not that we were all that great or perfect, but the protests of today seem more a result of an eruption of frustration with things like police brutality than identifying a perceived wrong and going out into the streets to change it. That is, today's protests and riots seem often triggered by a dramatic event. I suppose to some extent that was true of us. Those protests of an earlier era were when we went into the streets for things like ending the Vietnam war and not in response to a particular or specific incident. That does not make those events any less powerful, just a shift in attitudes and motivation from the past."

It wasn't too long before Brian drifted back to his host/bartender duties and Steve looked at his watch and said he had to meet his wife. The bar was full, but I was alone in a comfortable cocoon surrounded by the shuffling of chairs, the clinking of glasses, and the din of people unwinding after a day's work. I heard the sounds but didn't concentrate on the words. I was lost in my thoughts. I knew Emma would be home late so there was no hurry. I also knew I was getting a buzz and would have to order some food later, maybe a burger and fries.

What Steve had said had triggered thoughts in my head that pinged around in my mind. Why were we different and how were we different? The generation behind us didn't seem to want to invest the time and energy to protest what was wrong with our country. But then again, neither did many baby boomers at this stage in our lives. I certainly didn't. A common theme now was that we wanted to get out there and make the big bucks and get our share before things fell apart even more.

That fear was fairly common throughout the country. Many perceived Jimmy Carter as a nice guy but a weak president who was overwhelmed by the Iranian hostage situation and energy crisis. Some of my friends called him the bionic peanut.[78] And, they didn't use the term as a compliment.

---

[78] He was a peanut farmer, and this was a takeoff when combined with the popular TV show called the Bionic Man.

I wasn't sure why we were different beyond the fact that we had grown up differently, but how we were different seemed obvious to me in my alcohol-fueled state. Okay, unlike us when we were their age they didn't want to mobilize and take action to fix a system that seemed to be unraveling at an increasing rate. Mentally I started ticking off how we baby boomers were unique from not only our parents but from the generation that came after us.

Baby boomers were shaped as we became a generation of many firsts and lasts.

We were the first generation in America, and maybe the last, to make protesting a way of life, a way to be heard. We took to the streets regularly by the thousands as we sought to impact a range of issues.

We were the first generation to make nothing. Our parents made things you could touch, see, and use. This gave them a concrete sense of what they accomplished. This was not the case with us baby boomers as the American economy transitioned.

What did I produce? Nothing tangible. I became a paper man in a plastic world, helping to make an industry out of nothing but information. Upon reflection, killing trees to make paper a product probably had a lot to do with the overall widespread job dissatisfaction within our generation.

Not only did our folks make things, but they fixed them, too. In the early years, we briefly fixed things, but we ended up being the first generation not to fix anything. As we grew older everything from shoe repair to TV repair shops disappeared. We became a throw-away society. This made us the last to know what main street was as megastores and malls were replaced it. Ironically, those are now being replaced by online shopping. Proving once again that nothing stands still.

We were the first generation not to have a family bible. We lost history and a connection to the past because those before us recorded births, deaths, marriages, and family milestones on the inside cover. Bibles were passed along from generation to generation. And, regardless of the level of spiritual zeal or participation in the form of church activities a particular family had, it also was a tether to religion and a moral and ethical framework. We have lost that. It disappeared. Gone.

We were the last generation to dance. Oh sure, young folks still dance at events like weddings, but for us, our disco days meant we went regularly to clubs and spent hours making our moves. We strutted, gyrated, and swayed to the music. Our music was the last sounds about tender love, cool chicks, and hot cars.

We were the last generation to read physical newspapers. Whether we read the morning or evening editions, it was a daily ritual. We were the last generation to use classified advertisements in newspapers to find jobs. We were the last generation not to be bombarded with a 24-hour news cycle.

We were the last generation to not use f—k in casual conversation. During our youth, it still had shock value and was used sparingly, if at all, and seldom during mixed company conversations.

We were the last generation to write physical letters to communicate and stay in touch with family, friends, and loved ones. We bought stationery, wrote down our thoughts and messages, bought stamps, and hoped they would be delivered in a few days. It wasn't instant communication, but I believe it was lasting and more comprehensive.

As a kid, I had a cigar box full of treasured letters. I suppose today a kid could have an inbox full of emails they could click on if they wanted. When young, I would pull them out regularly and re-read them. They were a source of comfort and entertainment, a real connection to other people. A physical connection to memories. And, even though they were not a form of face-to-face time, you learned how to communicate on more than a superficial level. Writing and reading them helped you develop your vocabulary and syntax. Perhaps this is an unfair criticism because I have to admit that if I were a kid today, I wouldn't be writing letters but instead using the tools currently available.

We were the first generation to be liberated—or shackled, depending on your view—by the pill, making us the first to make shacking up and carnal delights mainstream. Yet, while this may have made us more uninhibited and free in many ways it also probably created other hang-ups and guilty feelings.

We were the last meatloaf and mashed potato generation. Lifestyles like being a vegetarian or a vegan were largely foreign to us and we certainly didn't indulge in things like sushi as many of our kids do. We mostly ate what I would consider diner fare.

We were the last generation to get our entertainment in discrete segments as opposed to today's dominant streaming formats. Our way made it easier for us to tune out and detoxify.

When we were coming of age, cars replaced bicycles as symbols of freedom. This is not the case nearly as much anymore. The love affair with the car seems to have come to an end with today's young.

My reverie ended when Ellison touched me on the shoulder. "Man, where were you? You looked a thousand miles away."

I smiled. "Just thinking."

"Is everything okay?"

"Yes, fine. I was just going over some things in my head."

"Anything you want to share?"

"Another time. It's a long story."

He shrugged good-naturedly and signaled for a drink.

I was still in a spacy state but stayed for one more beer I didn't need. Then I said my goodnights and walked slowly home, enjoying the night air. I hadn't eaten but planned to warm a can of soup when I got home.

# Chapter 9
# Me, Me, Me
# (1980 – 1984)

By now the oldest BBs were in their mid-thirties. If possible, we were becoming harder to shock. We were also becoming even more cynical and numb as computer errors in our national warning system triggered two false nuclear alarms. This happened in 1980 when US Command posts received a warning that the Soviet Union had launched a nuclear strike. In response, our bomber pilots began manning their aircraft. Monitor screens showed two hundred incoming missiles when someone realized it was a false alarm caused by a computer chip error.

This was not an isolated instance. It happened again in 1983 when the nuclear early-warning system of the Soviet Union reported the launch of multiple US Air Force Minuteman intercontinental ballistic missiles from bases in the United States. Again, fortunately, these were determined to be false alarms before the Russians responded.

I found it fascinating that even though our early years were shaped by the threat of a war that could destroy the planet that somehow, we still enjoyed and fostered a general sense of optimism and entitlement at that point in our lives.

Such issues as the false alerts were reported in the media and freaked out a lot of Americans. We BBs, though, mostly took it in stride. After all, we had grown up under the mushroom cloud threat, so it was nothing new. Besides, there were other threats to our existence. The Japanese, for instance, started to push U.S. electronics and auto industries to the brink. It was the beginning of the most fierce competition they had ever faced. The word "recession" was becoming too common.

Older BBs continued to sound more and more like their parents and wondered where all the "real" music had gone. Sugarhill Gang's *Rappers Delight* became the first rap hit. Wow, talk about radical. Although it made you tap your foot and the lyrics were clever, at the time some of us wondered if that genre was even music or just some sort of street poetry.

I paid less attention to new music and started to look for retro music stations and played my 60s and 70s music at home and in the car. On the contemporary scene, though, groups and singers like KC and the Sunshine Band and Michael Jackson were popular. As were Billy Joel, Blondie, and Dolly Parton, along with Culture Club and Police. Perhaps Tina Turner summed up our feelings best with her hit *What's Love Got to Do With It* or Madonna's *Like a Virgin*. Did we want to feel like virgins again? It was a little late for that.

Alvin Toffler told us about *The Third Wave* and Lester Thurlow's *The Zero Sum Society*[79] among other things reminded everyone that the world population was growing geometrically.

It was a time when uneasy signs never seemed to cease. For us BBs, like many people in the US, the late 1970s and early 80s were troubled and troubling times. Although we were focused on our lives and comforts, the radical and countercultural movements of the 1960s and early 1970s, Watergate, the Vietnam War that politicians tried to whitewash by calling it a police action, and

---

[79] The Third Wave was the sequel to Future Shock, and the second in what was originally likely meant to be a trilogy. It laid out the history of the internet and how it was going to permeate everything in our lives in an online world. The zero-sum book looked at where one person's gain would be another's loss. The term was derived from game theory. However, unlike the game theory concept, zero-sum thinking refers to a psychological construct—a person's subjective interpretation of a situation.

our confidence level was not high. Indeed, the instability in the Middle East and our economic crisis highlighted by gas shortages and high inflation at home undermined all Americans' confidence in both their fellow citizens and in their government. For BBs, this further drove us inward and towards becoming more about me, me, me.

The end of Jimmy Carter's presidency came, but it had pretty much finished destroying our idealistic dreams of the 1960s, which were worn down by inflation, gas shortages, foreign policy turmoil, and rising crime. In response, many Americans, including BBs embraced a new conservatism in social, economic, and political life during the 1980s. This was characterized by the policies of President Ronald Reagan. Although he was the oldest person ever to hold the office, it was us BBs who helped ensure that he was swept into office in a landslide.

In the back of our minds, of course, we knew he was old, but he didn't look, act, or sound old. So, we just sort of glossed over the fact. Surprisingly, what was lost on us during this time, was that we were embracing a conservative approach that was very much in line with our parents thinking.

The populist conservative movement known as the New Right appealed to a diverse assortment of Americans, including evangelical Christians, anti-tax crusaders, advocates of deregulation and smaller markets, advocates of a more powerful American presence abroad, disaffected liberals, and defenders of an unrestricted free market. And, yes, many BBs.

The decade started with the Cold War showing few signs of warming. In response, arms control advocates argued for a 'nuclear freeze' agreement between the United States and the Soviet Union. In 1982, almost a million people rallied in support of the freeze in New York City's Central Park. Many historians believe this was the largest mass demonstration in American history. It was a touchy-feely moment when John Lennon sang *Imagine*.

The rise of the New Right seemed to be in part due to the growth of the so-called Sunbelt as large segments of the population migrated to the Southeast, Southwest, and California, where the population had exploded during the 1970s. Many of these folks migrated from the older industrial cities of the North and

Midwest. The latter which continued to live up to its name the Rust Belt.

People were growing increasingly tired of the seemingly insurmountable problems facing aging cities, such as overcrowding, pollution, and crime. Perhaps most of all, many voiced frustrations at paying high taxes for social programs they did not consider effective and they were worried about the stagnating economy. Many were also frustrated by what they saw as the federal government's constant, costly and inappropriate interference. The movement resonated with many citizens who had once supported more liberal policies, but who no longer believed they represented their interests as the political pendulum continued its inevitable swing from side to side.

Us BBs were caught in the middle. We were starting to make big bucks. And, although we mostly wanted extensive liberal social programs, we were becoming more sensitive about the tax bite it was taking out of our paychecks. Hypocritical to be sure, but it was the dichotomy that we faced.

During and after the 1980 presidential election, these disaffected liberals came to be known as "Reagan Democrats." They provided millions of crucial votes for the Republican candidate.

President Reagan was a staunch anti-communist who believed that the spread of it anywhere threatened freedom everywhere. Not surprisingly he pushed for financial and military aid to anti-communist governments around the world, including Grenada, El Salvador, and Nicaragua. This was known as the Reagan Doctrine.

About this time, the press reported that the White House had secretly sold arms to Iran, an action that was not approved by the US Congress. This became known as the Iran-Contra affair. This was a secret U.S. arms deal that traded missiles and other arms to free some Americans held hostage by terrorists in Lebanon. It also used funds from the arms deal to support the Contras in the armed conflict in Nicaragua where they were fighting Daniel Ortega's fledgling communist government. The controversial deal—and the ensuing political scandal—threatened to bring down the presidency of Ronald Reagan. We BBs wondered if this was Nixon 2.0.

Instrumental in forming and implementing the secret deal were Reagan's national security adviser John Poindexter and

Marine Lieutenant Colonel Oliver North, a member of the National Security Council. They were summoned before the US Congress which provided months of televised drama as the hearings became polarizing entertainment for the country.

They were convicted but this was later reversed. Although the whole affair and its fallout were fascinating, it was yet another scandal we suffered through. We BBs were truly becoming immune to the scandal of the month. Many BBs admired North because he was cool, full of conviction, and essentially flipped off Congress.

The decade was also characterized by its materialism and consumerism. It saw the rise of the "yuppie." There was an explosion of blockbuster movies and the emergence of cable networks like MTV, which introduced music video and launched the careers of many iconic artists.

Our reactions, biases, and fears varied. As a generation, we were further splintering and becoming more diverse. The older we got the more fractured BBs became politically and culturally. Sure, we still shared much in common, but we were not the homogenous block we once were. I found it odd that our parents' generation, although older, was still largely consistent and cohesive in their view of the world. Not us as our perspectives and viewpoints started to span the spectrum of thought.

As a sign of imbalance and greed, Savings and Loan institutions continued to become insolvent, wreaking havoc on millions of investors and borrowers. This made us smug that many of us were spending 110 percent of our earnings and not being dopes by saving it or investing in the system.

S&Ls were specialized banks created to promote affordable homeownership. They typically offered higher rates on savings accounts to attract more deposits. This increased their ability to offer mortgages because at that time banks didn't lend money for residential mortgages. By 1980, they represented half of the approximately $960 billion in home mortgages outstanding at that time.

But dramatically rising inflation and interest rates caused chaos within the industry. First, the interest rates that they could pay on deposits were set by the federal government and were substantially below what could be earned elsewhere. This led savers to withdraw their funds. Second, S&Ls primarily made long-term fixed-rate mortgages. When interest rates rose, these mortgages lost a considerable amount of value, which essentially wiped out the S&L industry's net worth.

At that time, it was arguably the most catastrophic collapse of the banking industry since the crash of 1929. Thousands of S&Ls failed to end what had been one of the most secure sources of home mortgages and investment.

This financially hurt a lot of Americans, like my parents, although Emma and I didn't have any savings in S&Ls, or banks either for that matter, as taxpayers we helped foot the bill for the bailout that followed. Just like other bailouts, it wasn't the average man or woman who got help, it was those fat cats who had money.

We were spending and running up the balances on our credit cards. It is difficult to imagine now that the federal government encouraged this reckless personal spending by allowing people to deduct the interest paid on credit cards on their tax returns, but we did just that. Emma and I used to joke about it when we filed our tax returns.

IBM introduced the Personal Computer. Up to that point, computers existed as huge mainframes housed in large climate-controlled rooms at corporations and government offices. They were beasts and generated a lot of heat. They weren't personal or for the little guy. Their software was controlled by stacks of card punch cards.

*Vintage personal computer station.*

When I bought my first PC, it required two 5-inch floppy disks to boot up and had a storage capacity provided by a 20-megabyte hard drive. Today that memory wouldn't be enough to run almost anything. But for me, it was a marvel with its orangish-yellow writing on the screen of the clunky monitor. They were not glossy flat screens of today, but it was still magic and mesmerized me.

Pac Man foretold our coming fascination with joysticks and video games while staring for hours at video screens. I wondered if it was just me or did it seem like we had been staring at TV screens almost since we were born?

Jamaican reggae man Bob Marley died. Michael Jackson was strutting his stuff. The first few AIDS cases were diagnosed in LA. We didn't pay much attention. Later we would learn that this was the beginning of the end of casual sex. The Pill freed us, and AIDs brought us back to earth. Suddenly condoms became important again. John Belushi[80] died from drugs and reminded us that many BBs still had a problem with self-restraint and discipline.

There used to be only one telephone company in America and that was Ma Bell or AT&T. That changed when the baby bell telephone companies became orphaned from AT&T as the government broke up the communications behemoth that had held a monopoly on telephone service since its inception. This was mandated in 1982 by the federal government when they decreed that AT&T would relinquish control of the regional bell operating companies. AT&T would continue to be a provider of long-distance service and the regional bell companies would be independent and provide local service.

This had been festering since a 1974 filing of an antitrust lawsuit against AT&T. It was shocking since the iconic company was one of the most powerful American enterprises in existence at the time. Companies like Bell Atlantic came into their own as they became Verizon and other names. It was earth-shattering and the beginning of affordable long-distance service in the US as AT&T faced competition for the first time.

The world kept getting smaller. We watched on TV as a proud Britain gave Argentina a black eye over the Falkland Islands in a mini 10 week-long war. The Falklands War was the result of the Argentine invasion of the British-owned Falkland Islands. Located in the South Atlantic, Argentina had long

---

[80] He was an American actor, comedian and singer, and one of the original cast members of the NBC sketch comedy show *Saturday Night Live*. He was one of the first comedians to push the boundaries of traditional standup comedy. He was often raunchy but always outrageous and funny. We BBs loved his humor, our parents not so much.

claimed these islands as part of its territory. In 1982, Argentine forces landed in the Falklands, capturing the islands two days later. In response, the British dispatched a naval and amphibious task force to the area.

The initial phases of the conflict occurred mainly at sea between elements of the Royal Navy and the Argentine Air Force, but since the British launched its planes from an aircraft carrier on the far side of the island, its naval forces were at the limit of the Argentine planes. In May, British troops landed on the islands and by June had compelled the Argentine occupiers to surrender and leave.

For the first time since the Vietnam War, we watched a conflict on TV, and it became a form of entertainment for us.

The election to the U.S. Congress of a former activist turned mainstream citizen, Tom Hayden, typified how the radicals of the 1960s were starting to become the yuppies of the 1980s. He founded the Students for a Democratic Society, or SDS as it was known, and served as its president for two years.

The legendary auto man John DeLorean was arrested with 60 pounds of cocaine. We wondered how anybody could be that stupid. Some of us should have looked in the mirror. Most of us never knew that cocaine could cause so many of our lives to unravel during the 80s as coke became a "designer" drug.

The Vietnam Memorial was dedicated, and BB vets finally felt like they got their due and a little respect. Highly criticized at first, it would become a deeply stirring reminder of the sacrifices some BBs made during the turbulent 60s and 70s with over 57,000 names of those who fell inscribed on The Wall as it became known. Many of us visited the hallowed site and took paper and pencil and rubbed the name of classmates, friends, and relatives onto it as a way of remembering those who fell.

On the big screen, we watched the *Quest for Fire* and were visited by *E.T.* and *Poltergeist*. We also watched *Terms of Endearment, Flashdance,* and *The Big Chill*. Also, *The Elephant Man* and *The Blues Brothers*, starring John Belushi, were popular in theaters. A lot of vacant office space in major cities reminded us that the economy was still sputtering despite the uptick in optimism among BBs. Congress passed legislation to rescue the

Social Security System. We BBs scoffed because we were convinced we would never collect a dime of it anyway.

Times Beach[81] in Missouri was declared an environmental disaster due to dioxin contamination. The most cynical of us began to wonder how many more toxic eco landmines were out there. No matter, by this time many of us were so caught up in the almighty dollar that we no longer kidded ourselves. It started to be overtly all about money. A lot of us had become yuppies, complete with the BMW and gold American Express Card.

Those of us with blue-collar parents watched uncomfortably as they continued to be alarmed, confused, and hurt by the loss of manufacturing jobs. Many of us had become part of the services sector and information age so we coped a little better with the change. I'm sure academics and those in think tanks knew, but we didn't fully realize it yet. Unconsciously we were witnessing the transformation of the American economy and workplace. Maybe we should have paid more attention to Toffler's book about the third wave.

We were still uneasy as the seemingly unstoppable Japanese super economy continued to take over America, buying companies and real estate, including the iconic Rockefeller Center in New York City. They also acquired mainstream American companies like Firestone Tires and Columbia Pictures as they moved into Hollywood.

The AIDS virus was identified and cholesterol was linked to heart disease. We joked about everything being bad for you, including our mainstays burgers and sex, but we started to be a little alarmed as we looked in the mirror and saw ourselves aging and heading rapidly towards the big four o.

The homeless were becoming very visible to us. Yuppies were uncomfortable and tried to look the other way, but some younger BBs were angry with Reagan and conservatives. Yet, he still had his fans, like Brian. Life was mocking us because we were a major force in electing him.

---

[81] This resort community was located on the iconic Route 66 that ended up being one of the biggest environmental disasters in US history when motor oil used to control dust on the town's many dirt roads was laced with toxic waste, like dioxin, which was generated in the production of Agent Orange—a widely used chemical weapon in the Vietnam War. The area indirectly became another casualty of the war. The deadly pollution caused the town to be declared uninhabitable and abandoned.

We listened to Boy George and Springsteen sang *Born in the USA*. Break dancing was hot. We watched Harrison Ford in *Indiana Jones and the Temple of Doom*. For those of us who had become the material girls and boys of the day, one of our heroes got caught as Ivan Boesky[82] pleaded guilty to fraud on Wall Street.

By this time, crack cocaine was a national nightmare. Since many of us had kids and we had overindulged ourselves in the past, we were uneasy as we lectured on the evils of drugs. The first Generation Y kids were born. We pursued our careers with a vengeance and became such things as marketers and general managers—BB purists called it selling out, but most of us called it just plain selling.

All these events and thoughts continued to shape who we became as a generation and started to increasingly impact who we were and who we would become. This further eroded the idealism and optimism that had once characterized our generation. I suppose if I had thought more about it, it signaled the end of our dreams that we would change the world.

Reagan kept reminding us that our best days were still ahead of us, but we weren't so sure.

Sure I still dreamed at night, but my waking dreams were rapidly disappearing into thin air.

※

My marriage was growing colder or at least more sterile. I didn't want to dwell on it, but Emma and I were becoming like roommates, sharing living space but lacking in intimate personal time or any romantic connection. I didn't know what to do to address it and turned inward. I wanted more, but the only thing I seemed to control was my career. So, I quit my job and started a couple of years of job-hopping for more money. In some ways I guess I was a pioneer because this was long before job-hopping was considered okay and even smart in terms of career management.

---

[82] He was a former American stock trader who became infamous for his prominent role in an insider trading scandal that occurred in the United States during the mid-1980s. He was charged and pled guilty to insider trading, was fined a record $100 million, and became an informant and blew the whistle on other cheats.

I avoided discussing this with my dad because it would have horrified him. Usually, I just glossed over what I was doing in my conversations with him. Emma was aware of it and seemed to approve because it meant I was earning more and going up.

If possible, I became even more of a fixture at Brian's bar. Most nights I got buzzed. I wasn't falling down drunk but in the back of my mind, I knew I had a problem. It didn't affect my ability to get to work on time or perform, but it bothered me and lowered my self-esteem.

Instinctively Ellison seemed to read my habits and mind better than I did. More and more he invited me to join him, Rosa, and the kids for dinner and family activities. I became a regular at their house. I was Uncle Jimmy to his kids. If Emma noticed, she didn't express her thoughts. She was completely engrossed in her career.

Looking back, it seemed a little sordid, but while I slowly pickled my liver, Emma snorted the white stuff. That type of abuse seemed to be all too prevalent for us BBs in the 1980s, we were focused on ourselves and what made us happy. We didn't think about the toll it might eventually take on us or our loved ones.

By now snorting cocaine had become a regular habit for her. I hated that she did it. The prevailing attitude throughout the country, though, was that it was harmless. This was fueled in no small part by the media, many of whom wrote stories that tended to underestimate the dangers and even glamorize the lure of cocaine. It was the drug of successful young professionals and Hollywood types.

Specifically, there was a time in the 1980s when, just like the day of alcohol prohibition in the US, fashionable opinion was on the side of the smugglers. The thought being that where there was demand, there would-be suppliers.

Also, at least initially among the early users and even the general public, there was a widely held belief that cocaine was a non-addictive and harmless vice. It is difficult to envision such attitudes today, but it was considered a recreational and fashionable drug. Young professionals from lawyers and business types to movie stars and other celebrities were using it. It was upscale and widely accepted. With a lack of experience, as we had with drugs like heroin, it was glamorized to a high degree and thought to empower the user with energy and confidence.

Emma sure subscribed to that. It was prevalent at parties and gatherings wherever we went. Folks were even snorting up during the day in their offices or restrooms of trendy restaurants and bars. It simply didn't carry the grimy loser image of other drugs—like heroin—that society associated with junkies shooting up in back alleys. After all, as Emma pointed out, cocaine was pure white and usually snorted, not injected with dirty needles.

I didn't buy into any of that. I thought it was dumb and told her so. She threw my use of alcohol in my face and resorted to my standard retort was that at least it was legal. It finally all came to a boiling point.

It was dark, about 10 in the evening when I go home. The living room was shadowy with some filtered light from streetlamps and I didn't switch on any lights. Her voice was soft in the gloom.

"We need to talk, Jimmy."

I could just make out her silhouette in the murky light and sat down opposite her on the couch. And, even though I knew it wasn't, I asked, "Sure. Is everything okay?"

"No, it's not, but you already know that." I remained silent and she continued. "I don't know what happened to us, but this is not a marriage anymore."

"All couples go through rough patches," I said without much emotion and a little defensively.

"I want a divorce. I've already filed. Before you say anything, I have thought it through. I want the house but will buy your half. We can split the furniture any way you want. It will be a clean break."

I should have been stunned, but I wasn't. All I could think to say was, "I'll take tomorrow off and pack my things."

"Wow. I expected you to put up a bit of argument." She hesitated. "That's fine, but there is no rush. By the way, I've already had our place appraised and I can write you a check by the first of the month."

"So, this is final?"

"Tell me you are not relieved. No bullshit. Be honest."

I let out a deep sigh. "Yes, I suppose I am, but that doesn't mean I'm happy about it."

"I feel the same way, but we both know it's for the best."

She stood and said, "I'm going to bed. I hope you don't mind but I want you to sleep on the couch. I'll bring down some bedding."

I felt a little numb, but she was right—I was relieved.

As if to add to my heavy and disconcerting thoughts, Paul and Molly called me the following day to let me know that mom had died. She passed quietly in her sleep. I didn't cry but my heart was like lead. Well, at least I wouldn't have to tell her about Emma and me.

The following day I called Ellison and told him what was happening. He was thoughtful and said, "Not to make light of it, my friend, but perhaps a fresh start is for the best. You know while you are making other living arrangements you are always welcome here."

I thanked him and said I would let him know when I decided how I was going to resettle. Later in the day, I had almost an identical conversation with Brian. Their support gave me some comfort that I wasn't alone, even though I knew I was. That comfort was short-lived and eroded as I knew I had failed again. To dispel these thoughts, I got busy making new plans and moving on with my life.

## Chapter 10

# It's All About Money & Living in a Material World (1985 – 1989)

The oldest of us were turning the big Four O. We were well into our peak earning years and moving into key corporate positions and executive suites in record numbers—although most of us still hadn't taken retirement planning too seriously. After all, we never had, and it still seemed a long way off. Nonetheless, we knew retirement was lurking out there somewhere down the road.

Depending on our situation, we saw our salvation in different quarters. Sally, for instance, still had the feeling, albeit uneasy, that the union would stand behind her and her family. Brian railed against big government, but others saw Uncle Sam as the salvation of all. Many of us were earning big and charging and spending just as large.

Mikel Gorchov, or Gorby as he was known, was leading the Russians and continued to call for economic reforms. So, even for the Russians, it was all about money. The movie *The Killing*

*Fields* was in theaters. It was a true account of the civil war in Cambodia where the Khmer Rouge rebels conducted a genocide that killed millions.

In a revolution closer to home, the truth about the sexual revolution being over finally hit home when iconic movie star Rock Hudson died of AIDS.

First Lady Nancy Reagan kept telling us to just say "no" to drugs. Since some of us had college-age kids at this time, it seemed like there should be more than a two-letter word that we could provide in the way of advice. Plus, some of us had drug problems leftover from the excesses of our own youth.

When NASA's Space Shuttle Challenger exploded our space program was suddenly on the back burner. On some level, this event coincided with our feelings that we were not as adventurous as we once were.

In 1986, the stock market was hot and we tried to make a killing. Gorby[83] kept pushing Russia mainstream. We started to wonder if the world would finally become a safer if not saner place.

The nerds from our generation started to play God as genetically engineered animals were patented. The 1987 stock market crashed and reminded us that maybe we weren't smarter than our parents. It also reminded us how materialistic we had become. Movies like *Wall Street* and *Fatal Attraction* showed the dark side of the yuppy lifestyle of the 80s. AIDS continued to cause an outbreak of "safe sex" and the sale of condoms spiked as they were suddenly back in demand.

The anti-war and establishment protests were long gone, they had been replaced by kinder and gentler protests against us killing our planet. In 1988, the U.S. had the worst drought since the 1930s dust bowl days. There were a lot of forest fires and Global Warming became a concern. Hospital waste materials, like used

---

[83] He was the last leader of the Soviet Union, serving as the general secretary of the Communist Party of the Soviet Union from 1985 until 1991 before it broke up. Although he was committed to preserving the Soviet state and to its socialist ideals, Gorby believed significant reform was necessary, particularly after the 1986 nuclear disaster at the Chernobyl power plant that turned the site into a toxic environmental disaster. He engaged in summits with Reagan to limit nuclear weapons and these actions signaled the end of the Cold War. His enlightened policy, called Glasnost, allowed for freedom of speech and the press within the crumbling Russian empire. He also sought to decentralize—called Perestroika—the economic decision-making process, which undermined the country's one-party state.

syringes, were found on East coast beaches and some of us had the nagging thought that just maybe our materialism might eventually destroy the planet.

A federal Drug Czar was named to lead the war on drugs and we wondered if it would be as big a bust as LBJ's War on Poverty. The Exxon Valdez tanker oil spill helped to solidify the eco-movement when the oil tanker ran aground on a reef in Prince William Sound in Alaska. An eighteen-foot-wide hole was ripped into the hull, and almost 11 million gallons of crude oil spilled into the ocean. It was the biggest oil spill in United States history.

Terror took to the air when Pan American flight 103 was blown out of the sky over Lockerbie, Scotland, killing 243 passengers and 11 crew members. It was the deadliest terror attack in the history of Great Britain. It also killed 11 people on the ground as wreckage fell onto a residential street. After a long investigation, arrest warrants were issued for two Libyan nationals and Libyan leader Muammar Gaddafi handed them over for trial. They were found guilty and jailed for life. Years later one of the jailed Libyan intelligence officers was released on compassionate grounds after being diagnosed with cancer.

The more conservative of us BBs were outraged. Compassion for the terrorist killer. How about more compassion for all the victims?

No matter, the movie *Roger Rabbit* made us laugh, and *Stand and Deliver* inspired us. There were student demonstrations in Tiananmen Square in China as tanks rolled over and crushed students and we were reminded that we once protested to make things better. For older BBs, though, those days of protest seemed like a long time ago.

We started to wonder if we would be overwhelmed by technology, like our parents, as we aged. At first, we thought it was a joke, (asking ourselves if our computers had a cold while rolling our eyes) but computer viruses became a real threat to us. The Berlin Wall finally crumbled in 1989 and we felt like we had won the Cold War.

Since peace had broken out, liberal BBs joined the chorus for killing the Pentagon. This was tempered, though, when we realized that we not only had many enemies still out there, but many of us were working for industries that supported the military It was all part of our dependence on the money that supported our lifestyle. *Dangerous Liaisons, Born on the Fourth of July*, and *Sex, Lies, and Videotape* were at theaters. The fitness craze had started to run in high gear and vitamins and working out became important to many BB.

The S&L collapse and resulting fallout were still very much mainstream. The Keating Five epitomized the lingering scandal. It involved five sitting United States Senators who were accused of corruption. This ignited a major political scandal as part of the larger Savings and Loan crisis of the late 1980s and early 1990s. Specifically, the failure of the Lincoln S&L resulted in fraud charges later being brought against senators Alan Cranston, Dennis DeConcini, John Glenn, John McCain, and Donald W Riegle.

They faced serious accusations of having unethically involved themselves on the material behalf of banker Charles H. Keating, Jr. who was then Chairman of the Lincoln Savings and Loan Association. The Senate Ethics Committee launched an investigation into the conduct of the five heavyweight politicians who were seen as having improperly intervened with regulators to protect a campaign contributor. Not surprisingly, all five Senators denied improper conduct, claiming that it was Keating's status as a constituent rather than as a donor that motivated their actions.

We all said to ourselves, "Sure it was." Wink wink.

Keating himself was eventually convicted on 73 counts of fraud in 1993 and served 4 years in prison. Even though the Keating Five emerged from the scandal legally unscathed (only Cranston received a formal reprimand) the political consequences had more lasting effects. Cranston left office and Riegle and DeConcini opted not to run for re-election. McCain, for his part, said his involvement in the affair was "the worst mistake of my life," but that didn't stop him from later running for president.

None of these folks were BBs and we were smug that we wouldn't have acted in such an unethical manner if we had been bestowed with the public trust of an elected office. At the time we thought that accusations against us for being greedy were hypocritical. It turned out that we weren't better or above it all when later we starred in our own political scandals.

At the time, the whole thing reminded me of something Ronald Reagan once said, "Politicians and diapers need to be changed often . . . and for the same reason.

※

After Sally left, the office just wasn't the same. I was making more money but felt restless. I updated my wardrobe by adding a three-piece suit every month. I felt special. I started looking at other opportunities. When I mentioned this to dad when we chatted by phone, I could hear him shaking his head.

"As I've told you before, being a job hopper will hurt your career, Jimmy. Firms value loyalty."

"But I can make more money."

"Maybe, but you have to consider job security."

But under Reagan, the economy was continuing to gain momentum from the lackluster President Jimmy Carter years in the 70s decade. In the end, I took other jobs for more money at other non-governmental organizations. Even though we were no longer a couple, Emma was proud of me.

Although I spent a lot of time in our marathon group sessions, I also spend hours alone nursing a beer and musing on my life and my personal and the country's state of affairs.

It still stung that Emma hadn't wanted to have a family with me. She just didn't want any kids and I suppose that was just as well. I already had a daughter I barely knew. It had been all about us and success.

I still felt like somebody. With my snazzy wardrobe, I felt important in a city where everybody felt like they were indispensable and somehow key players in the running of the country. When you met someone, anyone, the first question always was, "What do you do?"

It was a time of not only greed but a wave of conservatism that continued to sweep over the country. When Reagan was elected, the Democrats were red and the Republicans were blue on the electoral map. I remember looking at election night on the news and the country looked like a swimming pool. It was a blowout. Hollywood's handsome leading man was the great communicator and much of the country seemed enthralled by his eloquent plan talk when he said, "Government is not the solution. Government is the problem."

The Democrats were beaten so soundly in that contest there was even talk by the pundits that they would not win an election again for decades. Looking back, of course, that was laughable. The political pendulum always swings from side to side.

Around dinner parties and happy hours, we continued to ponder the state of things, pronouncing our beliefs as though they were insightful and meaningful. We sounded like pundits on TV as we expounded on things.

Although the ultimate impact of what was happening escaped us. As Emma had pointed out, we were always two Americas—one left and one right—but we shared a common denominator, which was the good of the country. That started to change in the 1980s and its impact would contribute to the country's polarization and identity politics into the new millennium.

Some, or perhaps even many, would argue with me, but we and our parent's generations were the last generations of civility and compromise. Today, we are still two Americas, but no longer can even decide what is good for the country. One side wants to maintain the status quo, the other wants to radically transform America. We used to express ourselves in things like protests. Now we weaponize words and demonize each other. We have entered an era of extremism with no room for compromise. The seeds for this were sown in the 1980s.

Nothing can be moderate. We have abandoned common sense; for example, it is not enough that contraceptives must be covered by a government-mandated health plan, nuns must conform, too. It is not enough to be sensitive with word choice and language, we must punish those who say or think the wrong things. We cannot agree to disagree and move on. Regardless of one's politics or, heaven forbid religion, it is not enough that gay marriage is legal, bakers who disagree must be forced to bake the wedding cake or be punished. It just won't do that attention be paid to scientific arguments on the environment, we must surrender our rights to an all-knowing and all-powerful government. There is little room for debate about different or rational approaches to address such problems.

In the halls of power in Congress, no one reaches across the aisle anymore, including BBs. Instead, we hurl words at each other like stones. Whatever I'm for, the other guy is against and vice versa.

Perhaps our upbringing in a more innocent time made us more tolerant. Those times were far from perfect, but they did foster a certain sense of civility and courtesy we extended to others. It started with us as kids. We had to at least go through the motion of politeness. Yes ma'am and yes sir were instilled in our being. Certainly, our parents understood the power of dialog and the concept of you want this, I want that, so let's meet in the middle.

Although to some extent we may have been overcome with greed, we weren't overloaded with too much information. That all changed when Ted Turner launched his 24-hour CNN news network. This would forever change news coverage, and many would argue not necessarily for the better.

As reality changed, we continued to be obsessed with acquiring material things. Growing up our folks paid cash so nothing was bought that couldn't be afforded and paid for. You either had the money in your pocket, or you didn't. Not us. We had magic plastic. We bought stereos, cell phones, personal computers, upscale clothes, luxury cars. We ate out a lot, dining on expensive fare washed down with wine. It was "get rich, borrow, spend, enjoy." We wanted conspicuous opulence.

This was reflected in society and the business world at large. Much like today, for example, there were crooked wall street types who flourished in an age of deregulation. Personal freedoms rose, but economic inequality had started to set in as the gap widened between the haves and have nots.

For my part, and much to the horror of my dad, I changed jobs three times in about a year and a half. Each time it was about making more money, but not necessarily achieving more job satisfaction. Consumption continued to be the order of the day for too many of us. We no longer even pretended to seek equality but a me-first attitude. I'm getting mine and the devil with others.

I didn't think about it because it made me uneasy, so I kept it tucked away in the back of my mind. People like Emma who were completely focused on their careers and status didn't even give such things a second thought. While I didn't agree, I did admire their single-mindedness.

It was a time of big hair piled high and held in place with hair spray for women. For men, it was pastel polyester leisure suits, which were first popularized in the disco era of the 1970s. The times were also characterized by yuppies and the AIDs epidemic. Safe sex was in.

MTV provided a venue for singers like Madonna to parade across the stage half nude while they sang. For female entertainers especially, exhibition and flashing lights and flashy stage settings seemed as important as actual singing talent.

In addition to the excesses of our newly acquired material possessions, it was a time when technology was changing our lifestyles at a rate that made my head spin. Chips and microprocessors were shrinking our electronics. Where there had only been large room size mainframe computers, the personal computer was putting this power on our desks and in our homes. I felt like the king of the universe with that kind of power at my fingertips.

As technology pushed the boundaries it gave rise to the World Wide Web or the Internet as it would become known. It was the first step of us being an online virtual society. We would become more connected but eliminate a lot of people-to-people contacts.

I bought my first cell phone that was the size and weight of a brick. It turned out, of course, that we were not the masters of technology we thought we were when we were brought back down to earth when the explosion of NASA's challenger killed seven astronauts, scattering body parts and wreckage all over the sky. Graphic footage of this was televised and shocked us.

More of our excess during the 80s continued to be paid for with credit. "Fly now, pay later" had solidly become a way of life for many BBs. It would later cause a financial hangover for many of us. We made 100 percent and spent 110 percent. Much like our government with their revenues, whatever we made was never enough. Spend, spend, spend was the order of the day.

Original video games like Pac Man gobbled up ghosts like our credit cards gobbled up our income. The first clunky home video games, like Nintendo and space invaders, became more pervasive in our lives. For those of us who didn't buy them, there were new arcades where you could play anything. As a kid, I remember pinball machines with flippers and bumpers to send a steel ball bouncing around to score points, but video games were virtual and not physical at all. Looking back, I suppose this was just another step from all things physical to a digital world.

With the ever-increasing rise of credit cards and all things plastic, we were well on our way to creating a plastic world that would eventually threaten to overwhelm us with the indestructible stuff. If not plastic cards to drown us in debt then plastic bags, plastic water bottles, plastic cups, plastic straws, plastic toys, and plastic fast-food containers to drown us in plastic trash. It marked the beginning of today's plastic world. It doesn't decompose and never seems to disappear, just like our debt.

Recycling indeed helps solve some of the problems, but not nearly enough. There are currently trash islands, much of them comprised of plastic, around the world which are staggering in their scale. The great Pacific Island is estimated at 600,000 square miles or about twice the size of the state of Texas! About 80,000 tons of discarded plastic. This is overwhelming when as I try to comprehend it. It's a far cry from the fix and reuse world we BBs grew up in. Those of our parents who were still alive would be horrified if they could even comprehend the scale of this.

We continued to consistently get together often at dinner parties to "solve the world's problems." We were smarter than everyone else, including our politicians. If you didn't believe us, we would tell you so. One such Saturday's gathering at Emma's house saw us not only naively congratulating ourselves but making the inevitable comparisons between our generation and those before and after us.

Emma often hosted such affairs. Even though we were divorced. Indeed, our relationship was more relaxed now that we weren't a couple.

That night Brian held everyone's attention when he said, "Before reality set in, we were anti-war, anti-government, anything is possible. We were unlike our folks who didn't question authority and believed in duty before pleasure. So, we were different because too many of today's young people seem to lack that level of organizational loyalty or loyalty to a movement. They are more independent and self-reliant. That is not necessarily a bad thing, I'm just saying they are different than us."

This set off a flurry of opinions.

"Yes, attitudes are changing," said Emma. "For example, we felt that higher education was a birthright, today's kids just see it as a way to get there."

Then Ellison asked, "Are you saying our generation we felt more entitled?"

"Oh yes," said Emma.

"Well, I personally didn't, not to say others didn't feel that way."

I added, "Maybe so, but entitlement or not, we know that acquiring skills is important, they are just not as important as a good work ethic and face time. Our kids think work ethics are sort of important but not as much as skills. Do you see my point?"

"Are you saying we live to work and they work to live? asked Emma."

"Yes, I think to a large extent that is true," I replied. "Maybe they have it right."

Brian laughed and said, "Well our folks were certainly hard working and understood loyalty." He looked at me, "They weren't job hoppers like many of us."

"What are you saying, Brian?'

He smiled, "You know exactly what I'm saying, Jimmy. You are a mercenary."

"I'm just following the money." Then I chuckled, "We started out to change the world, but the world changed us."

"Speak for yourself, Jimmy."

"You don't think we are becoming establishment like our folks?" asked Ellison. "As a minority, my dad got screwed over a lot, but he was he was one hundred percent American, right down to the American flags on his boxer shorts."

I nodded in agreement. Then said, "Yeah, but he was military and a patriot."

Emma poured more wine. "Lighten up guys. Let's face it, we have gone from saying "never trust anyone over thirty to facing the big four O. It's called maturing or at least the passing of time.

You guys are no longer rebels. We are getting ours and we don't want that to change. That is what the establishment is all about, maintaining the status quo. Would any of you really want to go back to when we struggled?"

In a somewhat defensive tone, I said, "Well, we wanted to make a difference and I hope we did."

Somewhat condescendingly Emma noted, "Yes dear, but with time you stopped being so righteous and marching in the streets."

"Yeah, I can't argue with that."

And on and on it went into the night. Maybe we didn't solve anything, but it was a way for us to express ourselves and, at least in our minds, put our place in the world into some sort of context. I don't know if our kids indulge in these types of exchanges. I imagine they do to some extent. We covered the waterfront from politics and world affairs to culture and lifestyle, rationalizing and pontificating. I suppose a therapist would say such sessions were therapeutic if nothing else. Or maybe it would provide endless fodder for them to dissect and analyze our flawed generation.

Although we were soaring career-wise and entered the 1990s feeling successful but a little threatened as things kept changing. This was probably all normal because we had more to lose. The more we acquired the more evident this became. Like an investor who sees the market go ever higher we thought it would never go down. If we were being honest with ourselves probably deep in our minds we did, but we wanted to believe otherwise.

Perhaps Madonna's song, *Material Girl*, said it all with lyrics like *"Cause the boy with cold hard cash is always mister right. Cause we are livening in a material world. And I am a material girl...."*

I had dropped a note to Sally to see how she was doing and to mention that Emma and I had called it quits. Within a few days, she called me and suggested maybe it would be good for me to get out of town for a few days and asked if I wanted to visit. I didn't take this invitation as anything more than Sally treating me as a sort of big brother.

I took a few days off and planned my route for the drive to McKeesport, which was essentially a part of the Pittsburg metropolitan area. That Friday morning after rush hour died down, I got on the road. I stayed off the turnpike and interstate roads.

## Chapter 10

I enjoyed the two-lane road that passed through many a small town and village, bringing back fond memories.

As I finally passed over a picturesque river and into the little city, I felt good to be out of the sterile environment of the nation's capital. It exuded a smokestack industrial ambiance, a place where things got made and things got done.

Since Sally and I hadn't discussed my trip in any detail, I checked into a quaint downtown hotel. As I checked in the elderly clerk eyed me and asked, "Business? Or perhaps a trip home?"

"Neither I'm just in town to visit a friend."

That seemed to satisfy his curiosity and he handed over the key and I made my way upstairs to my room. I called Sally and we agreed to meet later for dinner, and she asked if I wouldn't mind if she invited her dad and one of her brothers. I told her that was fine with me.

It was a chophouse in the downtown section, and it had a warm inviting feeling. It was obvious by the host's greeting that they knew Sally. As I approached the table a tall man with the build of an ex-pro football linebacker rose and extended his hand.

"I'm Chuck, Sally's dad."

Her brother joined us a few minutes later and turned out to be a younger version of his dad. He was a fellow baby boomer, but I knew our lives were completely different.

We ordered drinks and fell into an easy conversation that centered on what I did and what they did. They were curious about life in Washington, DC and I enjoyed hearing about life at the local mill. Sally embellished what I did and I smiled politely but knew in my heart I was a paper man.

I admired their fundamental conservatism. They were not judgmental of others. It was just who they were. Although they probably never had protested or ever would, they stood tall and firm in what they believed in—family, morals, and America. Emma would not have connected with them. They probably owned guns, I didn't.

It struck me, as it had lately, that the fundamental divide within our generation did center, at least in part, around where we lived, urban versus rural, and what we did. The more abstract our work, the more liberal we tended to be. It seemed to me that those who produced things and worked with their hands tended to be more conservative. I chided myself because of my irritating tendency to categorize and simplify things. To put things in the right pigeonhole. All neat and tidy.

They seemed justifiably proud that they were part of generations of iron men working in steel mills. Although they did fret that the times were changing, and their industry was slowly but surely dying or being shipped overseas as they became part of rusting of American where whole sections of industrial areas consisted of abandoned brick factories and mills. Nothing made me sadder as I passed by these areas while driving or traveling by train.

Later, sitting alone in my room, nursing a drink in the dark, I thought about my early roots when I first started out in Cleveland as an administrator/bookkeeper. Yes, I pushed paper at the time, but I was part of efforts to make products that people could touch and use. I wasn't sure why this bothered me so much, but it did and always had. I felt I had lost my roots and it ate at me. This just served to reinforce that I was a paper man in a plastic world. I wondered how many of my generation realized, or even cared, about such things. Was I the exception and not the rule? How did my friends feel? And if I asked would they just scratch their head and wonder what in the hell I was even talking about?

It was a great couple of days of socializing and sharing food and drink with Sally and her kin and I promised to be back soon. It was comfortable and relaxing, but the drive back was bittersweet for me as it gave me too much time to think. I realized how much I loved the gritty charm of the factory towns where I had grown up. I made good money, but my jobs were short on job satisfaction and perhaps more importantly a sense of being connected and belonging to a community.

Not only that but my job-hopping had resulted in my almost pricing myself out of my job market for my level of education and experience. Although I would never admit that to dad.

Nonetheless, when I returned, I easily fell into old habits, especially my bar gabfests. By now our informal pub roundtable happened as a matter of routine. These sessions usually took place during happy hour and even into the night, but Saturday

## Chapter 10

afternoons were the marathon gatherings. Along with Brian, who frequently took a break from his barkeep duties to join us, Professor Steve was a regular, as was Ellison. The others floated in and out of our circle. Even Emma, in addition to hosting the occasional dinner party for the gang, would pop by.

By now she was dating a lawyer from her firm and our relationship had evolved into a classic ex-spouse situation. Neither of us was jealous or vindictive and we shared a history that was exclusively ours. Just a knowing smile was enough to communicate thoughts between us.

I didn't always agree with the good professor. He was a few years older than us and his views were unique with his academic's take on some of our BB characteristics. It was a Saturday and we were into our second pitcher of beer. We had ordered some potato skins and he was wiping his hands on a thick paper napkin.

"All I'm saying Jimmy is that the less a person produces in terms of a physical product the more progressive they are. Conversely, the more tangible stuff they produce the more traditional they are."

"I totally agree with you. Does that mean that as a college professor you consider yourself pretty liberal?"

He smiled, "Yup. It goes with the job. Regardless of my true feelings, I have to tow the party line or be criticized and ostracized by my fellow academics. That's the world I live in."

I felt like being the devil's advocate. "While I agree with you, how about people involved in manufacturing and service sectors that are unionized?

"Good point. They tend to want to be rewarded for longevity rather than for what they actually produce, which is hardly a conservative approach. But unions are dying in this country and except for certain industries, like some service sectors and auto and government workers, it's becoming a moot point." He eyed me, "For a guy who just produces paper you seem to be fairly conservative, proving there are exceptions to everything. I think my point holds up, though. Where do you do you think all those Reagan democrat voters came from?"

I just nodded. The guy was observant and smart. Both qualities I admired.

No matter how much we talked, I always learned something. If not about trends impacting the country, then things on a more personal level that resonated with my life. I suppose at the end of the day, it didn't matter as we marched into the end of the millennium.

# Chapter 11

# Scandals, Culture Wars & Middle Age (1990 -1999)

We started the last decade of the millennia with an all too familiar recession. Many BBs felt a slight shudder of guilt (or was it something else?) at the label that the 80s were purely a me, me, me, greed era because most of us were able to relate to the tag. But that seemed to pass as we settled into middle age. It seemed like a long ride from the hometown to the emerging global village everyone kept talking about.

Reagan's Evil Empire, the USSR, continued to unravel and Saddam Hussein became our new world villain as Iraq invaded Kuwait. We rallied around the flag to defeat him. In our hearts, though, we knew that it was more about oil than freedom for our Arab brothers.

The reunification of East and West Germany reminded us that we had won the Cold War. The European Union was created when the Maastricht Treaty was signed. This would mean the creation of a new currency called the Euro later in the decade. Closer to home, the North American Free Trade Agreement—NAFTA—was signed. Yet even as politicians congratulated themselves and celebrated, some of us realized that it signaled the further erosion of our shrinking manufacturing base.

The Internet also continued to gain power during the decade as it became available for unrestricted commercial use as business models transformed. By the end of the decade, the search engine Google was founded. We were becoming more addicted and dependent on technology. From 1991, when WWW first became available for public use, to the year 2000, there were about 300 million users on the Internet. Fast forward to today (2020) and there are over 4.5 billion users, including almost 95 percent of Americans. Add to that almost 5 billion smart and mobile phones in service worldwide and the impact on our culture and lifestyles is mind-boggling.

When I bought my first cell phone in 1998 it was a brick, but new models kept shrinking. The technology of the day was giving us a preview of what was to come.

In 1992, the power of video was vividly illustrated as we watched LA cops beat Rodney King, a Black man, and wondered how far we had really come in race relations. King's words, "Why can't we all just get along?" echoed in our minds. The event resulted in riots that were triggered after a jury acquitted four police officers accused of using excessive force in the arrest and beating of King. This turned into a series of riots and civil disturbances that occurred in Los Angeles County in the spring of 1992 when the unrest began in South Central Los Angeles and then spread.

Not since the 1968 assassination of civil rights leader Martin Luther King, Junior, which unleashed unprecedented violence around the country, had the smoldering embers of racism sparked into such an inferno. Again, it looked like we were at an all-out war as riots broke out in 125 cities nationwide. Our cities burned, including the nation's capital. Looting was rampant. It took tens of thousands of military personnel to quell them and resulted in over 21,000 being arrested. It was a cycle that was periodically triggered by racial incidents that kept repeating at regular intervals.

But that didn't mean that there were no signs of progress on the equality front as Nelson Mandela became the first black president of South Africa in the country's first multiracial elections.

On the big screen, Kevin Costner *Dances with Wolves* was a film depicting our racist treatment of Native Americans many decades before as history kept repeating itself or at least rhyming.

Also, in movie theaters, *Thelma and Louise* went on a liberating cross-country spree and ended up sailing off a cliff into nothingness. The women's movement was waning. For some of us, the myth that you could have it all at once was exposed as just that. Female BBs started to pursue a new strategy—work until 30 something and then do the family thing. But boundaries were being pushed as Madeleine Albright became the first female Secretary of State in a victory for women's rights.

We were saddened and sobered when we learned that basketball hero Magic Johnson had AIDS because in the early years of the disease it was a death sentence. In 1991, Freddie Mercury, the lead singer of the band Queen, did die from AIDS, further reminding us that celebrity was no protection from the dreaded disease.

But not all deaths were natural. Serial killer Jeffery Dahmer[84] was arrested. Just when we thought we had seen and heard it all. We further wondered what the world had become after we watched *The Silence of the Lambs* about cannibalism.

Sexual harassment became a very public issue as witnessed by Congressional hearings over Anita Hill's charges against Supreme Court nominee Clarence Thomas. Both male and female BBs began to look at and discuss comport in the workplace. The rules in the workplace started to change and some of us didn't even want to work with female co-workers alone. The risk to offend females was just too high. I was one of them. If you told someone they looked nice or you admired their outfit, would that make them uncomfortable? I wasn't sure at that time and didn't want to find out.

Finally, one of our guys made it to the White House when Bill Clinton beat the senior George Bush, who was running for a second term.

Race relations and our legal system were further rocked when O.J. Simpson was indicted for murder. An ex-professional football

---

[84] Dahmer, known as the Milwaukee monster, was not just a serial killer, but also a cannibal and rapist who, when caught, confessed to killing 17 young men.

player and actor, Simpson was accused of the grisly slashing deaths of his ex-wife Nicole Brown Simpson and her companion, Ron Goldman. His pursuit, arrest, and trial were among the most publicized events in American history. The trial itself was dubbed the 'trial of the century.' Despite a bloody glove found behind his house, he was acquitted in a controversial decision by the jury.

Singers like Mariah Carey, Paula Abdul, Michael Bolton, and Elton John and groups like Boyz II Men were popular with hits like *One Sweet Day, How Am I Supposed to Live Without You,* and *If Wishes Came True.* Madonna, Whitney Houston, Janet Jackson, Jon Bon Jovi, and George Michael were also popular and sang songs like *Praying for Time* and *The Promise of a New Day*. Rapper Notorious Big, with Puff Daddy, weighed in with *Mo Money, Mo Problems*. Maybe they knew something we didn't.

Many of the titles seemed to reflect our hopes and changing reality. Although I kept paying less and less attention to emerging sounds. My music indulgence was more focused on oldies. We also grooved on the surfer music of the 60s and 70s, but most of us had never actually surfed. No matter, by this time many of us were surfing the Internet.

On TV we watched the teen drama *Beverly Hills 90210* and *Sex in the City*. *Everybody Loves Raymond* was popular. *Will and Grace* broke ground with its gay characters as did talk show host *Ellen*. On the gritty side, we watched *Law & Order*. *The X-Files* with its otherworldly theme song fascinated us about the possibility of alien and extraterrestrial life. *The Sopranos* reminded us that the Italian mafia was still a part of the American scene.

*Friends* became the quintessential young person's buddy/roommate sitcom series and ran for years. *South Park* burst on the scene as a biting adult animated series that used four boys to explore cutting-edge topics of the day. Perhaps the most enduring sitcom was *Frasier* starring Kelsey Grammar. As a testament to its excellence, it garnered 37 Grammy Awards over its 11-year run.

By 1995 corporate takeovers were in full swing as Disney acquired ABC. Terrorism came home with the bombing of the Oklahoma City federal building—except this time it was American terrorists named Timothy McVeigh and Terry Nichols. The blast killed 68 people, injured more than 680 others, and destroyed more than one-third of the building, which had to be demolished.

In many ways, it was a sordid decade in which Bill Clinton, a fellow BB, was squarely at the center. We learned in 1998 that the 49-year-old president had carried on a sexual affair with 22-year-old intern Monica Lewinsky between 1995 and 1997. He was charged with lying under oath and obstruction of justice, which originated from a sexual harassment lawsuit filed against him by another woman, Paula Jones. He also lied in sworn testimony when he denied that he had engaged in a sexual relationship with Lewinsky. In 1998, he became only the second president to be impeached since Andrew Johnson was impeached in 1868. He was, however, never convicted when he was acquitted by the US Senate.

When he went on TV, though, and uttered his famous statement, "I did not have sexual relations with that woman, Ms. Lewinsky," while wagging his finger at the camera, most people felt embarrassment at the awkward moment.

Our human frailties were on full display in other ways, too. The 1990s saw a worldwide increase in the use of illegal drugs as they became more addictive and destructive. In the US drugs like cocaine flooded into American society by the ton. Government programs to stop it seemed unable to stem the flow. The best advice for combatting it seemed to be Nancy Reagan's, "Just say no." Simplistic, but it worked for me.

I never got tired of the ritual and always looked forward to getting together for happy hour with friends. It was nice to share what was on our minds until late evening. It seemed that the older we got, the more we reminisced and pontificated.

We pondered our impending retirement and I was uncomfortable because in my heart I knew I had squandered much of it on my current lifestyle. Ellison voiced his disapproval with many kids and their fascination with tattoos and body piercings. We all expressed our support and wondered what happened to "your body is a temple that shouldn't be defaced?"

We conveniently forgot how we abused our bodies when younger with tobacco, alcohol, and drugs. Many of us were still abusing our bodies with booze and cigarettes.

We all had our pet peeves and favorite subjects. Brian was prone to rants about such things as middle age, Viagra, and the need for a hair club. I mused how TV and the "desensitization" of our kids and grandkids were affecting our society in the form of school shootings and brutal teen crime. It was not lost on us that this was not our parents who were talking about the "good old days," it was us.

All these events, our reaction to them, and our experience continued to set us apart from those who went before us and those who followed. Some of us had to start grudgingly admitting that we bore more than a little responsibility if the system was screwed up and failing. This awareness kept increasing in the ensuing years.

Often those sessions centered on our folks when our favorite topic became advice our dads and moms gave us. We would go around the table and toss them out and often comment on whether we took such advice or not or wished we had. Regardless, as we got older our folks seemed smarter. These words of wisdom included the following, some of which seem timeless and still relevant. Boy, our folks had a thousand ways to brainwash us. They truly were the masters.

Heard many times as fathers advised their sons was, "The best way to love your children is to openly express your love for your wife. Let them see the love and respect you share by setting the right example."

One of my female friends said when she started dating her dad told her that sex wasn't bad, and she would have it throughout her life. She said his candor shocked her. Her dad added that her attitude towards herself would shape the attitude boys had towards her. He summarized his thought to her by telling her that if she didn't respect herself, others would not respect her.

Another friend told me her dad also helped shape her moral compass by telling her that before doing something she should ask herself if she would want her children to find out about it in the future.

For my dad's part, one of his pearls of wisdom was to praise in public and criticize in private.

But perhaps his best was there are wishbones, jawbones, and backbones. Translated it meant there are those who dream about doing things, those who talk about doing things, and those who actually take action and do things. I wasn't sure where I fell on that spectrum. Maybe all three, depending on the situation.

On marriage, their advice included that it takes a lot of work to make a marriage work and the most important thing is to learn how to bite your tongue. Based on my experience I'm sure this still works.

I think the most common one among our parents was the golden rule. That is, do unto others as you would have them do unto you. Somehow, as time passed, that evolved into those who have the gold make the rules.

In a break from my routine, dad came to spend a month with me. Paul drove him and his small suitcase to the modest townhouse I had rented in Washington, DC off Connecticut Avenue. It was close to the zoo and I loved the neighborhood. Plus, even though it was only a few minutes from Brian's pub, it gave me a little distance from Emma.

I told Paul I thought dad looked gaunt. He shrugged and said he hoped I could do better with his diet. I knew that since mom's passing, he didn't seem to have much interest in food. It was still shocking that he had seemed to shrink and age so much. I suppose in the back of my mind it was a reminder of my encroaching aging and mortality. Was I really middle age? I didn't want to think about it.

I invited dad to eat dinner at the pub. I thought a bar burger and some hot oily fries would do him good. Sure enough, he loved them. He did make me squirm a little when he brought up the subject of Abbie, his granddaughter.

"I know, dad. I haven't been able to have the level of contact with her that I want or should."

"You need to do better. I barely know her since you never bring her to visit. You have a responsibility, son, and it not just about providing support. You have an obligation and to be honest, I'm disappointed that you are not making more of an effort."

His words stung. "You are right, dad. The distance is a problem, but I need to find a way to do better."

"Plan some trips. Don't you remember when you were a kid and mom and I would plan a different road trip every summer? We went places like Mammoth Cave in Kentucky. You were impressed that it was the longest cave system in the world. I remember you bragging about it to your friends when we got home." He stared off into the distance. "Another summer we went all the way to top of Pike's Peak in the Rocky Mountains. You told me you could see forever. I still remember that. Do you?"

I smiled. He was right, of course, but I avoided looking him straight in the eye as I twirled my beer glass. Fortunately for me, Ellison showed up and Brian joined us almost immediately. I made the introductions, and, just like that, dad temporarily became part of our roundtable. I hadn't really thought about it beforehand, but I was grateful that it might provide some welcome diversion from his normal life. He seemed to hang on to every word and be genuinely interested. And, when the group started to ask him about his thoughts and views, he seemed to come alive.

Later he cleverly dubbed the events as "Nights of the Roundtable," in a twist on King Arthur's "Knights of the Roundtable. When I told the guys, we adapted it as our official name and it stuck for years.

That night he didn't hesitate when Ellison asked what we had been talking about.

"Jimmy and I were talking about his daughter earlier. Kids need both parents not just to spend time and know them, but to know their values as well. I think we are losing our way, not just at home but in schools, too." He hesitated. When I was young if you got caught with a rubber in school your parents got a call and you were probably suspended. Today schools hand out condoms like candy. Go figure. Do parents even talk to their kids about morals anymore?"

Brian said, "Yes, teenage pregnancy is a problem today. Society is more worried about unwanted babies than morals."

"Fiddlesticks!" dad said. "Boys need to learn some self-discipline and keep it in their pants. They might even find that when they do finally have sex that it is special and not just some animal act."

A little taken aback, we all looked at him. Unsure of what to say or if we should even attempt to respond. Finally, I said, "Things have changed, dad."

"For the better?" he shot back.

I busied myself topping off everyone's beer glass. Dad took a sip and said, "It's nuts. It is. A friend told me about a teacher in his grandson's school. A kid was mouthing off and called her a bitch. Imagine that? Well, she slapped him. Now the school board has suspended her, and the boy's parents are threatening to sue the school. In what world is that fair or sane? Jimmy, if you had called one of your teachers a bitch you would have been disciplined and kicked out of school. And, mom and I would have supported the school and marched you right back there to apologize to her."

He glanced around and looked a little sheepish. "Sorry I didn't mean to get on my high horse, but the world seems to have lost its mind."

Ellison smiled at him. "Yes sir, you are right. Things have changed. It is a real challenge today for people like us with kids in school. I'm not sure what they are learning in academics, but they certainly aren't learning much about how to act or personal responsibility for their actions."

Brian asked, "What was it like when you were a kid? We all hear the stories about you all walking miles through the snow to a one-room schoolhouse."

Dad laughed. "Yes, I've heard the stories and maybe even embellished a few of my own. Well, while that may have been true for some, it wasn't my experience. But I have to tell you, life was no picnic. We had no indoor plumbing and used an outhouse. You remember Jimmy when we visited your grandad?"

I smiled. He sipped some beer, "Maybe that's why we worked so hard to give you kids what we didn't have. But unlike today, we didn't do it at the expense of values. We always tried to teach you morals and personal responsibility and how to get it for yourself—although I don't think we succeeded very well on that last score judging on how some of you turned out."

I felt as if this was directed at me. As mom would have said, "if the shoe fits, wear it."

He looked thoughtful. "I hope you don't take this the wrong way, but one thing I don't understand is your generation's attitude about loyalty and lasting power. I mean, not only do you job hop, but half of your marriages end up in divorce. When we made a commitment we stuck to it." He grinned, "Sorry that is a curiosity of mine, but I know it came out as a criticism."

Brian shrugged, "Well, you can't argue with the truth."

"I suppose the question we all wonder about is how do we make things better?" Ellison asked.

Dad shook his head. "Please don't shoot the messenger, but that is up to you because you baby boomers are essentially the establishment now. My generation is largely gone from the workplace. Increasingly, you are the teachers, the politicians, and policymakers. You are certainly in control of whether you make your marriages work or not. If you want change and wonder who is responsible for making it happen, look in the mirror."

We just stared at him. Damn, I thought, he is right. At that moment it hit me that we all bitched about the system and talked about "they" and "them." That was us now, not our parents or some mysterious force out there.

We all let that sink in. I looked at dad. "Well, maybe we should get going. Dad and I have to get our beauty sleep."

We said our goodnights and I had Brian call us a cab. It wasn't that far home, but I was buzzed and knew I shouldn't be driving. I also thought it might be a little far for dad to walk after a few beers.

After we were settled in the backseat, dad turned to me in the dim light. "I'm sorry, son. Did I talk too much or embarrass you?"

"Not at all, dad. I think everyone enjoyed hearing about your views and experience. We kind of get in a rut with our sessions so it was nice that you made us think about things a little more. Not to mention the cool name you gave us. Nights of the Roundtable has a ring to it."

"Well, it fits and I'm glad you like it."

Dad turned in shortly after our return home. I laid down but my mind wouldn't stop working. I finally switched on my bedside lamp and slipped into my bathrobe and went to the kitchen. I got a cold glass of juice and wandered out to my tiny backyard. The stars were out, and the neighborhood was silent except for the passing of the occasional car.

   I sat in the dark and sipped my orange juice as my mind wandered back to a recent conversation I had with my daughter, Abbie. I couldn't believe she was legally an adult. I hadn't been much older than that when she was born. For some reason, the conversation had stuck in my head like a tape recording. One that I had already played over and over in my mind.

   I had been making excuses why I couldn't visit and said, "Maybe I can get out there the next long weekend."

   "Whatever, dad. I'm not holding my breath."

   That stung, so I lied. "It's just that things are busy at work right now and it's hard to get away. Things will lighten up but it's budget season and I'm trying to protect our funding right now."

   When I said that, I remember that she had grown so silent I thought I had lost the connection. Then she said, "Mom said you would find an excuse. Is that what happened to you guys? Did your work get in the way? I would love to know why my parents just split up. It's something I've always wanted to know."

   "It wasn't like that. Your grandma got sick and your mom wanted us to move to the West Coast."

   "Why couldn't you have made that sacrifice, dad? Hell, would it have been a sacrifice? It's not like California is the end of the world."

   "Believe me, honey, I often wish I had."

   "But you didn't," she said accusingly.

   "What has your mom been telling you?"

   "Oh, don't worry, she protects you, but I can tell it hurt when you didn't support her and let her go."

   "It's complicated. One day perhaps you will understand."

   "I talked to grandad."

   "Whose? Mine or your mom's?"

   "Your dad. He said he hoped that I knew that family came first even if I didn't learn that from you."

   "Oh, he did, did he?"

   "Yes. He also said there were times when he and your mom could have taken the easy way out and just called it quits, but they didn't. I hope when I fall in love it's with a guy who is willing to go the extra mile."

Unsure what to say, I said, "So do I, honey. It seems the older you get the more you resent me." There it was out in the open.

"Do you blame me? I never really see you or spend time with you. I mean, you are my dad after all.

"I didn't ask your mom to move three thousand miles away."

"Don't you understand why she did?"

"Of course, but I had a life, too."

"It was a partnership, dad. A compromise."

"When did you grow up and get so smart?"

"I've been doing a lot of thinking lately."

"Well, you are scaring me."

"These are exciting but scary times for me. I look at my friends and what they are doing. I have questions about drugs, sex, and lots of other things and I need two adults in my life more than ever."

Wow. I was stunned. Whatever happened to the little girl with pigtails who worshipped me? This coupled with what dad had said freaked me out a little. Had I made an irretrievable mess of my personal life? God, I hoped not. On a whim, I told her, "When can you come and visit me. I'll get you a ticket."

"That would be nice, but I don't want to inconvenience you."

No, honey, you are right. We need to catch up and it's my fault we haven't."

"Sounds good. Let me look and I'll send you some dates."

That's how we had left it. Just like then, I sat there long after she hung up that night and played my life through my mind like an old black and white movie. Had I been so self-centered and selfish? It didn't seem like it at the time, but in retrospect, I suppose I had. I had let my relationship with my only daughter grow weeds just like I had with my siblings, Paul and Molly. I tried to shrug it off and vowed to do better. That night thoughts of Sally intruded. I envied her close and solid relationship with her family.

Soon my world would be further rocked when I received a late-night call from Emma. I had never heard her so frantic and stressed. Her rock-solid confidence was gone.

## Chapter 12

# Becoming Senior Citizens & the New Millennium (2000 – 2008)

It was exciting to start a new thousand years. The millennium also brought a lot of hysteria for what our computers would or wouldn't do. Called Y2K, no one seemed to know if computers would stop working. Up until that point, computer programs used two digits to represent the year. So, 1970, for example, was just 70. The fear was that for 2000 it would be 00, which the machine would think was 1900. Banks, government agencies, insurance companies, hospitals, and just about all other sectors were worried and spent millions of dollars to ensure the machines kept working.

    The fear that the computers in banks and other key institutions would go offline never materialized. But me, like others, held our breath as the old year counted down. Then we laughed and told each other we were never really worried.

    Another baby boomer, George W. Bush, succeeded Bill Clinton. Despite some nagging thoughts about who we were and what our future held, we thought we were firmly in control of the business world, the government, and the world at large.

This illusion changed in a heartbeat in September of 2001 when terrorists flew planes into the World Trade Center in New York and shattered our delusion that we were insulated from terror. They also crashed a plane into the Pentagon and a field in Pennsylvania, wreaking havoc. Three thousand Americans lost their lives that day and 25,000 more were injured.

The country was paralyzed. All air travel in the US was grounded and the nation held its breath not knowing if more was to follow. For a moment Republicans and Democrats stood shoulder to shoulder in solidarity to present a united front in this shocking attack on American soil. It may have been the last time we put politics aside and joined hands.

Despite everything, the country slowly returned to normal, but across the board it was a somber time.

If that was possible, to me even music became more nondescript and fragmented in the 2000s. It became a collection of sounds, including Hip Hop, Rhythm and Blues, Teen Pop, Latin, and Grunge. Part of this was driven by technology—something we were still struggling to become proficient and comfortable with as we were caught between the memory of our freedom that a total lack of smart devices had given us as we came of age to being overwhelmed by the capabilities technology made available on a routine basis as we aged. We functioned but were never as good as our kids with smart devices. Instinctively they seemed to master things. We didn't.

We were stuck in the past with the songs that had shaped us and our view of our world. We listened to this retro music because it was the soundtrack of our lives. This made us further distanced and out of step with our kids and grandkids. They thought we were dinosaurs.

The Internet facilitated unprecedented access to music and enabled artists to distribute music easily without big record label backing. Music genres became sub-genres and sub-sub-genres. But it also provided direct access to our golden oldies.

We didn't get things like hip hop or gangsta rap, so we stuck exclusively to oldies stations and watched oldies revivals on public television. It was familiar and comforting. We also couldn't relate to the young boy bands like New Boyz. As others listened and hummed to the top 40 pop tunes, many of us didn't. Music videos further complicated things. Scanty costumes and suggestive moves seemed to enable a whole generation of singers with marginal talent to flourish. Even though many of them had genuine talent, it seemed to me that it was flash over flair and glitter over real talent.

No matter how much we tried to shrug it off, we were getting old. We had built a culture of worshipping youth that was now turning on us big time. This combined with another significant financial meltdown, which was perhaps the most significant in our lifetimes, took a lot of wind out of our sails. It was further evidence that we were not invincible. Life touched us—we aged, we got sick, we lost jobs and money. It was like a 'welcome to being an adult class 101' as it exposed how sheltered we had been in our lives.

Among the triggers for the most severe recession since the Great Depression was excessive risk-taking by banks, mortgage companies, and individuals. If you were a banker or loan officer, the prevailing attitude was, "No problem. If you make $50,000 a year that qualifies you to buy a $500,000 house." At the time no one said, "Right. Sure, it does." What were any of us thinking?

It was a house of cards as lenders told marginal borrowers, "We will just estimate and exaggerate that you make a lot of overtime and that your job situation is solid." Reality didn't enter into the equation at all. Everybody made money upfront with no thought of what was going to happen down the road when people couldn't pay for what they had been sold.

At the time there were hundreds of billions of dollars worth of mortgages given to people with poor or marginal credit ratings and insufficient income. When the crash came it not only wiped out them but wacked the rest of us, too. It became increasingly clear that we could easily start to become irrelevant like some of our folks were becoming.

For the moment, though, it was another stark reminder that we didn't have half the financial savvy our folks did. As house prices stopped rising and started to fall, we baby boomer homeowners could no longer refinance and remortgage our houses for cash, and defaults started to soar. Our folks knew that what goes up, eventually comes down. Lacking their experience, though, we apparently didn't know that. We only had seen the upside, not the real downside.

The downturn was global. Here at home, several major brokerage houses collapsed. The net effect on us was a collapse of whatever investments we had in our day trading accounts and 401K retirement accounts. Many of us were upside down with our houses. That is, we owed more on them than they were worth on the market. I lost almost 50 percent of my retirement funds that I held in high yield but risky portfolios. I didn't mention this to dad but just stoically swallowed the loss.

Emma was also a prime example. We had bought the townhouse we once shared for about $200,000. It had then escalated up to over $400,000 as Washington, DC enjoyed a robust real estate bubble. After our split, Emma had taken this largely imaginary paper equity out and invested it in a hot stock market full of overheated tech stocks. Rumor had it that when things went south, she lost about half of her investments like I did. Apparently, none of us were immune or as smart as we thought we were.

That doesn't mean my life wasn't enriched during this time. In an unexpected twist of fate and life, I had a second chance at being a dad. After my daughter Abbie became a divorced mother with two young children, she moved east to live with me. It was a nasty breakup and she needed lots of hugs. It allowed me to catch up and bond with her and share my life's lessons with grandkids. It was wonderful and rekindled my appreciation of family. One thing I think this proves is that most of us do get second chances.

Abbie stayed with me for several years and I loved every minute of it. When her kids were older and she was back on her feet she moved out even though I wanted them to stay. She gave me a hug and a look that said it all. I felt like I finally had achieved fatherhood as I enjoyed that special feeling of pride.

But I didn't kid myself that I had been her first choice because Kathy had passed on after a lengthy bout with breast cancer. I was it, the only option. I remember her service and standing at the gravesite apart and alone from the other mourners as thoughts swirled through my mind. Thoughts about what might have been. I didn't allow these thoughts to intrude for long and shrugged them off. I was good at shrugging things off.

It was an era of pop dominance by the likes of Lady Gaga, Katy Perry, and Justin Bieber. Outrageous costumes and behavior continued to be the in thing. Singer Britney Spears became the bestselling female performer of the 2000s with songs like *Oops! I Did it Again*, along with Christina Aguilera singing hits like *Come on Over Baby*.

This teen pop trend, though, kept giving way to modern R&B and hip hop. Boy bands started the decade strong but faded, except for a few groups like the Backstreet Boys. Some members, however, like Justin Timberlake from N'Sync went on to enjoy solo success. Girl groups like Destiny's Child and the Pussycat Dolls remained popular, too. Singer Miley Cyrus also sold lots of music and shocked us with her wild behavior. Other girl pop-rock artists topping the charts included Hilary Duff and Selena Gomez. Singer and actress Jennifer Lopez remained at the top of her game. The TV show *American Idol*, which was a new type of talent show, became a part of generating new faces on the music scene.

In 2001, the king of pop, Michael Jackson, released his final album called *Invincible*. It turned out he wasn't indestructible at all when he died in June 2009. The passing of the King of Pop was mourned by millions. Alicia Keys became the bestselling R&B performer of the decade, selling 30 million records. Norah Jones was hailed as the greatest jazz singer of the decade, ringing up sales of 37 million records worldwide. Beyoncé Knowles sold a whopping 160 million records worldwide and Rihanna also enjoyed the rise to music stardom.

Carrie Underwood, was the first American Idol winner to amass eight number one songs—primarily in the country genre but also including some pop and R&B. Some traditional country singers, like George Jones, complained that real country music had been hijacked and was no longer pure. It seemed like a changing of the guard as legendary country singers like Waylon Jennings, Johnny Cash, Buck Owens, Porter Wagoner, and Eddy Arnold died during the decade. White rapper Eminem was named the best artist of the decade, joining Elvis, The Beatles, Elton John, Michael Jackson, and Mariah Carey in their respective decades.

We watched all of this but didn't care about any of it. For the first time in my life, there were wildly popular celebrities whom I knew nothing about or had never heard of.

In 2008, the first BB became eligible to collect Social Security. She launched what would become the silver tsunami as over the following two decades almost 80 million would become eligible for social security payments—more than 10,000 a day.

Her name was Kathleen Casey-Kirschling, a retired teacher born shortly after midnight on January 1, 1946. She applied at age 62, foreshadowing the strain that BBs would eventually put on the system. After all, by 2030 it is estimated that there will be 84 million people on Social Security and Medicare—compared with 50 million in 2008.

Increasingly, many BBs are having to deal with meager retirement savings and a scale back in their lifestyles. Surprisingly, this comes at a time when the largest intergenerational transfer of wealth ever is now underway as our parents pass away or become incapable of caring for themselves. Estimated at trillions, many BBs are wondering if a windfall from their parents—the frugal depression-inspired generation—lies ahead. This expectation is tempered as we also realize that much of this money will be spent caring for our aging parents or paying exorbitant college tuition for our kids.

If consumerism drives the American economy, then we are front and center because, despite our often-shaky financial situations, we still spend money freely. According to some data, it is estimated that people over the age of 50 account for half of all discretionary spending power in the U.S. Alas, too much of this is on credit.

As the first of us BBs entered our 60s, we were confronted with some of the same issues we faced in our youth. Our generation was still fighting over the legacy of the 1960s. We BBs never fully resolved the questions raised by the Vietnam War, about what America's role in the world should be, and about our personal sense of responsibility and obligation to provide for national security or the wellbeing of society in general.

BBs remain divided about involvement in Iraq and Afghanistan wars but find our opinions have shifted in conflicting ways. Some who refused to support Vietnam are now hawkish on Mideast wars. Some who were hawkish on Vietnam are now critical of U.S. policy in Mideast. The issues are slightly different, but the questions about whether there has been an erosion of our national moral authority or whether we need to try and impose a sense of right or wrong have remained remarkably similar.

If war and civil rights left their mark on BBs, modern technology has also had a profound impact. Where TV once helped BBs forge a sense of generational identity and unity, the Internet, cell phones, and other technology are pulling them apart by allowing us to live in our own little worlds. As for the future, that can be found in the past because what the 1960s did was expand the range of choices people have about the way they live their lives.

One of the challenges for our generation is to be able to communicate with people who are having different generational experiences. We also need to learn how to gracefully let go and pass power and responsibility on to the next generation. It's still up in the air as to how successful we will ultimately be in doing that.

There is so much irony in our lives; for example, it's ironic that we were a people-to-people generation and are now part of a time when we live in a virtual world. The power of the Internet to deliver instant news, gossip, video, pictures, and all sorts of media means people are even more removed from any type of physical contact with others or things. We are fed the stuff of life from a cyber pipeline that reduces our need to interact with people. Indeed, with the advent of sexting, we can even have virtual sex.

Even though we contradictorily and simultaneously praise and criticize our digital world, millions of us have become voyeurs to life—able to sit at a terminal and tap into everything from social media, chat rooms, and forums to porno. Also, millions now experience sports in this manner, instead of playing something or going to the ballpark or stadium and interacting with others.

We also are increasingly meeting potential partners or dates through electronic means. In the past, this was done through finding clubs or social activities where you could meet someone. Millions more experience sex through online porno or adult and sex chat rooms. So instead of the physical experience of having a relationship, we find gratification by watching at home while sitting in subdued lighting and staring at a monitor.

We lament that actual conversation and social skills are becoming lost arts. We are reduced to reminding ourselves to help our children or grandchildren be aware that while technology has transformed the world in many wonderful ways, they should foster ways to avoid becoming virtual voyeurs, void of a whole dimension of humanism. That is, the ability to interact with others where there is real conversation, laughter, and physical contact.

And, while we are at it, we must encourage them to actually pick up and read a book. The feel and smell of paper can be a wonderful experience, not to mention allowing yourself to use imagination to be transported to a different place or to experience a new adventure. Just the physical contact with a book, rather than a plastic keyboard or mouse, seems to help what you are reading come more alive.

Achieving this is the need to find ways to substitute 'actual' for 'cyber' as we live our lives in what has become a digital virtual world. Who knows, it might just help prevent a forgotten art from becoming a lost art by keeping us in physical contact with our world.

In addition to the great war on terror that encompassed the planet and an ever-expanding global economy, BBs were faced with a significant slump in housing prices and rising commodity prices during this time. Declining housing costs meant that the BB piggy bank was broken. It is not known if the transfer of wealth from our parents will save us.

A survey by the American Association for Retired Persons (AARP) indicates that almost 30 percent of BBs may end up putting their retirement on hold because of poor planning coupled with economic conditions. It is a case of a financial system meltdown and volatile markets just when we want to cash in. Add to this that many of us are working longer to pay for skyrocketing healthcare and health insurance costs. A couple over 60 can expect to pay up to $1000 a month for comprehensive coverage.

Even though he wasn't a baby boomer, I think foul-mouthed, grouchy comedian George Carlin captured the unfolding challenges and changes in our culture and lifestyles that were and are impacting us and our fellow Americans when he observed that, "We laugh too little and get too angry. He further noted that, "We have multiplied our possessions but reduced our values. We talk too much, love too seldom. and hate too often. We have learned how to make a living, but not a life. We've added years to life not life to years. We've been all the way to the moon and back, but have trouble crossing the street to meet a new neighbor. We conquered outer space but not inner space. We've done larger things, but not better things. We've cleaned the air but polluted the soul. We've conquered the atom, but not our prejudice. We write more but learn less. We accomplish less. We've learned to rush, but not to wait. We build more computers to hold more information, and produce more copies than ever but we communicate less and less."

But he didn't stop there, he went on to say that "These are the times of fast food and slow digestion, big men and small character, steep profits and shallow relationships. And, they are the days of two incomes, but more divorce, fancier houses, but broken homes. Quick trips, disposable diapers, throwaway morality, one-night stands, overweight bodies, and pills that do everything from cheer, to quiet, to kill. It is a time when there is much in the showroom and nothing in the stockroom."

His observations seemed to sum up things, especially for BBs. His thoughts also reminded us that we BBs were fortunate enough to have straddled both a frugal and a wasteful culture. We saw how our parents fixed, reheated, and renewed the things, including relationships, in their lives. Despite that, we learned to be wasteful all by ourselves. Waste meant affluence. Throwing things away meant there would always be more.

We started learning sorrow as we entered an age when we started to lose loved ones. When that happened to me, I was struck with the pain of learning that sometimes there just isn't anymore. Whether life or material things, they get used up and go away—never to return.

When I talked to my friends, I realized I wasn't the only BB who was becoming reflective, if not downright philosophical. We started our journey before the pill, credit cards, ATMs, copy machines, ballpoint pens, and computers. For us, time-sharing didn't mean a condo to use at the beach a few times a year but spending time together. We eventually used technology that we didn't grow up with, so it was forced on us and not inherent in our beings. I'm still more comfortable taking a piece of paper and making a to-do list rather than put it into my electronic notes on my smartphone. I prefer to have a physical calendar book than an electronic one. I can touch them, tap my pen and think. I'm connected in my way.

Today's younger adults will spend 34 years of their lives staring at screens (phones, tablets, computers, and TV) according to a British study by Vision Direct! There were no computers in our early world. A chip meant a piece of wood. Hardware meant nuts and bolts and hammer and nails, hard wear referred to everyday use, today hardware refers to a piece of equipment, and the word software hadn't even been coined yet when we were young.

Women wore dresses, men wore slacks, women wore earrings, men did not. People got married then lived together. Closets were to store clothing, not to come out of. We thought cleavage was something butchers did in their shops. We thought fast food was something you did during Lent when you abstained from eating. Smoking was fashionable, grass was for mowing, Coke was a refreshing drink, and pot was something you cooked in. We experienced all those changes and more. Things today change, but for us, we felt like everything changed. It was overwhelming.

During this time, I also noticed that we were increasingly beginning to struggle to remain relevant. That didn't mean we hadn't always found ways to feel good about ourselves. We were in charge of our jobs, but we started to feel like has-beens. We started to measure our worth not just by our waning careers but losses in our portfolios and the lines and creases we saw when we looked in the mirror.

By this time, our culture of worshipping youth had completely turned on us. We had spent our lives celebrating young film stars, singers, and athletes and casting them aside as they grew old. Now it was our turn to experience aging and how it can make you invisible.

Oh sure, society pretended age was just a number. After all, it was illegal to ask a job applicant their age. But those of us who were downsized and found ourselves sitting across the desk from a 30 something couldn't hide our age. We were too often politely escorted out with excuses like you lack the required computer skills.

As the nature of work continued to change, making fewer physical things and the rise of information as a product, meant people moved around more. Or you worked in the service sector. We were ill-equipped as the economy shifted towards Me Inc even though we were the me me generation. It was the beginning of our kids creating their own futures, telecommuting, and becoming contract workers and consultants. Even retail jobs started to disappear as shopping became more of an online thing. To add to this drama, we kept losing our greatest fans—our parents.

*

I missed having dad stay with me when he went to stay with Paul or Molly. It was too quiet around my place. After Abbie and the kids moved out, I had a few one-night stands and long weekend relationships, but it was superficial and hardly satisfying. I went to visit Sally and her family several times. Those were the times I felt most at home and at peace.

I even fantasized about moving back to such an environment. The sterile BS environment of the nation's capital had never really been my cup of tea. Oh, I enjoyed the money and the pseudo sense of feeling important, but it was at odds with my roots.

It was a Sunday and I had returned from a Sally visit and before I went home, I stopped in the pub. My absence was duly noted as the guys teased me that I had gotten lucky and was shacked up. I told them my absence was a family matter, which in a manner it was.

It was after ten and I was considering heading out when my cell phone buzzed.

I had never heard Emma sound like she did. "Oh, thank God, Jimmy, I got you. You are my only phone call."

"Where are you?"

Her voice was shaky. "I've been arrested."

"What happened?"

"I'll tell you when you get here. Can you bail me out? I'm in the 4th precinct."

"Of course. I'll be there shortly. How much money do you need?"

"Two hundred and fifty."

"Don't worry, I'll take care of it." I heard a voice tell her to hang up and then there was a click.

Brian was behind the bar and I walked over and whispered in his ear. "I need a big favor. Emma is in jail and I need to post bail."

He jerked his head around. "Oh wow. How much?"

I told him and he was already ringing the cash register drawer open. He counted out a stack of bills then folded them neatly and slid them into my shirt pocket. "I'm going to want to hear all about this."

"Sure, when I get her out and know more details."

I was sitting on a wooden bench with a very drunk man in a rumpled suit when a uniformed officer led her into the room. She was dressed in a party dress but looked awful, mascara streaked down her face from crying. I was shocked. Her face brightened a little when she saw me. She stood beside me looking embarrassed while I paid the bail then I helped her collect her purse and personal items.

As we exited into the night air, she slipped her arm in mine. "Thank God I got you. Brian said you were out of town for a few days."

"Yeah, I was. I just got back. Now tell me what happened."

"I was at a private party and most of us were snorting a little coke when the cops busted the place. Which, by the way, was a someone's home, not a public place."

"So, the charge was doing drugs?"

"Yeah. And don't go saying 'I told you so.'"

"Well, I did."

"Don't start with me. I'm embarrassed enough."

The moment passed. "Do you want me to take you home? Or maybe you should spend the night at my place."

"Home, please."

## Chapter 12

We rode in the backseat of the taxi in silence and when I dropped her in front of the house, she gave me a quick kiss on the cheek and slid out. "Thank you. I'll call you once I sort this all out."

"I'm here if you need me." She gave me a wan smile and then was gone as she disappeared into her house. I had my travel bag stowed at the bar but decided just cab home.

The following day I didn't hear from Emma, but she called a day later. "Can you meet me for coffee?"

"Sure."

It turned out that the lawyer she had been dating from the firm had taken on her defense and was confident that the police raid had been flawed and he would win in court or maybe even get the DA to drop the charges. It looked like she was going to get off unscathed. It was even unlikely that she would be reprimanded at work. Of course, it helped that her boyfriend was a senior partner.

Later privately she told me that she knew she was lucky, and she had given up the white stuff and was even going to counseling and outpatient rehab. I told her how happy I was and that it was the right thing to do. I noticed that she started hanging around more with me and the guys at the pub. Brian knew the whole story, but nothing was ever said among the group. I did see her slip Brian an envelope and knew she had settled accounts with him.

During this time, a lot of friends and people I knew got caught up as the cops cracked down on baby boomers. Some like Emma were lucky but for many tens of thousands of others, it destroyed careers and marriages. Young professionals snorting the white stuff was one of the hidden and quickly forgotten scandals of our generation.

Yet, race relations still dominated much of the news and our thoughts.

It was a quiet weekday. Ellison was there as Rosa was visiting her parents with the kids. He was talking in his quiet but forceful manner. "You can't legislate a cure for racism. People are demanding laws to stop it, but while necessary, that won't fix the problem. It is only part of the solution. People have to look into their hearts and consciousness to make it disappear. In my opinion, unlike our protest era, today everyone is shouting, few are listening, and even fewer are offering real solutions. More needs to be done to fix the system but tearing everything down is downright dumb. It has to be internal to our souls."

Professor Steve sauntered over, catching the tail end of the comments, and said, "You'll get no argument from me."

Ellison glanced up. "Hey, Steve, pull up a chair."

"You guys sound so serious. What did I miss?"

"I was telling Jimmy that every time there is an incident involving real or perceived police brutality towards Blacks that everyone makes a lot of noise, but no one articulates a plan to make it better—whether that be better screening, or better training, or whatever. It's just hysterical screaming followed by silence until the next time."

"Amen, brother. Right on."

Ellison rolled his eyes and laughed.

"I'm sure there are many who mean well, but for others, it's just an excuse to loot," said Steve.

"Yeah, it's complicated. These things tend to happen in poor neighborhoods, making some folks feel entitled to get a little something for themselves. Classic haves versus the have nots."

Like always, though, we explored such issues as we searched for some context of how our generation fit in. It was part of us trying to articulate how we were different and maybe even special. Even our obscure rites of passage were different.

Like our parents, for example, we tended to have substantial furniture. It was not bolted together out of a box from a box store like Ikea.

Did this give us a sense of permanence—solid and sturdy? Perhaps. Things like china cabinets filled with multiple sets of dishes. We had everyday use and good china with classic patterns. We had dining room tables with leaves we could add to accommodate more people for a good meal. We used those on such occasions as dinner parties, Thanksgiving, and family gatherings.

Young couples planning to marry were usually gifted their good china by family members. They would usually spend considerable time selecting a dish pattern that they would keep for life.

It was part of the process of a couple compromising and bonding. Often the china would be passed along to their children much later in life. These traditions developed family history, heirlooms, and a sense of continuity and permanence.

When my folks passed, I remember sitting in the dining room with Paul and Molly as we divided up such things as family china and silverware, Mom's modest jewelry was handed down to Molly. Upon reflection, I suppose we are going to be the last generation to honor those traditions. I don't think our kids will want either our furniture or our dishes. That will end with us. In general, the younger generation won't do this because you don't pass bolt-up furniture or plain china along.

This might sound judgmental on my part, but it's not a case of one thing being better than the other. It's just changing norms caused by our different tastes tempered by upbringing and roots.

These things increasingly occupied our quiet moments of thought as leading-edge BBs started to become senior citizens. Most of us didn't feel like we were becoming elderly, but it was a fact as time ticked by.

# Chapter 13

# The End of Normal and the World as We Know it
# 2009 – Present

Despite often looking inward throughout my life, as I got older, I have increasingly sought to put my life and my actions into sharper focus to define the journey. I believe this is something I have in common with most BBs do as we age, especially as our world becomes more strange.

As Ellison is fond of reminding me, "The end of anything we think is normal is merely the beginning of new norms."

Despite his observation, that doesn't mean though that our world hasn't morphed into a place that few of us recognize or could have imagined a few years ago, not just for BBs but for everyone. It is a place of dramatically changing reality characterized by a form of journalism that is foreign to us, the dramatic appearance of a pandemic, and unimaginable political polarization making things shift in new and often strange directions. A world where changing habits such as smartphones and other electronic devices have replaced cigarettes as the addiction of younger generations.

Even late-night comedy and comedians have become skewed and polarized. Where is Johnny Carson when we need him? Wouldn't it be nice if we could watch a comedian today and not know if he or she was a liberal or a conservative? One who pokes fun at everyone. After all, politics and life provide plenty of humor of all shades on the political spectrum.

We wonder who is to blame for a world gone mad? We know it's complex with many contributing factors, but the only thing that seems clear is that it is taking a startling toll on our national psyche.

For BBs, the fallout from the 2008 financial crisis continues to impact us unabated into this time frame. As a country, we seem to keep going backward—or at the very least going in the wrong direction. In 2008, for instance, for the first time in modern American history, more businesses closed their doors than opened them. Unfortunately, the so-called "recovery" saw banks bailed out while millions of ordinary Americans lost their homes, savings, retirements, and jobs. Some of those bailed-out bankers were BBs who had made it big. Many others, though, like me, were middle-class BBs who got screwed and stuck with the bill.

In typical American fashion, the finger-pointing always starts as we search for someone to blame. It is becoming like a circular firing squad as we all point at each other. For good reason, because if we are being honest, we all share some of the blame. It's spread across generations.

Somewhere along the line, all of us forgot that just because we disagree we don't have to be disagreeable.

BBs didn't get us into Vietnam, for example, which came with a staggering price tag that saddled the country with years of debt, that was Presidents Kennedy and Johnson. The BB sacrifice was more personal as we lost many lives fighting another generation's unwinnable war.

For our part, we didn't save enough for that rainy day our parents warned us about. Instead, we leveraged the equity in our homes like piggy banks. To our credit, though, in general, we didn't take out mortgages we couldn't afford. When we bought our homes, the rules were different and governed by firm income to debt ratios. But we did all indulge and share in the evolution towards exaggerated and increasing levels of consumption—too much of it on credit. The list goes on, but our demise and blame cannot be pinned on a single generation, including ours.

No one acted unilaterally when it came to creating massive government overreach or passing budgets and laws where, as a country, we spent $1.40 for every dollar collected in revenue. In the words of Brian, "Good grief! Who thought that was a good idea or sustainable?"

We criticize our elected officials for that type of behavior, but somehow conveniently ignore that we voted them into office. Moreover, as individuals, many of us indulge in the same kind of fiscal irresponsibility in our personal lives. I certainly did as did many of my friends.

Every generation has its share of sinners, saints, and scandals. That is a given. Politicians since the founding of our republic have found creative and often devious ways to benefit financially and abuse their positions. But again, as citizens, we elected these folks. For our part, we also wanted to get ours without a lot of thought about the cost to ourselves down the road or to future generations.

There is no doubt that because of our parents, we were part of the broadest middle class in American history. This helped make us different. Never had the middle class encompassed such a wide swath of our country. Since that peak, it has shrunk as more Americans struggle to earn livable wages and manage debt. We were the most privileged generation in history. As such, we each much ask ourselves if we plundered the present while tending to sacrifice our kids' futures.

I, and most of our generation, must look inward for answers to what our impact has had on the system as a whole. If, for nothing else, then to place things into context in our minds.

Trying to place blame almost always gives rise to lies we tell ourselves and others as we try and pinpoint those responsible. In reality, though, every demographic group and political sector has their agendas that we all try to use to blame others. We don't use guns to do this, but rather things like weaponized words and statistics. Unfortunately, these are tainted and distorted by generational, political, and lifestyle ideologies.

As Mark Twain once muttered, "There are three kinds of lies: lies, damned lies, and statistics."[85]

He was referring to the use of statistics to push an agenda or to bolster weak or faulty arguments by twisting them to fit what you want to prove. It is noise and data without context or sound logic.

Our national decline started with little things that people, including us, got used to and ignored. Things as simple as driving past empty construction sites and not wondering why people weren't working there. Or, seeing rusting bridges and potholes but not questioning why and on and on in a thousand ways

I remember riding on the train to places like New York city and passing by abandoned factory after factory—often solid-looking red brick structures with weeds sprouting in parking lots and broken windows as we made less and less under the guise of globalism and a result of questionable trade agreements that sent millions of jobs overseas. It always nagged at the back of my mind but didn't fully register at the time.

Such factors as economics are well beyond the scope of this book because it is the story of how we grew up and we lived our lives. Nonetheless, the impact of these other factors on our psyche, our lives, and our nation, although often subtle in appearance, has been profound over time. Like other Americans, we started to accept things like a crumbling infrastructure and slick but incompetent politicians we should have rejected or at least questioned. Suffice it to say, almost every systemic economic and other advantage we enjoyed in the world community is under threat.

We sometimes look in the mirror and have doubts that we could have done more or done it better. But who doesn't look back during quiet times of reflection and doubt or question what was or might have been? Like other BBs, was I, Jimmy Bennett, a model citizen who always cared for our planet or the economic future of our kids? Nope, far from it.

Other factors, like uncontrollable immigration, threaten our national stability in terms of the economy and our national identity. But are me and other BBs responsible for the dismal,

---

[85] It was popularized in the US by Twain who mistakenly attributed it to British Prime Minister Benjamin Disraeli; however, it appears to have been written in 1891 by an anonymous writer.

inequitable conditions in countries like Mexico, which drive millions of illegal immigrants north to the US? Of course not.

So, speaking as a BB, I wonder where does all of that leave us standing?

Sure, the US has problems, but so does everyone else. Like them, we don't have a perfect past or a perfect track record, but one generation is not exclusively responsible for our imperfections. We weren't the only ones who started wars and programs we couldn't afford or who indulged in unsustainable lifestyles.

I believe we still stand with the best. Despite our problems and issues, there is a reason why millions clamor to enter the US by any means. Also telling is that the vast majority of BBs I have interacted with would not seriously want to live anywhere else.

Other factors contribute to and amplify our increasing national angst. We are bombarded with information 24 hours a day, much of it sensationalized and exaggerated. Along with social media, the news occupies the stage of our lives more than the immediacy of our families, workplaces, and neighborhoods. As we pass more and more time checking and rechecking our phones and tablets and other smart devices most days, we are probably more familiar with the headlines before we have exchanged a word with another human in the morning. Plus, we can Tweet soundbites endlessly.

Our shortcomings, divisions, and problems also seem to be intensified and amplified by the nature of today's journalism. Traditional journalism is dead. Slanted and biased news is the order of the day. Both progressive and conservative news sites indulge in this practice. If nothing else, it's good for ratings and revenue. Success is now measured in the number of 'clicks' not the quality or accuracy of the material presented.

Years ago, in universities across the land, budding young journalists were taught to report the who, why, what, where, when, and how. That is no longer the case. Journalists today too often try and make themselves and their thoughts part of the story instead of reporting facts.

The media has blended into a venue where opinion and news are no longer separated. Many younger readers may have trouble believing this, but there were once journalists like Walter

Cronkite. He was a TV news anchor from the early 1960s until the early 1980s. He would just read the news on-air every weeknight. He didn't seem to have an agenda or try to make anybody look good or bad.

He once remarked that, "Our job is to hold up the mirror. To tell and show the public what has happened." Not what he wished had happened or thought happened. He would end each broadcast by saying, "That's the way it is on . . . " and give the date. Imagine a news anchor who would do that today?

When reporting the news, he always retained a neutral demeanor. He didn't roll his eyes or raise his eyebrows and his voice wasn't sarcastic, disbelieving, incredulous, or anything else. As Cronkite said, "It is our duty to be sure we do not permit our prejudices to show. That is simply basic journalism."

That type of reporting doesn't happen enough anymore. The result is that not much of what we hear today is to be believed. News and commentary have blurred to the point where we make the old Soviet Union propaganda machine look like amateur hour. The news has regressed into a 24-hour spin cycle, depending on one's politics. All of this has tended to erode our individualism, freedoms, and thought processes. Many don't notice because it's gradual.

Not surprisingly, as we have tended to wander off the path and lost our way, we have become skeptics of not only what is reported and how it's reported but the government as well. In 1964, just 29% of Americans believed the government was "run by few big interests looking out for themselves." By 2013, 79% believed it. In Rasmussen polls in 2014, 63% thought most members of the US Congress were willing to sell their vote for either cash or a campaign contribution and 59% thought it likely their representative already had.

Despite those gloomy observations, though, I don't think that means that our children can't find a way to get the country back on the right path. If they demand better and are willing to get involved in public service, they can. We can help by sharing our experiences and lessons learned with them. In the end, though, they are entitled to make their own mistakes and not repeat ours.

Today BBs are in the crosshairs of the coronavirus pandemic.

It is not lost on us that medical experts say we are the most vulnerable group to get the dreaded virus or to suffer death because of it. This has dramatically altered our lifestyles. We avoid going out. We avoid socializing with our friends. The Nights of the Roundtable is gone.

Baby Boomer couple shopping with masks during the corona virus pandemic.

The word I hear too often from BBs is "unreal." We just can't wrap our heads around it. We never thought we would be wearing masks and going into banks and asking for money unless we were robbing them, or obediently following arrows like lab mice through a maze as we shop for groceries.

That most of us BBs haven't been frugal is a given. Indeed, consumer debt jumped from 22% in 1946 to over 110% by 2002. Also, consumer credit has increased almost 50% from 2002 until the present. This is a reflection of our indulgent lifestyles.

We think we experienced record-breaking political and social upheaval, from race riots to the Civil Rights Movement, Vietnam protests, the assassinations of JFK, MLK, and RFK, the man on the moon to free love and drug experimentation, but today's issues are unprecedented and unexpected as we enter uncharted territory.

As BBs settle into encroaching old age, too many of us are left wondering what happened to what was supposed to be our golden years.

Today's issues feel overstated, including the current race riots triggered primarily by the actions of a few ill-trained and unscrupulous cops. At my age, I no longer go into the streets, but when I watch on the tube my mind wanders. In hindsight, I wonder if in our protest time, the issues were clearer cut. We marched against war, nukes, and racial equality. We wanted change but I don't think we advocated total anarchy. Yes, there were small splinter groups like the Black Panthers and the Weathermen who did want a revolution, but they were the underwhelming minority.

Is that my imagination and just wishful thinking that things were different back in the day? While I don't think so, I'm not sure. Now things seem to shatter into a thousand sub-issues. So many agendas. Tear down the system. Abolish things like the police—although I can't imagine how that would work in terms of public safety—universal income for all, free healthcare, and on and on and on...

So much to ponder. When did right and wrong go out the window? Now they don't seem to matter because it is more about being sensitive. While sensitivity certainly is paramount, how can we just ignore what is right or wrong? I thought all three were important. Without standards, it is too easy to lose our perspective and our way.

Perhaps that is just me being idealistic. After all, looking back, we wanted it all: rewarding work, personal satisfaction, unlimited energy, low taxes, lots of government entitlements, including free retirement, ageless youth, a forever rising standard of living, peace, racial harmony, and other utopian desires. But idealism is not a bad trait. Our parents said we were special, and they wanted a better life for us. So, we ended up being not only dreamers but doers as well. Not a bad combination.

The good we did mixed with the bad. When I put on my "the glass is half full," hat we prevailed. Of course, as a BB I'm prejudiced that, on balance, we changed the world more for the better than than the worst.

When I put on my "the glass is half empty hat," I'm troubled because we inherited a country with lots of resources and what we will leave behind are large national debts, a damaged environment, the threat AI and robotics poses to jobs, an inequality that is negatively impacting us as well as driving mass migration that we, and other nations, are ill-equipped to handle.

Also, race relations are still far from ideal. Add to this the myriad of associated problems, like an unending wave of global terrorism, a pandemic, and the challenges are formidable for our children and grandchildren. It is little comfort that you can always look back and say we could have done more or done things better.

Does that mean we failed as the most privileged generation ever? I don't think so. It means we were human. We were an integral part of navigating some of the most turbulent changes in human history, starting with a basic shift in the family structure. We were the result when the number of children for the average American family declined from seven to three as the country transformed from a nation of farmers into an urban manufacturing powerhouse. Our parents were part of that and the impact on our world was profound.

After this wave, as manufacturing jobs shifted to countries with cheaper wages, we saw the rise of consumer and information services that powered the economy, and the evolution goes on.

As we enter the age of hyper technology where AI and robotics emerge as driving forces, we have raised children as parents and grandparents, who are well qualified to find ways to manage the future. Perhaps all those video games they played, that we tended to criticize, were necessary.

We were into cars, but today's kids are more fascinated with technology. They don't share our love of autos, which in an era of dwindling oil reserves is probably just as well. They are going to need those computer skills to figure out the way ahead as they develop tools and models to solve many of today's issues. But the racism part is going to take something more internal, like a change of heart and attitude by many.

We know that the nature of families has changed since our parent's time. Today about half of all marriages end in divorce. Many of us remarry and end up raising stepchildren. Some of us, like me, have essentially failed as parents. Others, like my siblings Paul and Molly are great parents. We have become a nation of blended families, raising other people's kids and trying to make it all work.

Despite our current condition, we should look forward with confidence that our kids will rise to the challenges they face. The world is not ending. It is merely undergoing the endless waves of change that all generations have always faced.

For BBs, our lives have been characterized by two great contradictions. First, we were afraid our world would go BOOM! because of nuclear weapons. Hiding under our desks at school was a constant reminder of this. Fortunately, there was the concept of MAD or mutually assured destruction. This kept a hot war at bay because of the simple fact that if the Russians launched an all-out attack against the US, we might be destroyed but they would perish, too.

Second, despite that gloomy scenario, we somehow all shared an exaggerated sense of optimism. We were privileged and special. Our parents told us we were, and we felt it.

These conflicting emotions or feelings of fear and optimism somehow coexisted within us. The thing is, we wanted to believe and embrace the optimistic side of things. Despite current conditions, I believe this is still true. Our underlying optimism still creates and fosters hope as we face the future.

So, while I don't have a crystal ball, I have something better because despite it all if there is one word that captures our spirit it is "optimistic." And, for me, that optimism creates hope. After all, no matter what happened in the past we have been privileged and lucky all our lives. Sure, we have had our share of hard knocks in recent years, but not winning is something we are unfamiliar with. Things happen, but we somehow plow through and land on our feet. Our world didn't end with a mushroom cloud. We want our charmed life to continue and have confidence, which has created hope, that it will. Even if we don't know exactly how. I believe that will come to characterize our children's lives as well.

I believe the words of iconic actor and fellow baby boomer, Samuel L. Jackson, sum up who we were and who we are. He said, "Our capacity to make huge mistakes was equaled by our tendency to find creative solutions and seek social justice."

So, I say these things with hope and confidence, even though lurking in the backs of all our minds is our mortality. Something which we view with a mixture of fear and fascination.

✳

Brian sold the bar but never left the city. Ellison, Rosa, and their children, also still live in Washington, DC, although I've lost track of Professor Steve and many of the others in our circle. Emma married her lawyer beau, and they are now retired and living in Florida. Paul and Molly have solid and successful lives in Ohio and are a source of great pride for me. I think of them as all American families.

We all stay in touch via cell phones, email, social media, and the occasional visit as we share our experiences of the challenges we face as we continue to age and reminisce about the good old days.

I retired in 2014 at the age of 68. Social security and some modest investments have afforded me a comfortable lifestyle despite some of the less than intelligent choices I made in my life.

In a wonderful twist of fate, my friendship with Sally eventually turned into something deeper. We are married. I finally got it right and have my life partner.

After I hung up my calculator, I moved to Mckeesport and have returned to my past roots, living in the gritty industrial environment I always loved. Although I no longer go to an office and too much industry has been shuttered or lost, it makes me feel connected to a place where things get made and done.

Abbie and my grandkids visit often. The peace this brings me is immeasurable. She and Sally have developed a close mother-daughter friendship. Equally rewarding is the closeness we share with Sally's family.

As I look back, one thing that still surprises me, though, that is, I thought it would take longer to get old. I was wrong. I blinked and it was there but, like most BBs, I'm still excited to see what happens next. Things have a lot of room to get better, so our children and grandchildren have a lot to work with.

I have a favor to ask you as a valued reader. I hope you enjoyed this book, but no matter, if you would please take a few moments of your time and write a review, even a line or two would be appreciated, especially on book sites like Amazon.com, Goodreads, and other popular online hangouts. Good, bad, or indifferent, your candid thoughts would be appreciated. Also, I love to hear from readers and make every good faith effort to respond. You can email me at michael@michaelkastre.com

www.ingramcontent.com/pod-product-compliance
Lightning Source LLC
LaVergne TN
LVHW020926090426
835512LV00020B/3218